The 5 Types of Wealth

The 5 Types of Wealth

A Transformative Guide to Design Your Dream Life

Sahil Bloom

BALLANTINE BOOKS

NEW YORK

Published in the United States by Ballantine Books, an imprint of Random House, a division of Penguin Random House LLC, New York.

BALLANTINE BOOKS & colophon are registered trademarks of Penguin Random House LLC.

Images © Sahil Bloom

LIBRARY OF CONGRESS CATALOGING-IN-PUBLICATION DATA
Names: Bloom, Sahil, author.
Title: The 5 types of wealth: a transformative guide to design your dream life / Sahil Bloom.
Other titles: Five types of wealth
Description: First edition. | New York: Ballantine Books, [2025] |
Identifiers: LCCN 2024050105 (print) | LCCN 2024050106 (ebook) |
ISBN 9780593723180 (hardcover) | ISBN 9780593723197 (ebook)
Subjects: LCSH: Success. | Wealth. | Happiness. | Self-realization.
Classification: LCC BF637.S8 B55 2025 (print) | LCC BF637.S8 (ebook) |
DDC 158—dc23/eng/20241122
LC record available at https://lccn.loc.gov/2024050105
LC ebook record available at https://lccn.loc.gov/2024050106

International edition ISBN 978-0-593-98352-2

Printed in Canada on acid-free paper

randomhousebooks.com

2 4 6 8 9 7 5 3 1

First Edition

Book design by Caroline Cunningham
Watercolor swash: AdobeStock/Elena Panevkina

For my wife, Elizabeth, and my son, Roman.

With the two of you by my side, I always feel like

the wealthiest man alive.

CONTENTS

Social Wealth · 127

Mental Wealth · 203

Physical Wealth   259

Financial Wealth   311

The 5 Types of Wealth

PROLOGUE

The Journey of a Lifetime

"YOU'RE GOING TO SEE your parents fifteen more times before they die."

All of what follows is the story of how those simple words changed my life—and how they may change yours.

On a warm California evening in May 2021, I sat down for a drink with an old friend. As we settled in at our table, he asked how I was doing. At first, I gave him the standard response that we've all grown so accustomed to: "I'm good. Busy!" I said it with all the unintended irony of the modern era, where *busy* is a badge of honor, as if being *more stressed* is something to be proud of. When I asked the same of him, instead of replying with typical busyness one-upmanship, he replied that he was "making time for the important things," since his father had gotten sick the prior year. The unexpected vulnerability in his words knocked me off the typical conversation track that defines these "catch-up" encounters. He had opened a new track, and rather than resist, I walked down it, adding that living in California had begun to wear on me, it being so far from my aging parents on the East Coast.

This rare emotional honesty sparked the interaction that altered the course of my life:

FRIEND: How often do you see your parents?

ME: Maybe once a year right now.

FRIEND: And how old are they?

ME: Mid-sixties.

FRIEND: Okay, so you're going to see your parents fifteen more times before they die.

Gut punch.

I had to take a deep breath to avoid an instinctively angry response. This was an old friend, one who knew my parents well. It wasn't meant to be insensitive—it was just . . . math. The average life expectancy is approximately eighty years; my parents were in their mid-sixties, and I saw them once per year. The math said I would see them fifteen more times before they were gone.

This was the math that broke me. It was the math that *changed my life.*

PLAYING THE WRONG GAME

I was born of an unlikely collision of two worlds—a rejection of common convention is in my DNA. In 1978, my mother, Lakshmi Reddy, born and raised in Bangalore, India, hopped on a plane with a one-way ticket to study at Mount Holyoke College in South Hadley, Massachusetts. Her parents were, understandably, worried that she'd never come home. Their friends told them she'd meet an American guy, fall in love, and build a life in that faraway land. They were right.

My father, born and raised in a Jewish household in the Bronx, New York, had a life mapped out for him by his overbearing father, one that involved marrying a Jewish girl and settling down for a stable career in academia. Fortunately for me, fate (if you believe in that) had different plans.

In a made-for-the-movies twist, they crossed paths in 1980 at a Princeton University library, where my mother was working to pay her way through a master's program and my father was in the final stages of writing his dissertation. Her parents' concerns nine thousand miles away, my mother worked up the courage to ask him on a date. As they enjoyed their ice cream, my father, never one to beat around the bush, told her, "My family will never accept us." My mother, too blinded by excitement at the use of the word *us*, completely missed the message.

Sadly, he was right; for a variety of reasons that seem impossible to understand today, my father's family was not accepting of the budding courtship. The fight grew so contentious that he was ultimately forced to choose between his family and my mother. I never met my father's parents, and he never saw them again, but the legacy of his decision—to choose true love above all else—set the stage for the world that I was born into.

My childhood and young-adult years were a steady, monotonous march toward a textbook definition of *success*. I did well in school—maybe not according to my discerning Indian mother, who continues to this day to ask, "Why not try for medical school?"—but my thoughts were always on the baseball field. With some natural ability and a hell of a lot of hard work, I earned a scholarship to pitch at Stanford University. I'll never forget the look on my mother's face when I told her the news. Her disbelief that her ne'er-do-well, always-playing-never-studying son had been accepted to Stanford was priceless.

I flew out to California with dreams of a glory-filled career in professional baseball, but when a junior-year shoulder injury derailed those aspirations, I was forced to find my footing in the classroom and plan for an alternative future. The problem was that I had no idea what future I wanted to build.

To try to solve that puzzle, I did what I thought any ambitious young person would do—I went to the richest people I knew and asked them about their work and how I could get into it. I vividly recall a formative conversation with a family friend who had made a fortune in the world of investing. He suggested I join an investment firm straight out of school, and his case was simple: "You'll make a hundred thousand dollars a year right away, five hundred thousand a year soon after that, and by the time you're thirty, you'll be making more money than you know what to do with." That sounded pretty damn good to me on the basis of one simple, foundational assumption: Money will lead directly to success and happiness.

To be clear, I'm not sure when I formally adopted that understanding as my own. My father was in academia and my mother was a small-business owner—we always had enough, but we certainly weren't rich, particularly not on a "making more money than you know what to do with" measuring stick. When I was a kid, I had one very rich friend. He had an incredible house, all the newest toys, and he was constantly getting the latest and greatest sports equipment. I was envious of his life. I never questioned whether all that stuff actually made him happy—whether he would trade the chef-prepared dinner he ate *alone* for a takeout meal at a table *surrounded by love*. I proceeded to attend college with high achievers who frequently measured status by who got the highest offer from Goldman Sachs or McKinsey, so it's safe to say my foundational assumption about the nature of success and happiness was firmly entrenched by the time I was ready to enter the real world.

Mark Twain is often quoted as having said, "It ain't what you don't know that gets you into trouble, it's what you know for sure that just ain't so." Well, when I took the advice of my family friend and accepted a job in California where I would earn well into the six figures in my first year, I *knew for sure* that this was the beginning of my road to the good life—that if I put in my time, I'd eventually reach that stress-free future filled with money and happiness.

What I knew for sure *just wasn't so;* I simply hadn't realized it yet.

By the time I turned thirty, I had achieved every marker of what I believed success looked like. I had the high-paying job, the title, the house, the car—it was all there. But beneath the surface, I was miserable. I began to think something was wrong with me. I had spent years with my head down, embracing the long hours, believing that the idyllic land of success was well within reach. At every step along the way, I told myself that I was just one bonus, one promotion, or one fancy bottle of wine away from arriving in that land.

Then, one day, I realized I had achieved all of it, and all I could think was *Is this it?*

The *arrival fallacy* is the false assumption that reaching some achievement or goal will create durable feelings of satisfaction and contentment in our lives. We incorrectly assume that we will finally experience the sensation of having *arrived* when we reach whatever we have propped up as our destination. I was thirty years old and making millions of dollars. I had *arrived*. But the feelings of happiness and fulfillment I expected were nowhere to be found. Instead, I just felt that familiar dread of needing to do more, of never having enough.

I'm willing to bet I'm not the only person who's had this experience. How many times has the thing your younger self dreamed of become the thing you complain about once you've gotten it? The house you longed for becomes the house you grumble is too small, the house in need of repairs. The car you obsessed over becomes the car you can't wait to trade in, the car that's constantly in the shop. The engagement ring that made your eyes sparkle becomes the ring you need to upgrade because of its imperfections.

Worse yet, the incessant quest for more had blinded me to the great beauty of what I had right in front of me. In a fable recorded in Plato's early works, a philosopher named Thales of Miletus is walking along obsessively gazing at the stars, only to fall into a well that he did not see at his feet. A poetic retelling by Jean de La Fontaine concludes,

> How many folks, in country and in town,
>   Neglect their principal affair;
> And let, for want of due repair,
>   A real house fall down,
> To build a castle in the air?[1]

I was chasing that *castle in the air,* blind to the reality that I was allowing my *real house* to fall down: My health had deteriorated from my lack of sleep and activity, my relationships suffered from my absent energy, and, as my friend's piercing math had made clear, my time with those I loved most was depressingly finite and quickly slipping away.

My exclusive pursuit of money was slowly, methodically robbing me of a fulfilling life.

Sitting there on that warm May evening, polishing off several more drinks after my friend left, I knew for sure that something had to change. I had prioritized *one thing* at the expense of *everything*.

From the outside looking in, I was winning, but if this was what winning felt like, I began to wonder if I was *playing the wrong game*.

THE SCOREBOARD PROBLEM

The greatest discoveries in life come not from finding the right answers but from asking the right questions.

If I had been playing the wrong game, what was the right one?

This question was where my journey to discovery began. I had to define the *right game,* the one that would actually lead to the life I wanted. I read everything I could get my hands on—hundreds of books and tens of thousands of pages—that might help me make sense of the maze I found myself in: ancient self-help classics and modern self-help hits. Biographies of great men and women throughout history. Religious texts, epics from a diverse array of cultures, and legendary tales of the hero's journey.

But reading, I found, can take you only so far—to understand something deeply human, you need to immerse yourself in the human experience.

I had conversations with people from all walks of life. I sought them out. I flew to them. I sat with them. I listened to them. From recent college graduates to CEOs of Fortune 100 companies. From stay-at-home parents to those working multiple jobs to make ends meet. From professional athletes living out of suitcases to ski bums and digital nomads. From life coaches and spiritual guides to factory workers and auto mechanics. I became a student of the human experience.

I spent hours with a man who was reeling from the recent loss of his wife, which had left him alone with their young daughter as he navigated the waves of grief; he shared his profound understanding of the greater depths of love accessible to us all. I grew close to a twenty-eight-year-old who, on the verge of starting his dream job, was diagnosed with an inoperable brain tumor that derailed his plans and forced him to reset his expectations to an entirely new baseline. I spoke with a new mother navigating the difficult balance of career and maternal ambitions, her CEO title and responsibilities weighing heavily on her desire to be a deeply present figure in her son's life. I interviewed a man recently released after a twenty-five-year prison sentence and was engrossed by his words on the dynamic, fluctuating nature of time and how his pursuit of a higher-order spiritual purpose had provided him with the stability to endure. I met a forty-six-year-old barber who grinned as he told me, "I can pay my bills and I take my girls on two vacations a year. If you ask me, I'm a rich man." I shared a meal with a ninety-year-old woman who had recently decided to take up painting and who smiled broadly as she told me that the creativity and community were life-giving for her. I spoke to countless young people who were deciding how to navigate their early career years, wrestling with the tension of family and societal expectations against their personal path of meaning. I sat with a father who had tragically lost his twin boys but who, amid the incomprehensible sadness, had found healing and even joy in daily walks in nature.

In each conversation, I walked through a beautiful visualization exercise that had been recommended to me by a mentor. Close your eyes and imagine your ideal day at eighty years old (or one hundred, in the case of the ninety-year-old!). Vividly imagine it. What are you doing? Who are you with? Where are you? How do you feel? The exercise forces you to begin with the ideal future end in mind—it establishes a personal definition of a successful life that can be used to reverse-engineer the actions in the present to achieve that desired end.

Through this exercise, and through the hundreds of books and thousands of hours of conversations filled with smiles, tears, laughter, and silence, I arrived at a powerful realization:

We all want the same thing—and it has very little to do with money.

From the young entrepreneur to the old retiree, from the new mother to the empty nester, from the rich attorney to the middle-class teacher, the ideal future end looks remarkably aligned:

Time, people, purpose, health.

Without fail, every single person I guided through the exercise had some combination of these pillars at the center of the ideal future day. Spending time surrounded by loved ones, engaged in activities that create purpose and growth, healthy in mind, body, and spirit.

Money was an enabler to these ends, but not an end in and of itself.

With this realization, it hit me: I wasn't playing the *wrong game,* I was playing the *game wrong.*

The scoreboard was the problem.

Our scoreboard is broken. It forces us into a narrow measurement of wealth, success, happiness, and fulfillment entirely defined by money. And what you measure matters. In a famous articulation often attributed to Peter Drucker, the Austrian-born management guru, "What gets measured gets managed." The statement implies that the metrics that get measured are the ones we prioritize. In other words, the scoreboard is important because it dictates our actions—how we play the game.

Your broken scoreboard may say you're winning the battle—but trouble awaits:

* Your time slips through your fingers.
* Your relationships show cracks.
* Your purpose and growth wither.
* Your physical vitality atrophies.

Broken scoreboard, broken actions. If we measure only money, all of our actions will revolve around it. We'll play the game *wrong.*

If we fix the scoreboard to measure our wealth more comprehensively, our actions will follow. We'll play the game *right.* Right scoreboard, right actions.

With this insight in mind, I began a journey to build a new tool with which we could measure our lives, one grounded in the timeless pillars that had appeared again and again across my readings, conversations, and experiences: time, people, purpose, health. It wasn't enough to know that these pillars were important; I needed a way to measure them—a way to track my progress and assess the impact of my daily actions toward building them.

This book is the manifestation of that journey.

Whoever you are and wherever you are in life, this book is for you:

The recent graduates wrestling with how to prioritize their careers in the context of everything else in life. The new mothers struggling to balance career ambitions with the desire to be present in their children's early years. The retirees contemplating how to spend the last third of their lives. The seasoned executives beginning to question if the sacrifices are worth it. The immigrants grappling with the career opportunities of a new country and its distance from family. The young fathers navigating their prime career years as their kids grow up. The rising corporate stars feeling the tension between the required long hours and a desire to meet a life partner. The middle-aged empty nesters pondering how to build a new phase of life together.

While the lens through which you view the stories, questions, and frameworks in this book will be unique, the tools are universal.

The 5 Types of Wealth offers a new way to measure the right things, make better decisions, and design your journey to wealth, success, happiness, and fulfillment. Importantly, it also provides a guide to the high-leverage principles, ideas, systems, and frameworks that will enable you to progress toward these goals.

This will be a journey—but it's one that you can start today and one that can change your world faster than you ever thought possible.

In one week, you can jump-start your actions. In one month, you can see and feel the impact. In one year, everything will be different.

Your entire life can change in one year. Not ten, not five, not three. One. One year of asking the right questions. One year of measuring and prioritizing the right things. One year of focused, daily effort on the right actions.

Trust me, I've lived it.

In May 2021, I was silently miserable, my broken scoreboard and priorities slowly marching me toward the point of no return.

In one week, I had jump-started my actions. My wife and I had the deep, painful conversations about how we wanted to measure our lives, and we aligned on the priorities and values that would guide us going forward.

In one month, I could see and feel the impact. I had made the difficult yet important decision to embark on a new professional journey built around my higher-order purpose of creating a positive impact. I reprioritized my health, focusing on the boring basics of movement, nutrition, and sleep. Most important, my wife and I sold our house in California and started our move to the East Coast to be closer to our parents, a decision that turned "You're going to see your parents fifteen more times before they die" from a harsh reality into a memory of a former life.

In one year, everything was different—my entire life had changed. My new energy-creating entrepreneurial endeavors were thriving, and I had the freedom to go for multiple daily walks, find time for a robust health routine, and focus on the projects and people that brought me joy. And while we had struggled to conceive in California, soon after arriving in our new home in New York, we were blessed with the news that my wife was pregnant. She gave birth to our son, Roman, on May 16, 2022. As we returned from the hospital and pulled onto our street, I saw both sets of Roman's grandparents cheering in the driveway, our family all there to welcome him home—to welcome *us* home.

On a warm Friday afternoon that month, I was out on a walk with Roman when an old man approached me on the sidewalk. He said, "I remember standing here with my newborn daughter. Well, she's forty-five now. It goes by fast—cherish it." It hit me hard. The next morning, I woke up and brought my son into bed. My wife was still peacefully asleep. It was early, and the first glimmers of the spring sun were starting to slip through our bedroom window. I looked down at my son, whose eyes were closed, a small, perfectly content smile on his lips. In that moment, I had a profound sensation: I had arrived, but for the first time in my life, there was nothing more that I wanted.

This was *enough*.

Never let the quest for *more* distract you from the beauty of *enough*.

My name, Sahil, means "the end of the journey." For me, this book marks the end of my first journey, all made possible because I rejected the broken scoreboard and centered my life on the new one. In the pages that follow, I will show you how to do the same.

It is the journey of a lifetime. I hope you enjoy it.

Designing Your Dream Life

1.

One Thousand Years of Wisdom

What Advice Would You Give to Your Younger Self?

IN LATE 2022, I asked this question to a dozen eighty- and ninety-year-olds as part of my annual birthday ritual. Every year, I conduct a new and (hopefully) interesting exercise that will push me to think and grow. In past years, I had written gratitude letters to all my family and friends, gone on a twelve-hour silent walk, and attempted my version of a misogi challenge (a Japanese ritual that involves doing something so challenging on one day that it has lasting benefits for the rest of the year).

But 2022 felt different.

The birth of my son in May had altered my relationship with the most fundamental reality: time. Observing the passage of time—both in his daily changes and in the juxtaposition of the newness of his life with the suddenly apparent maturity of my parents' lives—had left me wrestling with its very nature.

I decided to explore the wisdom that time has to offer by talking with those who had experienced much more of it. My younger, naïve self had sought advice from the richest people he knew when charting his life course. My older, (slightly) more enlightened self would seek advice from the wisest people he knew to do the same. I wondered how older people would reflect on what they had learned.

What did they regret? Where had they been led astray? What had brought them lasting joy and fulfillment? What detours had proven to be better than the original route? What had they known for sure that just wasn't so?

What did they know at ninety that they wished they'd known at thirty?

I had these conversations with a diverse and fascinating group. A video call with my ninety-four-year-old grandmother in India, born a princess of a small kingdom prior to her family being run out by the British colonists, yielded this beautiful insight: "Never fear sadness, as it tends to sit right next to love." An email from a ninety-eight-year-old family friend who had spent his career as a Hollywood writer yielded a personal favorite: "Never raise your voice, except at a ball game." His eighty-eight-year-old wife, a former soap opera star whom he had met on set and fallen desperately in love with, added, "Find dear friends and celebrate them, for the richness of being human is in feeling loved and loving back." In a text message, the eighty-year-old father of a close friend expressed regret over his body's deterioration over the years: "Treat your body like a house you have to live in for another seventy years." He added, "If something has a minor issue, repair it. Minor issues become major issues over time. This applies equally to love, friendships, health, and home." A ninety-two-year-old who had recently lost his beloved wife of seventy years said something that brought tears to both of our eyes, his poetic ode to their evening practice: "Tell your partner you love them every night before falling asleep; someday you'll find the other side of the bed empty and you'll wish you could tell them." My last conversation was with the ninety-four-year-old great-aunt of one of my dearest friends, and she delivered this beautiful closing insight: "When in doubt, love. The world can always use more love."

The responses ranged from playful and witty ("Dance at weddings until your feet are sore") to deeply moving ("Never let a good friendship atrophy"). Some were common tropes repeated over the years ("Always remind yourself that your track record for making it through your bad days is perfect"); others were original and thought-provoking ("Regret from inaction is always more painful than regret from action"). The wisdom I gathered was the product of 1,042 years of lived experience.

I hadn't steered the dialogue in any way—I had simply posed the question and let each of them take it as they wished. They had independently focused on a variety of things: build lasting relationships, have fun, invest in your future mental and physical wellness, raise well-adjusted kids, and more. There was certainly immense value in what I heard but perhaps even more value in what I didn't. In all the advice, insight, and wisdom shared, there was a notable omission.

No one mentioned money.

THERE'S ALWAYS GOING TO BE A BIGGER BOAT

Before we go any further, I want to make an important point: This book will not argue that money *doesn't matter,* that you should give up your worldly possessions, go live as a monk in the Himalayas, and spend sixteen hours a day meditating in silence. If you want to do that, great, but I won't be joining you!

Money isn't *nothing*—it simply can't be the *only thing*.

Three core insights summarize the body of research on the topic of money and happiness:

1. Money improves overall happiness at lower levels of income by reducing fundamental burdens and stress. At these lower levels, money *can* buy happiness.
2. If you have an income above these levels and are *unhappy,* more money is unlikely to change that.
3. If you have an income above this baseline and are *happy,* more money is unlikely to drive increasing happiness.

The second and third insights point to the same critical conclusion: Once you've achieved a baseline level of financial well-being, more money is unlikely to meaningfully affect your overall happiness. In other words, the default scoreboard—focused on money—may be a useful asset in the earliest days of your journey, but it is a liability when you're attached to it in the later days. Arthur Brooks, a bestselling author, a professor at Harvard Business School, and a leading authority on happiness science, agrees. "When it comes to money and happiness, there is a glitch in our psychological code."[1] He argues that this glitch is driven by our flawed extrapolation of the early-in-life happiness gains from increases in income—that we experience some of the positive impact of money on our well-being as children and young adults and then spend the rest of our lives "[salivating] in anticipation of good feelings when the bell of money rings."

The glitch keeps us on a metaphorical treadmill, always running, never getting anywhere, chasing the early-in-life happiness that money once provided.

In a 2018 paper published by Harvard Business School professor Michael Norton, researchers asked a group of millionaires (1) how happy they were on a scale of 1 to 10 and (2) how much more money they would need to get to a 10 on the happiness scale. Commenting on the results, Norton said, "All the way up the income-wealth spectrum basically everyone says [they'd need] two to three times as much."[2]

I decided to test this notion by asking a group of financially successful people I knew to answer those same two questions. The responses were surprisingly consistent: A technology app founder worth thirty million dollars said he would need two times more to be perfectly happy; a software entrepreneur worth one hundred million said he would need five times more; a venture investor worth three million said she would need three times more. With the exception of one enlightened investor worth twenty-five million who replied, "Honestly, I'm happy where I am" (although he added, "But if I had twice as much, I could probably fly private a lot more, which would be nice"), everyone up and down the net-worth spectrum said that two to five times more money was all they needed to reach the land of perfect happiness.

I'll never forget a conversation I had with a friend who had recently sold his manufacturing company and made one hundred million dollars. I asked if he was happier now than he'd been, given that he was richer than most people could imagine, expecting him to say, *Of course!* His response surprised me. He told me that after he closed the deal, he had taken a group of friends and family for a weeklong trip on a rented yacht to celebrate. He was excited for the moment when everyone would board the beautiful vessel, which he had paid for with his hard-earned sale proceeds. But when everyone arrived, something peculiar happened. One of his friends looked over to the next mooring where an even bigger and more luxurious yacht was docked and commented, "Whoa, I wonder who's in that one!" The happiness and satisfaction that my friend had felt around the moment quickly deflated at the comparison.

There's always going to be a bigger boat.

Through the notable omission of money by the wise elders, the scientific research on money and happiness, and the anecdotal accounts from financially successful people, we can derive the most important lesson, the one that sits at the heart of this book:

Your wealthy life may be *enabled* by money, but in the end, it will be *defined* by everything else.

2.

The Five Types of Wealth

If you do not change direction, you may end up where you are heading.

—LAO TZU

IN THE THIRD CENTURY B.C., King Pyrrhus of Epirus rose to power as the little-known leader of an expanding territory in Greece. A second cousin of Alexander the Great, he developed a reputation as a strong and strategic military leader. By 280 B.C., he had waged successful wars all over the peninsula and consolidated his power across much of the region.

But his military fortune would soon change.

In 280 B.C., King Pyrrhus received a request for support from the southern Italian city-state of Tarentum, which was at war with the Roman Republic. While Tarentum was not an explicit ally, King Pyrrhus recognized the threat that an expanding Roman Republic would pose to his power. Seizing upon the idea that "the enemy of my enemy is my friend," he sailed to southern Italy with his large and well-trained army, ready to beat back the Roman invaders.

The battle, which was fought on a plain near the town of Heraclea, was initially quite lopsided, with King Pyrrhus's forces overwhelming the ragtag Roman army, whose generals had clearly been expecting to walk over their tiny Tarentum foe.

The Romans rallied, however, and pushed back to great effect, staining the plain red with days of bloody hand-to-hand combat. By the end of the battle, King Pyrrhus was able to declare victory, but at an exceptionally high cost, losing many of his best soldiers, including his lead general.

Despite the losses, King Pyrrhus sensed an opportunity to extend the influence of his kingdom into southern Italy, and he decided to press forward, engaging the Roman enemy for the second time near the town of Asculum.

Yet again, King Pyrrhus was able to declare victory, but only after days of painful combat that left his army physically and mentally decimated. At the end of the battle, King Pyrrhus is said to have exclaimed, "Another such victory and we are undone!" His hand effectively forced by the cost of these "victorious" battles, King Pyrrhus of Epirus withdrew from Italy and returned home, where he would wage a few inconsequential campaigns before dying in relative obscurity in battle five years later.

But it's not all bad for King Pyrrhus, whose desire to leave a legacy led him into those ill-fated battles against the Romans. His name indeed does live on, though perhaps not in the way he intended.

The term *Pyrrhic victory* now refers to the victory won at such a steep cost to the victor that it feels like a defeat. The victory damages the victor beyond repair. He wins the battle but loses the war.

This is not just a random history lesson. This is important: A Pyrrhic victory is what you need to avoid in your own life. And unfortunately, a Pyrrhic victory could be where you're headed if you don't change direction.

You're walking this perilous path because of one simple mistake: You're measuring the wrong thing.

Money.

When a measure of performance becomes an explicit, stated goal, humans will prioritize it, regardless of any associated and unintended consequences. You blind yourself to everything else, focusing on the single measure, no matter the costs elsewhere. Every new promotion, pay raise, and bonus feels like a win as you ignore the painful losses of a war slowly slipping through your fingers. Money has become not only the measure but the explicit, stated goal.

The war you wage is about happiness, fulfillment, loving relationships, purpose, growth, and health. If all the battles you're fighting are exclusively about money, you *may* win these battles, but you *will* lose the war.

The warning signs on the path don't involve loss of life and limb like they did for King Pyrrhus, but they aren't pretty:

- You hit another quarterly profit target but miss another anniversary dinner.
- You earn a record bonus but fail to make it to a single one of your child's sports games.
- You say yes to every single work call but can't find time to reconnect with an old friend.
- You stay in a job for the security but allow your higher-order purpose to wither and die.
- You host five client dinners per week but can't walk up the stairs without feeling winded.
- You never leave money on the table but won't think twice about leaving your peace of mind there.

If you march ahead, eyes fixed on the financial horizon, the Pyrrhic victory awaits.

YOUR NEW SCOREBOARD

Your new scoreboard is the *five types of wealth*:

1. Time Wealth
2. Social Wealth
3. Mental Wealth
4. Physical Wealth
5. Financial Wealth

Where the old, default scoreboard was entirely based on financial wealth, the new scoreboard is grounded in the diverse pillars that define a truly wealthy existence. With the five types of wealth, you are no longer waiting to arrive, because happiness and fulfillment—previously a hoped-for destination—are embedded in the journey itself. You don't have to wait to arrive; you can feel like you've arrived every single day.

This new scoreboard dramatically outperforms the old across three major domains:

1. MEASUREMENT: Incorporates all the pillars of a happy, fulfilling existence into your point-in-time measurement, which sets the stage for appropriate actions. Measure the right thing and you'll take the right actions. Measure for the war and you'll never lose sight of it amid the chaos of the battles.

2. DECISION: Provides a dynamic lens through which to evaluate minor and major life decisions. Rather than being narrowly focused on Financial Wealth, you can evaluate a decision based on its impact on all five types of wealth. A daunting decision on the old scoreboard (one that will have a negative impact on Financial Wealth) may prove exciting on the new scoreboard (because it will have a positive impact on several other types of wealth).

3. DESIGN: Provides a model for proactive life design that considers your changing priorities across the years and enables you to focus on specific individual battles without sacrificing your victory in the longer-term war. It creates clarity as you evaluate the trade-offs you are willing (and unwilling) to make to prioritize specific areas.

Each of the five types of wealth are individually important, but it's the relationships across them—the interplay and prioritization—that are critical in building a comprehensively fulfilling existence.

TIME WEALTH is the freedom to choose how to spend your time, whom to spend it with, where to spend it, and when to trade it for something else. It is characterized by an appreciation and deep understanding of the precious nature of time as an asset—its value and importance. It is the ability to direct deep attention and focus to the highest-leverage activities. It is the control over your time, the ability to establish your own priorities—to set the terms on which you say yes or no to opportunities. If you have a life devoid of Time Wealth, you are trapped in a perpetual loop of busyness, running faster and faster but never making progress, with little control over how time is spent and whom it is spent with.

SOCIAL WEALTH is the connection to others in your personal and professional worlds—the depth and breadth of your connection to those around you. It is the network you can rely on for love and friendship but also for help in times of need. It provides the texture that allows you to appreciate the other types of wealth. What good is the freedom to control your time if you don't have anyone special to spend it with? What joys can physical vitality bring if you can't enjoy physical pursuits with people you love? What satisfaction can money provide if there is no one to dote on? Social Wealth is defined by a few deep, meaningful, healthy relationships and a fulfilling breadth of surface ties throughout your community or culture. If you have a life devoid of Social Wealth, you focus on acquired social status and lack the consequential, weighty relationships that provide lasting satisfaction and joy.

MENTAL WEALTH is the connection to a higher-order purpose and meaning that provides motivation and guides your short- and long-term decision making. It is grounded in a pursuit of growth that embraces the dynamic potential of your intelligence, ability, and character and an engagement in lifelong learning and development. It is the health of the relationship with the mind, the ability to create space to wrestle with the big, unanswerable questions of life, and the maintenance of rituals that support stillness, balance, clarity, and regeneration. If you have a life devoid of Mental Wealth, you live a life of stasis, self-limiting beliefs, stagnation, low-purpose activities, and perpetual stress.

PHYSICAL WEALTH is your health, fitness, and vitality. Given its grounding in the natural world, it is the most entropic type of wealth, meaning it is more susceptible to natural decay, uncontrollable factors, and blind luck (positive or negative) than other types. Physical Wealth is defined by a focus on the controllable actions around movement, nutrition, and recovery and the creation of consistent habits to promote vigor. If you have a life devoid of Physical Wealth, you lack the discipline to maintain these habits and you are at the mercy of the natural physical deterioration that robs you of enjoyment, particularly in the latter half of life.

FINANCIAL WEALTH is typically defined as financial assets minus financial liabilities, a figure often referred to as net worth. On your new scoreboard, there is an added nuance: Your liabilities include your expectations of what you need, your definition of *enough*. If your expectations rise faster than your assets, you will never have a life of true Financial Wealth because you'll always need more. Financial Wealth is built upon growing income, managing expenses, and investing the difference in long-term assets that compound meaningfully over time. If you have a life devoid of Financial Wealth, you exist on a treadmill of matching inflows and outflows, a never-ending chase for *more*.

With these five types of wealth, you have a new scoreboard—one that will allow you to win the battle and the war.

THE SEASONS OF YOUR LIFE

As you start to walk on the way, the way appears.
—RUMI

The 5 Types of Wealth is designed to help you thrive *within* and *across* the seasons of your life. But thriving does not mean you have to achieve some utopian state of bliss and perfect balance. Thriving is about information and action—understanding the role of each type of wealth, considering the levers to affect it, and acting on the appropriate levers in line with your long-term values and goals.

Thriving is not an end state—it is a continuous journey.

Your life does not follow a single, steady straight line through time. It ebbs and flows and has natural *seasons,* each characterized by different wants, needs, priorities, and challenges. Each season must be embraced for the good and the bad. When we embrace the current season, with all its imperfections and opportunities, and when we think of balance on multi-season time horizons, we find a way to thrive.

The ideal approach for the foundation-building season of your twenties may not be well suited to the compounding season of your thirties, the family-building season of your forties, the purpose-finding season of your fifties, or the retiree season of your sixties and beyond. Similarly, the ideal approach for your later seasons may not work for your earlier ones. There's no predetermined guide for this journey. Everyone's seasons are unique. Everyone's definition of *balance* is unique. There are no fixed timelines on which you change, fail, learn, grow, and adapt. There are no requirements; there is no right or wrong.

You may have a season of professional growth, a season of divorce, a season of readjustment after a family tragedy, a season of inner health, or a season of new love. These five types of wealth will orient you within and across each and every season, through life's great highs and its most challenging lows—a durable idea that provides value on the micro, zoomed-in level of the present season's battle as well as on the macro, zoomed-out level of the multi-season war.

When you experience a pain, a rock-bottom moment, a tragedy, an end, there is a light that shines through from that darkness. The light is the blinding insight—the aha moment of clarity—that comes through when you see the other side. It's the light I saw when my old friend told me I would see my parents only fifteen more times before they died. It's the light an old man sees when he regrets never pursuing his passion in life. It's the light parents see when their kid no longer wants to get tucked into bed. It's the light a dying woman sees as she realizes her kids are the only people who remember the late nights she put in at the office.

It's the light you hope you never see, the light you eventually will see, the light you need to see now.

You know the light exists—you even know what it looks like. You hear the stories, nod at the takeaways, and go on living the exact same way.

But to ignore the light is to live in the dark.

You need to act on the light, embrace what it can bring to your life.

That is what *The 5 Types of Wealth* is all about: a new way to measure your life, because when you measure the right thing, you take the right actions and create the best outcomes.

The journey is just getting started. Allow the light from the other side to shine on the path.

Now start walking.

3.

The Wealth Score

YOUR *WEALTH SCORE* IS your performance on the new scoreboard.

Everyone should take the quiz to establish a baseline Wealth Score prior to continuing with the book. This baseline will be what you measure your progress against as you build and balance your life across the seasons to come. You can and should come back to this assessment in the future to track your progress, just as you might once have tracked your financial net worth using an online tool.

To establish your Wealth Score, you take a simple quiz. There are five statements for each type of wealth; for each statement, respond with 0 (strongly disagree), 1 (disagree), 2 (neutral), 3 (agree), or 4 (strongly agree), then add up your score for each section and the total across the sections.

The maximum score for each type of wealth is 20 (you strongly agree with each of the five statements), and the maximum score overall is 100.

THE WEALTH SCORE QUIZ

TIME WEALTH:

1. I have a deep awareness of the finite, impermanent nature of my time and its importance as my most precious asset.
2. I have a clear understanding of the two to three most important priorities in my personal and professional lives.
3. I am able to consistently direct attention and focus to the important priorities that I have identified.
4. I rarely feel too busy or scattered to spend time on the most important priorities.
5. I am in control of my calendar and priorities.

SOCIAL WEALTH:

1. I have a core set of deep, loving, supportive relationships.
2. I am consistently able to be the partner, parent, family member, and friend that I would want to have.
3. I have a network of loose relationships I can learn from and build on.
4. I have a deep feeling of connection to a community (local, regional, national, spiritual, and so on) or to something bigger than myself.
5. I do not attempt to achieve status, respect, or admiration through material purchases.

MENTAL WEALTH:

1. I regularly embrace a childlike curiosity.
2. I have a clear purpose that provides daily meaning and aligns short- and long-term decision making.
3. I pursue growth and consistently chase my full potential.
4. I have a fundamental belief that I am able to continuously change, develop, and adapt.
5. I have regular rituals that allow me to create space to think, reset, wrestle with questions, and recharge.

PHYSICAL WEALTH:

1. I feel strong, healthy, and vital for my age.
2. I move my body regularly through a structured routine and have an active lifestyle.
3. I eat primarily whole, unprocessed foods.
4. I sleep seven or more hours per night on a regular basis and feel rested and recovered.
5. I have a clear plan in place to allow me to physically thrive into my later years.

FINANCIAL WEALTH:

1. I have a clear definition of what it means to have *enough* financially.
2. I have income that is steadily growing alongside my skills and expertise.
3. I manage my monthly expenses so that they are reliably below my income.
4. I have a clear process for investing excess monthly income for long-term compounding.
5. I use my financial wealth as a tool to build other types of wealth.

VISUALIZING YOUR WEALTH SCORE

Using the results from your quiz, fill in the template to get a unique visual perspective on your baseline. The visual will provide a clear understanding of the strengths and weaknesses in your starting point and allow you to create goals to work toward a life of comprehensive wealth.

WEALTH SCORE

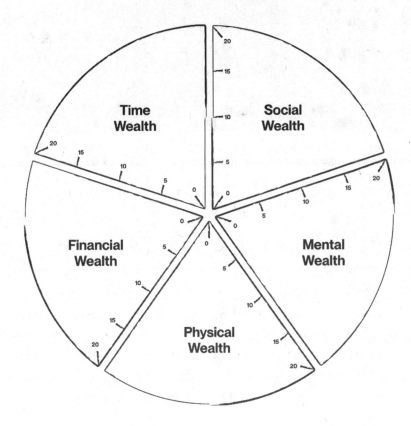

You can also take and share the assessment online at the5typesof wealth.com/quiz.

4.

The Life Razor

Keeping the Earth in the Window

ON APRIL 11, 1970, the Apollo 13 mission rocket launched from the John F. Kennedy Space Center on Merritt Island, Florida. It was meant to be the third human landing on the moon's surface, but that plan was derailed just three days into the mission when a short circuit led to an oxygen tank explosion that critically impaired the ship's ability to complete the round trip back to Earth. The three astronauts—Jim Lovell, Fred Haise, and Jack Swigert—were forced to use the tiny lunar lander as a makeshift space lifeboat, living for multiple days in near-freezing temperatures to conserve power for their hoped-for return home.

The entire saga was detailed in *Apollo 13*, Ron Howard's 1995 Academy Award–winning docudrama. In the climactic scene of the film, the three astronauts are faced with an impossible challenge, one with life-and-death consequences. As they approach atmospheric reentry, they are told by the mission operators that achieving the appropriate angle is essential—too shallow and their ship will skip off into space like a rock off a pond; too steep and their ship will ignite like a piece of dry kindling in a fire. To avoid these fates, they have to burn the engines and execute a correction to get themselves onto an optimal course and ensure their survival.

The problem: Given the state of the impaired ship, the correction must be manual, without benefit of the onboard computers usually used for such a maneuver. Without the computers managing the series of complex math and physics equations that govern orientation and alignment in space, the move is risky at best and doomed at worst.

In a moment of chaos, Commander Jim Lovell (played by Tom Hanks) proposes a solution: "Now, look, Houston, all we need to hold attitude is one fixed point in space. Is that not correct?"

He receives a quick affirmative reply from the mission command center. Holding the controls and peering out a small triangular window to his left, Lovell slowly moves the spaceship, and a familiar blue planet comes into view.

"Well, Houston, we've got one," he says, staring intently at the Earth in the center of the small triangle. "If we can keep the Earth in the window, fly manually, the co-ax crosshairs right on its terminator. All I have to know is how long do we need to burn the engine."

The bold strategy works, and the astronauts execute the daring manual burn and successfully reenter the atmosphere at the appropriate angle. They splash down in the ocean safely in one of the most heartwarming and dramatic movie endings of all time.

It was a historic final scene of survival and triumph that wowed audiences around the world, but the real insight from the scene has nothing to do with the movie, space, science, or even Tom Hanks.

The real insight has everything to do with the Earth and that tiny triangular window.

THE LIFE RAZOR

In the study of philosophy, the term *razor* denotes any principle that allows you to quickly remove unlikely explanations or avoid unnecessary steps. It allows you to metaphorically shave away unneeded explanations or actions. Today, the term is broadly applied as a rule of thumb that simplifies decision making.

There are many well-known razors:

* Occam's razor, named for fourteenth-century philosopher
  William of Occam, states that when weighing explanations for
  something, the one with the fewest necessary assumptions is
  generally the correct one. The simplest explanation is the best
  one. Simple is beautiful.
* Hanlon's razor, a tongue-in-cheek adage stating that one must
  never attribute to malice that which is adequately explained
  by stupidity. It's best applied to politics, relationships, and
  general online discourse.
* Hitchens's razor, created by and named for the late author
  Christopher Hitchens, states that anything asserted without evidence can also be dismissed without evidence. A useful rule
  that will save you from wasting time on pointless arguments.

Keeping the Earth in the window was, in an abstract sense, a razor
for the Apollo 13 astronauts. In the chaos of the moment, facing an
impossible challenge with hundreds of variables that might send
them to their graves, the astronauts identified a beautifully simple,
single point of focus, a rule of thumb that allowed them to shave away
unnecessary actions and simplify the complex manual correction.

This story offers a powerful metaphor for your life.

Inevitably, you will encounter opportunities, chaos, challenges,
and complexity that will test you:

* A shiny new job that tempts you to leave the company you love
* The death of a family member or dear friend
* A job loss that takes your financial situation from good to bad
* Health problems that affect those closest to you
* Relationship struggles with someone who once felt like your
  rock
* A critical decision that feels too heavy and difficult to make

It's easy to allow your priorities to fall victim to these encounters,
to lose yourself in the chaos. In these moments, you need your own

single point of focus—your own rule of thumb to simplify your decision making, a foundational decision-making heuristic that will allow you to navigate the uncertainty and trials of life with the confidence of an experienced explorer. You need to keep the Earth in the window.

You need a *Life Razor.*

NEVER MISS A TUESDAY DINNER

In January 2023, entrepreneur Marc Randolph, the cofounder and first CEO of the streaming pioneer Netflix, posted a photo of a short, handwritten note with the caption "My definition of success." In it, Randolph described a weekly nonnegotiable ritual that he had maintained throughout his ultra-successful technology career:

"For over thirty years, I had a hard cut-off on Tuesdays. Rain or shine, I left at exactly 5 P.M. and spent the evening with my [wife]. We would go to a movie, have dinner, or just go window shopping downtown together."

I spoke to Randolph a few months later and asked him about the origin of the Tuesday-dinner rule and its importance to his life.

Early in his career, he told me, he was working eighty-hour weeks, completely immersed in the start-up world. When his relationship began to suffer, Randolph said, "I realized that I was the problem, because I was expecting her to take the leftovers of what I was able to offer, and that felt wrong to me." But rather than ignoring the problem or expecting it to solve itself, he took matters into his own hands. "Everything comes from what you put first," he said. "I needed to reprioritize my allocation of time."

The Tuesday dinner became a nonnegotiable ritual. Even as he was starting one of the most transformative technology companies of the modern era, Randolph stuck to it. "Nothing got in the way of that. If you had something to say to me on Tuesday afternoon at four fifty-five, you had better say it on the way to the parking lot. If there was a crisis, we were going to wrap it up by five."

But the Tuesday-dinner rule wasn't about the dinner—not really.

"It was all about symbolism, ripple effects into every other area of my life. The ritual illustrates to me and everyone around me—my family, my partners, my employees, my friends—what my priorities are." It was a small, consistent weekly display of respect and admiration for what he valued most in life, a strong signal through action, not words. His wife sees his commitment to their relationship and love, which strengthens her own commitment to the bond. His children see his dedication to their mother and the family unit, which makes them secure in their understanding of their role in his world. His employees see his priorities and boundaries with his family and are encouraged to set their own, which makes them more loyal and focused during the hours at work.

One action—a weekly Tuesday-evening dinner—with ripple effects that extend well beyond.

"I resolved a long time ago to not be one of those entrepreneurs on their seventh start-up and their seventh wife. In fact, the thing I'm most proud of in my life is not the companies I started, it's the fact that I was able to start them while staying married to the same woman; having my kids grow up knowing me and (best as I can tell) liking me, and being able to spend time pursuing the other passions in my life. That's my definition of success."

Most important, that idea ("I will never miss a Tuesday dinner") is an identity-defining statement for Marc Randolph. It is clear, controllable, and serves as a reminder-to-self of the *type of person* he is. When a new situation or opportunity arises, good or bad, he can ask himself, "What would the type of person who never misses a Tuesday dinner do in this situation? How would he handle it?" This is where the true power lies—in the connection of a single, elegant statement to how your ideal self shows up in the world.

"I will never miss a Tuesday dinner" is Marc Randolph's Life Razor, his single point of focus that allows him to cut through the noise, maintain perspective and balance, make decisions in line with his core identity, and create positive ripple effects throughout his world. Without one, you're leaving life to chance; like a mountain climber caught in a blizzard, you'll become blinded by it, lose all points of reference, and wander aimlessly, praying for the storm to subside. With one, you'll see clearly—the storms won't be any less turbulent, but you'll be well equipped to navigate through to the other side.

Marc Randolph found his Life Razor. Now let's help you find yours.

SHARPENING YOUR LIFE RAZOR

Your Life Razor is a single statement that will define your presence in the current season of life.

A powerful Life Razor has three core characteristics. It is:

1. CONTROLLABLE: It should be within your direct control.
2. RIPPLE-CREATING: It should have positive second-order effects in other areas of life.
3. IDENTITY-DEFINING: It should be indicative of the type of person you are, the way your ideal self shows up in the world.

To bring this to life, let's look at an example from my own life. "I will coach my son's sports teams" is my Life Razor:

1. CONTROLLABLE: I am in control of making the time to coach my son's sports teams. I can take the actions necessary to have freedom to participate in these activities and to be the type of father who he is excited to have around him as a coach.
2. RIPPLE-CREATING: By taking these actions and making this commitment, I will show my son the value I place on our relationship. He will feel empowered by my support. My wife will see my dedication to our son and family and strengthen her dedication to us. My team and business partners will see my family priorities and feel encouraged to establish their own personal priorities, which will make them focused and loyal.
3. IDENTITY-DEFINING: I am the type of person who coaches my son's sports teams. This person is present, connected to his family and community, committed to his purpose as a father

and husband; he takes care of himself and others and declines opportunities that may infringe upon freedom or jeopardize reputation.

When new challenges appear, I use my Life Razor to navigate the situation:

- An interesting professional opportunity arises. It will mean more money and prestige but require more travel and time away for the next two years. I pause and ask myself, *What would the type of person who coaches his son's sports teams do here?* The answer: *He would be committed to prioritizing his most important relationships over additional money or prestige.* This helps me think through the trade-offs on time and freedom so I can either adjust the opportunity to fit my life or turn it down.
- A challenging family situation arises. It would be easy to ignore or outsource the struggle. I ask myself, *How would the type of person who coaches his son's sports teams step up here?* The answer: *He would confront the struggle, face it head-on, and stand as a pillar of strength for his loved ones.* This helps me clarify my response and encourage resilience in our family unit.
- A potentially life-changing financial opportunity arises but it carries reputation risk. I might be tempted by the money, but I know that the type of person who coaches his son's sports teams would never jeopardize his son's respect and admiration for money. I pass up the opportunity.

The simple statement "I will coach my son's sports teams" becomes a dynamic defining rule for life—my Life Razor.

It's time to define your Life Razor.

The goal is to complete this sentence: "I am the type of person who [blank]." To do so, write down the actions and character traits that capture your ideal identity. If you were able to attend your own funeral, what would you want everyone to say about your actions, about who you were and how you lived? List them. Then zoom out and contemplate the bigger picture. What single action from the list would imply all the others?

Here are a few examples from real people who've completed this exercise to spark your thinking:

- **MID-FORTIES INVESTMENT PROFESSIONAL:** I am disciplined. I delay gratification; I never chase the shiny thing. I wake up early and train my body and mind. I take care of myself and others. I work hard on things that matter to me and take pride in punching the clock for people who are counting on me. "I wake up early and do hard things" is my Life Razor.
- **MID-THIRTIES STAY-AT-HOME MOTHER:** I am a caregiver. I am the mother that I wish I had when I was growing up. I always have energy for my kids, no matter how tired I am. I am in a season where I prioritize their growth and development. "I always tuck my kids into bed" is my Life Razor.
- **MID-TWENTIES CONSULTANT:** I am fiercely loyal. I am trustworthy. I have high emotional intelligence. I am always there to sit with a friend in need. I prioritize my relationships and the people on the journey with me. I never let someone down if they're counting on me, professionally or personally. "I never let a friend cry alone" is my Life Razor.
- **MID-THIRTIES ENTREPRENEUR:** I prioritize my family and friendships above all else. I show up for the people I love. I am protective, supportive, and giving. I always make it to the game, concert, parent-teacher meeting, or doctor's appointment. I take care of myself physically and mentally so that I can take care of others. I am focused and get things done efficiently to make these priorities work. "I never miss a recital" is my Life Razor.
- **MID-SIXTIES RETIREE:** I am a servant leader. I believe in the world-changing power of good deeds. I always take care of others, both in my inner circle and in the extended circles of

my community. I value reputation, goodness, and legacy
above all near-term pleasures. "I do one good deed each day
(and never tell anyone about it)" is my Life Razor.

In each example, the single-statement Life Razor becomes a
broad, identity-defining rule for life that covers the entire range of
traits and actions. It's easy to see how the identity the rule shapes
can be used to clarify the appropriate, identity-aligned response in a
wide variety of life situations.

Pause here and walk through the exercise. Give yourself time to
think deeply and reflect. Write down a few options. Test each against
the three core characteristics (controllable, ripple-creating, identity-
defining). Narrow down the options to select your starting version.
Place it somewhere visible—it should always be top of mind as you
face life's opportunities and challenges. When they come, turn to it.
What would the type of person who [blank] do in this situation?
How would that person handle it?

Your Life Razor can (and will) change across the seasons of your
life. It may look very different when you're a single twenty-four-
year-old than it does when you're a married forty-year-old—and it
will certainly look different when you're a parent to young children,
a parent to adult children, or a grandparent. Revisit the exercise
every few years to assess its continued value and relevance. Adjust
and redefine it accordingly.

I've never met Tom Hanks, but he changed my life. If you identify
your Earth in the window—your Life Razor—and keep it top of
mind, I'm willing to bet he'll change yours too.

5.

Your True North

Climbing the Right Mountain

There is no favorable wind for the sailor who doesn't know where to go.

— SENECA

ON MY THIRTY-SECOND BIRTHDAY, my parents gave me a small silver compass. Inscribed inside was a short message:

*Sahil—So you may always know where
your true north lies. Mom & Dad*

A photo of the compass gifted to me by my parents

Their deeper message: Life is about direction, not speed.

When our old friend King Pyrrhus of Epirus charged into fevered battle with the Roman Republic in the third century B.C., he did so with a desire to crush his enemy as quickly as possible. He emerged victorious from the battle, only to realize his "victory" had set him on an inevitable course to lose the war. Far too many people are destined for a similar fate.

To avoid it, you need to focus on direction. You need to keep your compass pointed at your true north.

GOALS AND ANTI-GOALS: CALIBRATING THE COMPASS

In each section summary to follow, you will be asked to use a goal-setting framework to clearly calibrate your compass associated with that specific type of wealth. This compass works synergistically with your Life Razor: Your Life Razor establishes your identity—who you are and what you stand for—while your compass defines where you're going, your vision for the future. You will turn to your Life Razor when challenges or opportunities arise, but your compass will dictate your direction as you build toward your dream life.

The goal-setting framework you will use has two connected components:

1. Goals
2. Anti-goals

Goals are the things you want to happen on your journey. This should include your big, audacious, long-term ambitions and your medium-term "checkpoint" objectives. If the long-term ambition is the summit of the mountain, the medium-term objectives are the mid-climb campsites—you can't get to the summit without reaching these checkpoints along the way. To establish your goals, reflect on what you really want to achieve in each area of life. Identify one big, ambitious summit, then work backward from these long-term ambitions to establish medium-term objectives that represent the two to three logical "campsites" along the climb to that summit.

Anti-goals are the things we *don't want to happen* on our journey to achieve our goals.

The concept of anti-goals is derived from entrepreneur Andrew Wilkinson, who cites a 2017 conversation with his business partner as its origin. "Our true goal was actually pretty simple: We wanted to enjoy our time at work, but without the same problems—jammed calendars, constant travel, no time with kids, not enough sleep—that plagued many of our successful friends."

Andrew and his partner were longtime admirers of the late investor Charlie Munger, who famously said, "All I want to know is where I'm going to die so I'll never go there." That quote sparked their thinking: They needed to invert the problem. Just as they set goals for what they wanted to happen, they needed to set anti-goals: *things they wanted to avoid.*

To paraphrase Munger, anti-goals are about knowing where you're going to (metaphorically) die so you never go there. If the goals are your summit, anti-goals are the things you don't want to sacrifice while climbing—like your toes, your sanity, and your life. You want to reach the summit, but not at the expense of these things.

For example, if your long-term goal is to become a CEO, your anti-goals might be spending more than ten days away from your family per month, allowing your health to suffer from stress and travel, and loosening your moral standards to achieve profit targets. You want to achieve your goal, but not if it means having these three negative outcomes.

To establish anti-goals, look at your goals, but rather than think about this great outcome, invert the problem—flip it on its head:

- What are the worst possible outcomes that could result from your pursuit of these goals?
- What could lead to those worst possible outcomes occurring?
- What would you view as a Pyrrhic victory—winning the battle but losing the war?

Using your answers to these questions, select one to three specific anti-goals for each long-term goal.

Once your goals and anti-goals are established, your compass is calibrated for the journey.

HIGH-LEVERAGE SYSTEMS: BUILDING THE ENGINE

If your goals and anti-goals establish your direction, the high-leverage systems are the engine that drives you forward into that envisioned future. In his bestselling book *Atomic Habits,* author James Clear famously wrote, "You do not rise to the level of your goals. You fall to the level of your systems."

Systems are the daily actions that create forward progress. *Leverage* amplifies the output of a single unit of input. Combining the two ideas, *high-leverage systems* are the daily actions that create amplified, asymmetric forward progress. To understand this, we briefly turn to a legendary soccer star and the most famous investor of all time.

It's December 18, 2022, and Lionel Messi walks slowly around the pitch of Lusail Stadium in Doha, Qatar. He looks around, gazes off into space. It's easy to imagine this is a scene from a pregame practice or following a game's conclusion—but it is not. Lionel Messi is walking slowly around the pitch in the 107th minute of the most important match of his life—the World Cup final against France—with ninety thousand screaming fans in the stands and over one billion people watching worldwide.

Suddenly, he sparks into action. As if possessed, he sprints forward at an angle, receives a pass from teammate Lautaro Martínez, and quickly routes the ball to teammate Enzo Fernández, who sends it back to Martínez. Martínez shoots, but a spectacular save by France's goalkeeper Hugo Lloris deflects the ball straight to Messi. As he has done so many times in his career, Lionel Messi controls the ball and fires a shot into the goal, giving Argentina the lead in extra time. They would go on to win the match in a penalty shoot-out, cementing Lionel Messi's case as the greatest soccer player of all time.

Messi's almost incomprehensibly long list of professional accolades includes (at the time of this writing) a record eight Ballon d'Or awards and six European Golden Shoes, given to the best player of the year and the leading goal scorer, respectively; he also holds the records for the most goals in La Liga, the Supercopa de España, and the UEFA Super Cup, and the most officially recorded assists in soccer history. In a world of sports dominated by perfect physical specimens who outrun, outjump, and outhustle their opponents, Lionel Messi stands out as an anomaly. He is just five foot seven and weighs under 160 pounds, and if you watch him play, he often appears sluggish, even lazy. A Google search of *Lionel Messi lazy* yields about five hundred thousand results, most of them noting his propensity to walk around the soccer pitch while his teammates and opponents are sprinting feverishly in various directions. It is the most talked-about walking habit in the world. In the run-up to Argentina's 2022 World Cup final, *The New Yorker* published an article with a subtitle that said Messi "can often be found off the ball, strolling and dawdling and looking mildly uninterested."

But it turns out Lionel Messi's walking is far from laziness—it's strategy. Interestingly, it's the same strategy employed by the world's most successful investor.

Warren Buffett is known as the Oracle of Omaha for a reason. Over an investing career spanning more than seventy years, he has achieved compounded annual returns of over 20 percent, an astonishing feat over such a long time. To put this figure in perspective, if you had invested $10,000 in Buffett's Berkshire Hathaway in 1965, it would be worth an eye-watering $300 million today. In a world of investing dominated by high-frequency trading and high-tech algorithms designed to outmaneuver the markets and competition, Warren Buffett stands out as an anomaly. He generated these results while making fewer investments than the average casual day trader. Commenting on his strategy, he once quipped, "The trick in investing is just to sit there and watch pitch after pitch go by and wait for the one right in your sweet spot."[3]

So what do the young soccer star and the old investing whiz have in common? Both focus their energy on a few key moments and ignore the rest. When they're on, they deploy their energy in a concentrated, glorious burst. When they're off, they wait, conserve, and position themselves slowly and strategically into locations that will be advantageous in future moments. They work smart—not hard.

Lionel Messi and Warren Buffett understand the power of high-leverage systems. Whereas most people operate in a fixed, symmetric loop of inputs and outputs—with one unit input for one unit output—Messi and Buffett identify and focus their energy on the actions and decisions that are likely to generate one hundred units of output for their one unit of input. They fundamentally break the fixed relationship of inputs and outputs to create asymmetric outcomes.

If the greatest soccer player and the greatest investor of all time share this common trait, we should take heed. The guides at the end of each section will arm you with proven high-leverage systems for each domain. To establish your high-leverage systems, consider the guides and select the actions that will create meaningful progress toward your envisioned future.

THE DIMMER SWITCH: AVOIDING THE ON/OFF TRAP

An old school of thought would contend that your focus on each type of wealth exists in a binary state: on or off. It would say that you can have, at most, two types flipped on at any point in time and that the other three types would have to be flipped off.

The fundamental problem with this is that if one remains off for too long, it can never be turned on again. If you don't nurture and cultivate your relationships in your twenties and thirties, you won't have them in your forties. If you don't invest in your health in your forties and fifties, you won't have it in your sixties. If you don't take care of your mind in your sixties and seventies, you won't have it in your eighties.

This book rejects that old school of thought and offers a new one: If you have the appropriate goals, anti-goals, and high-leverage systems, your focus on each type of wealth can exist on a *dimmer switch* rather than an on/off switch. This shift is important. It allows you to prioritize your values and goals for the present season without turning off any one area, something that leads to atrophy that proves painful (and difficult) to reverse.

Let's consider an example of a potential life arc to bring this new school of thought into focus:

SEASON 1: You're just beginning your career. You want to establish a solid financial foundation and build marketable skills. Financial and Mental Wealth become the primary goals. Your anti-goals are allowing Time, Social, and Physical Wealth to atrophy in the pursuit of these goals, so you adopt a few high-leverage systems for maintenance. During this season, you dramatically improve your Financial and Mental Wealth and maintain the others.

SEASON 2: You're starting a family. You want to prioritize your relationship with your family but worry that the progress you've made in your career and finances will suffer. Time and Social Wealth become the primary goals. Your anti-goals are allowing Financial and Mental Wealth to diminish after the progress from Season 1, so you adopt a few high-leverage systems for maintenance. During this season, you have the freedom and energy to be an active figure in your family's formative years, and while you may not have accelerated your career trajectory, you have certainly kept it from deteriorating.

SEASON 3: Your family is less of a demand on your time and energy. You want to prioritize your purpose and improve your health. Mental and Physical Wealth become the primary goals. Your anti-goals are allowing Social and Financial Wealth to deteriorate, so you adopt a few high-leverage systems for maintenance. During this season, you find new energy for life from your purpose-imbued days and improved vitality, and your most important relationships and financial needs are preserved.

SEASON 4: You're retired. You've managed to navigate a thoughtful, dynamic balance across the seasons of your life and are ready to enjoy the fruits of your efforts. You want to prioritize

your relationships in this final season. Social Wealth becomes
the primary goal. Your anti-goals are allowing Time, Mental,
Physical, and Financial Wealth to meaningfully recede from
the levels you have built in your thoughtful approach across
the prior three seasons, so you adopt a few high-leverage systems for maintenance of these areas. During this season, you
find deep joy and fulfillment in human connection and flourishing relationship depth while the other areas are maintained
at previous levels. You sail off—literally or figuratively—into
the sunset years of life.

The concept of a dimmer switch should also mitigate much of the
undue personal and societal pressure to make constant forward
progress in *every area of life*. When my son was born, my wife, Elizabeth, was deeply certain of her desire to be as present as possible
during the first few years of his life. But doing so would have meant
stepping off the track as a star fashion designer rapidly rising through
the ranks in a competitive industry. It wasn't the decision itself that
was challenging—she knew what she wanted—but the weight of the
external perception of the decision gave her significant pause. She
felt the cultural pressure to do more, to make more, and to impress
more. It was the same weight that I felt when I left my high-paying
job to pursue a different path. I endured the confused looks from
friends and colleagues, the assumption that I must have burned out,
and a comment from a mentor, who remarked, "This will either
work out, or it'll be the worst decision of your life." For both me and
my wife, the idea that this was one season among many—that we
could prioritize certain things and maintain others—was deeply empowering.

Consider the mentality of surfers riding a wave. They fully enjoy
this wave, with the wisdom and awareness that there are always
more waves coming. They know they don't have to ride every single
wave that comes their way. They are aware that patience and proper
positioning are all that matters for when the next wave inevitably
comes. They know the only way to live is by putting themselves out
there in the water, because they can't catch any waves sitting on the

shore. You need to adopt the surfers' mentality with respect to the seasons of your life. There will be seasons of growth and seasons of maintenance for each type of wealth. Enjoy each season for its individual beauty, position yourself for future seasons according to your values and goals, and always place yourself in the water.

COURSE CORRECTION: RECALIBRATING THE COMPASS

Tiny deviations from the optimal course can be catastrophic. You need a process for real-time course recalibration—constant evaluation, correction, and adjustment on your journey.

At the end of each month, ask yourself three tactical questions:

1. WHAT REALLY MATTERS RIGHT NOW IN MY LIFE, AND ARE MY GOALS STILL ALIGNED WITH THIS? Assess the quality of your goals and ensure that they still serve as true north.
2. ARE MY CURRENT HIGH-LEVERAGE SYSTEMS ALIGNED WITH MY GOALS? Assess the quality of your high-leverage systems and whether they create the appropriate momentum.
3. AM I IN DANGER OF RUNNING AFOUL OF MY ANTI-GOALS? Assess the quality of your environment and decisions to evaluate any changes that need to be made.

The monthly ritual takes thirty minutes and creates an opportunity for regular reflection and minor course corrections that are essential on your journey.

At the end of each quarter, add these four questions to your regular ritual:

1. WHAT IS CREATING ENERGY RIGHT NOW? Review your calendars from the prior quarter. What activities, people, or projects consistently created energy in your life? Did you spend ample time on these energy creators, or did they get neglected? Recalibrate to spend more time on these in the quarter ahead.

2. WHAT IS DRAINING ENERGY RIGHT NOW? Review your calendars from the prior quarter. What activities, people, or projects consistently drained energy from your life? Did you allow energy drainers to persist, or did you cut them off in real time? Recalibrate to spend less time on these in the quarter ahead.

3. WHO ARE THE BOAT ANCHORS IN MY LIFE? Boat anchors are people who hold you back from your potential. They literally create a *drag* on your life. Boat anchors are people who belittle, put down, or diminish your accomplishments, laugh at your ambition and tell you to be more realistic, harm the quality of your environment through negativity and pessimism, and make you feel bad by consistently showing off what they have. Recalibrate to minimize or eliminate the energy you give them in the quarter ahead.

4. WHAT AM I AVOIDING BECAUSE OF FEAR? The thing you fear the most is often the thing you most need to do. Fears, when avoided, become limiters on our progress. Recalibrate to get closer to your fears in the quarter ahead.

By implementing this regular adjustment ritual, you'll keep your compass calibrated and stay on the right path.

THE ANSWERS ARE ALREADY WITHIN YOU

On January 1, 2014, as I was graduating from college, I wrote a letter to my future self. I sealed the letter in an envelope that read *Open on Jan. 1, 2024* and placed it in my small personal safe. Over the years, I forgot about the letter and was reminded of its existence only when I found it while storing some family documents following my son's birth. On January 1, 2024, as I was about to turn in the final draft of this book, I opened the letter and was knocked off my feet.

January 1, 2014

Hey Old Man —

If you're reading this, it means you're alive, so congrats on that, I guess.

I'm about to graduate and enter the *real world,* whatever that means, so it feels like an appropriate moment to lay out some hopes for my future:

1. I hope you married Elizabeth. Seriously, I hope you didn't fuck that up. She's the best thing that ever happened to you.

2. I hope you've got a kid by now. I don't want kids, but I imagine I might grow up at some point and change my mind on that. If you do have kids, I hope you're a good dad. If you're even half as good as your dad was to you, you'll be great.

3. I really hope you've worked on yourself and grown up. You have a lot you hide from the world. You're insecure. You compare yourself to everyone but yourself. You're so afraid to fail that you always seem to choose the safe path. You've got work to do—don't run away from it.

4. I hope you tell your parents you love them more often. They don't know how much they mean to you, and that's a shame.

5. I hope you live closer to family. You made your mom really sad when you took that job in California. She smiled and said she was happy for you, but it was that sad smile that her parents gave her when she left for college in America. The smile of losing a child to a new world. Don't let that be the case.

6. I hope you got closer to Sonali. Sibling love is special, but you've allowed your competitiveness to get in the way of that at times. I hope you've gotten past that and embraced each other in a new light. You can learn a lot from her.

7. I hope you're working on something that feels meaningful. I don't even know what that means, to be honest, but I guess it's something like enjoying a random Tuesday.

8. I hope the friends you love and care about are all healthy and thriving. I know that's probably impossible, so I guess I hope

the friends you love and care about [know] you love and care about them. That's all that matters in the end.

9. And finally, I hope you've had a little bit of fun along the way.

That's all for now. I don't know how you sign off a letter like this. Goodbye for now, I guess.

Sahil

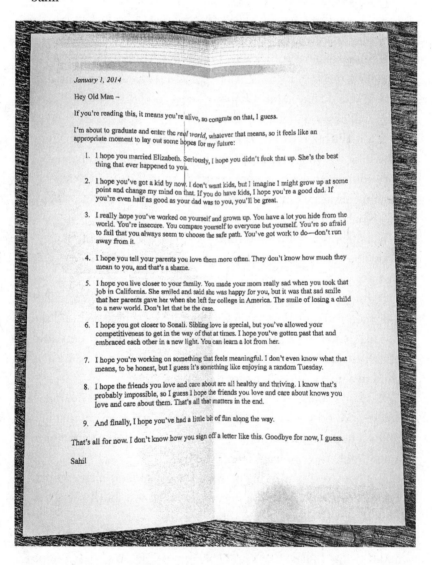

January 1, 2014

Hey Old Man –

If you're reading this, it means you're alive, so congrats on that, I guess.

I'm about to graduate and enter the *real world*, whatever that means, so it feels like an appropriate moment to lay out some hopes for my future:

1. I hope you married Elizabeth. Seriously, I hope you didn't fuck that up. She's the best thing that ever happened to you.

2. I hope you've got a kid by now. I don't want kids, but I imagine I might grow up at some point and change my mind on that. If you do have kids, I hope you're a good dad. If you're even half as good as your dad was to you, you'll be great.

3. I really hope you've worked on yourself and grown up. You have a lot you hide from the world. You're insecure. You compare yourself to everyone but yourself. You're so afraid to fail that you always seem to choose the safe path. You've got work to do—don't run away from it.

4. I hope you tell your parents you love them more often. They don't know how much they mean to you, and that's a shame.

5. I hope you live closer to your family. You made your mom really sad when you took that job in California. She smiled and said she was happy for you, but it was that sad smile that her parents gave her when she left for college in America. The smile of losing a child to a new world. Don't let that be the case.

6. I hope you got closer to Sonali. Sibling love is special, but you've allowed your competitiveness to get in the way of that at times. I hope you've gotten past that and embraced each other in a new light. You can learn a lot from her.

7. I hope you're working on something that feels meaningful. I don't even know what that means, to be honest, but I guess it's something like enjoying a random Tuesday.

8. I hope the friends you love and care about are all healthy and thriving. I know that's probably impossible, so I guess I hope the friends you love and care about knows you love and care about them. That's all that matters in the end.

9. And finally, I hope you've had a little bit of fun along the way.

That's all for now. I don't know how you sign off a letter like this. Goodbye for now, I guess.

Sahil

The raw voice of my younger self coming through the words felt jarring. As I reread the letter, one conclusion screamed off the page:

The answers are within you—you just haven't found the right questions yet.

I was as dumb, arrogant, and insecure as they come when I wrote those words in 2014, but the letter reveals a wisdom and clarity that I had yet to act on. I *knew* there was a brighter path ahead. I just had to start asking the right questions to begin walking it.

This book does not have the answers—you already have them within you.

It will help you ask the right questions.

Before you continue, sit down and write a letter to your future self—ten years from now, five years from now, three years from now, whatever. Reflect on where you are and where you hope to be when you open the letter. Vividly imagine that desired future.

The letter is your true north.

This imagined future is yours to create. You have the answers; it's time to start asking the right questions to turn this imagined future into reality.

Time Wealth

6.

The Big Question

How Many Moments Do You Have Remaining
with Your Loved Ones?

The years go by, as quickly as a wink
Enjoy yourself, enjoy yourself, it's later than you think

—GUY LOMBARDO, "Enjoy Yourself (It's Later Than You Think)"

IN EARLY 2019, ALEXIS Lockhart was living a happy, ordinary life in Houston, Texas. The mother of three boys, ages twenty-three, nineteen, and eleven, she possessed a rare stoic awareness that her time with her sons was fleeting.

"Since they were young, I had been saying that you don't get your children for eighteen years, you get them for about twelve or thirteen, if you're lucky. After they cross that line, you become a chauffeur, a taxi, and a hotel—they need food, a bed, and transportation to events with friends, sports, school activities, and, soon enough, jobs and dates."

It was that awareness that led Alexis to take advantage of every moment—of the precious time she did have with her growing boys. During spring break of that year, she surprised them with a ski trip to Colorado, a trip she called "a huge treat," since her older sons were either working or in school at the time. Reminiscing about the adventure, Alexis broke into a smile. "It was the trip of a lifetime; many memories were made."

A few weeks later, following her mantra of embracing every moment, Lockhart threw a small birthday party for her middle son,

Jackson. "Even though he was 'too old' for cakes and parties, we had a family celebration with presents, a cookie cake, and candles. We celebrated *him*."

Everything was right in her world. Until it wasn't.

On May 23, 2019, the unthinkable happened: Jackson was killed in a tragic motorcycle accident, just days after celebrating his twentieth birthday.

When I received an email from Alexis in April 2024 telling me this story, it stopped me in my tracks. As a new father, I could not even bear to imagine the pain she felt in losing a child. When we spoke later, she shared photos of her boys, pausing on a photo of a four-year-old Jackson and smiling broadly. "I cannot tell you how happy he was as a little kid. He never lost that.

"Always remember," she said, "everyone we love, they are on loan to us for a short period of time. *They are gone in the blink of an eye.*"

IT'S LATER THAN YOU THINK

The American Time Use Survey is a comprehensive national survey conducted annually by the U.S. Bureau of Labor Statistics since 2003. The aim of the survey is to provide information on how people allocate their time across a variety of activities, including paid work, household work, caregiving, active and passive leisure, personal care, and more. It's unique in that it records real-time responses from participants throughout the day, meaning it comes as close as possible to logging how people spend their time—and whom they spend it with—on an average day.

In November 2022, I discovered the dataset[1] and was hit by a tidal wave of emotions.

The discovery came at the right moment: My son was six months old, and becoming a father had changed a lot of things about my life. My relationship with time—specifically, my awareness of the *passage of time*—had fundamentally morphed, from one of naïve ignorance to one of anxious understanding. As a parent, you learn to track and measure time in the weeks and months of your children's lives. You grow so accustomed to reciting their ages in these terms that it becomes second nature.

These markers create a stark awareness of lost time—of the moments *you will never get back.*

For me, the data further illuminated a harsh reality of the fading, ephemeral character of time—that the passage of each week and month brought us closer to the end of a chapter of life that we would never be able to reopen.

There are specific windows—much shorter than you care to imagine or admit—during which certain people and relationships will occupy your life. You may have only one more summer with all of your siblings, two more trips with that old group of friends, a few more years with your wise old aunt, a handful of encounters with that coworker you love, or one more long walk with your parents. If you fail to appreciate or recognize these windows, they will quickly disappear.

Here are the six graphs of the data that everyone needs to see:

TIME SPENT WITH FAMILY

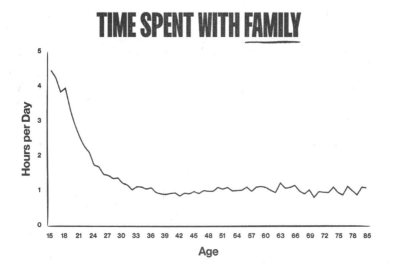

Time spent with your parents and siblings peaks in childhood and declines sharply after you reach age twenty. As you leave home and get caught up in your own life, you often fail to recognize that the time you have remaining with your family is so very limited. Cherish these relationships while you can.

TIME SPENT WITH CHILDREN

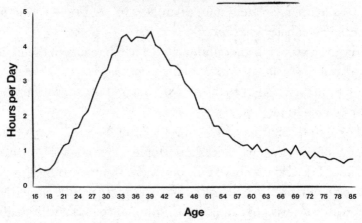

Time spent with your children peaks in the early years of their lives and declines sharply thereafter. There's a devastatingly short window during which you are your child's entire world. Don't blink and miss it.

TIME SPENT WITH FRIENDS

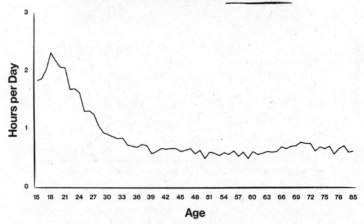

Time spent with your friends peaks when you're eighteen and then declines sharply to a low baseline. In your youth, you spend a lot of time with a lot of friends. As you enter adulthood, you spend a little bit of time with a few close friends. Embrace the breadth of friendships that comes with youth and prioritize the depth of friendships that should come with age.

TIME SPENT WITH PARTNER

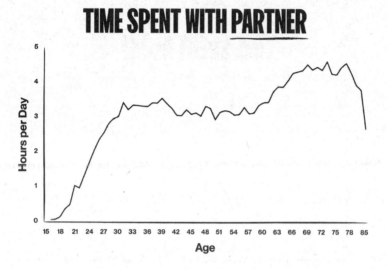

Time spent with your partner trends up until death. The person you choose to confront life's ups and downs with will have the largest impact on your happiness and fulfillment. Choose wisely.

TIME SPENT WITH COWORKERS

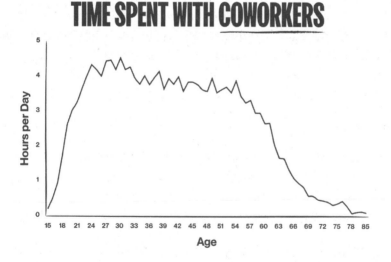

Time spent with coworkers is steady during the traditional prime working years, from age twenty to age sixty, and declines sharply thereafter. Work will pull you away from your family and loved ones throughout your life. If you have the luxury of choice, make sure you choose work—and coworkers—that you find meaningful and important. Aim to have coworkers who create energy in your life.

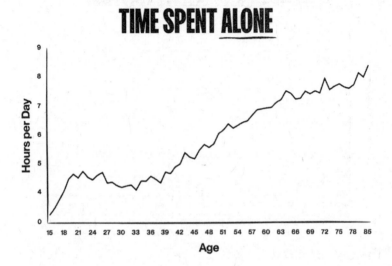

TIME SPENT ALONE

Time spent alone steadily increases throughout your life. When you're young, you tend to view time alone as a sign of not fitting in. You come to fear time alone, to fear boredom. But you need to learn to cherish it. Find happiness and joy in the time you have to yourself—there will be more of it as you get older.

Here are six key lessons for life:

1. Family time is finite—cherish it.
2. Children time is precious—be present.
3. Friend time is limited—prioritize the real friends.
4. Partner time is meaningful—never settle.
5. Coworker time is significant—find energy.
6. Alone time is abundant—love yourself.

It doesn't matter where you're from, how old you are, or whether you're rich or poor—time is a universal truth and struggle.

In 2015, author Tim Urban published a blog post titled "The Tail End" in which he framed time in the context of the limited number of opportunities you'll have to see someone again. His conclusion, which is echoed by the lessons of the American Time Use Survey graphs: "Despite not being at the end of your life, you may very well be nearing the end of your time with some of the most important people in your life."[2]

Writer and philosopher Sam Harris once said, "No matter how many times you do something, there will come a day when you do it for the last time."[3]

There will be a *last time* your kids want you to read them a bedtime story, a *last time* you'll go for a long walk with your sibling, a *last time* you'll hug your parents at a family gathering, a *last time* your friend will call you for support.

How many moments do you really have remaining with your loved ones? It's probably not as many as you'd like to believe. All the tiny moments, people, and experiences that we take for granted will eventually be ones we wish we had more of.

Once you embrace this harsh reality, investing in your Time Wealth means using the **awareness** of time's impermanence to *spark action.* It is building the power to direct your **attention** to the things that truly matter (and ignoring the rest). It is achieving **control** over your time—how you spend it, where you spend it, and whom you spend it with.

Alexis Lockhart had embraced time's reality well before she experienced the unthinkable loss of her son. Allow her closing wisdom to shine a light on your path, as it did on mine:

"I once saw a challenge that said, 'It's your time to shine! You've got the stage, ten thousand people are waiting for you to walk out, you get one sentence. What do you say?' My answer was and still is 'It's later than you think.'"

So it is that we end the chapter where we began, with the lyrics from that poignant song by Guy Lombardo:

Enjoy yourself, enjoy yourself, it's later than you think.

7.

A Brief History of Time

I'll tell you a secret. Something they don't teach you in your
temple. The gods envy us. They envy us because we're mortal,
because any moment might be our last. Everything is more
beautiful because we're doomed. You will never be lovelier
than you are now. We will never be here again.
                                    —ACHILLES, *Troy* (2004 film)

IN ANCIENT ROME, EXTRAVAGANT celebrations were thrown to com-
memorate the military victories of the burgeoning empire. The con-
quering military hero was paraded through streets lined with adoring
citizens on an elaborate golden chariot. This special treatment might
have made the hero feel untouchable, even immortal. Aware of the
human tendency to fall victim to our own pride, the Romans developed a solution to mitigate this immortal sensation: They placed a
person alongside the hero in the chariot whose sole responsibility
was to whisper an ominous warning in the hero's ear throughout the
parade:

Respice post te. Hominem te esse memento. Memento mori!

Translation: "Look behind. Remember thou art mortal. Remember that you must die!"

A continuous, not-so-subtle reminder of the hero's own mortality.

The concept of memento mori is a staple of Stoic philosophy, a
reminder of the certainty and inescapability of death—of time's inevitable victory over man. In recent years, memento mori has gained
a bit of a cult following. The most hardcore use a memento mori
calendar to track the passage of the weeks of life. The calendar is a

large rectangle made up of tiny circles, fifty-two columns wide and eighty rows long. Each circle represents one week of life; each row represents one year. Followers shade in the circles for each week they have lived, and the calendar provides a stark reminder of the time that has passed and the (average) time remaining.

MY LIFE IN WEEKS

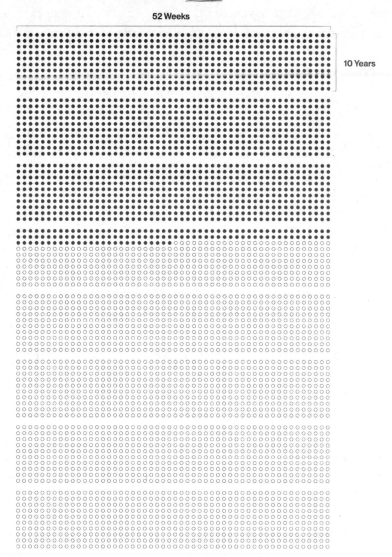

Here is what my memento mori calendar looks like at the time of writing. Gulp!

This may seem dramatic—even morbid—but it's hardly new. For as long as humans have walked the planet, we have wrestled with the nature of time, a journey that has taken us from worship to measurement to understanding and, now, to a modern desire for control.

The earliest human societies came to worship and respect the flow and passage of time. In ancient Indian cultures, time was believed to be a circle, a natural, infinite flow from creation to destruction to rebirth. This "wheel of time" (or *kalachakra*) concept is found across several religious traditions, including Hinduism, Jainism, Sikhism, and Buddhism. The ancient Mayan civilizations of South and Central America had a similar, cyclical view of time. They believed that sunrise represented renewal, and that the journey of the sun through the sky represented the natural cycle of life and death.

Many ancient cultures created gods based on the fear of the passage of time and the desire for longevity and personal extension into infinity. The ancient Egyptians worshipped the god Heh, whose name means "flood," a reference to the watery chaos that they believed preceded the creation of their world. This chaos was understood to be infinite in nature, and the world that followed it was finite, so Heh was viewed as the personification of eternity. In the ancient Zoroastrian tradition, the deity Zurvan was associated with infinite time and space, the creator of the world and all existence. Zurvan was believed to oversee the orderly flow of time and the natural cycle of birth, growth, and death.

The Vikings, known for their physical vitality, often pondered the withering effects of time. Elli was their mythical personification of old age. In a famous tale from Viking folklore, the all-powerful Thor, god of thunder, encounters Elli, an old woman, who challenges him to a wrestling match. Despite the considerable strength difference between the two, Thor is unable to defeat Elli, which is taken as a symbol that old age will eventually triumph over youth. The Vikings believed this was a striking reminder that the passage of time would eventually bring everyone, even the strongest, to their knees.

As human civilization progressed, humanity's relationship with time transitioned from worship to *measurement*—with a focus on tracking and management. The earliest known clocks were sundials used by the ancient Greeks, Romans, and Egyptians. These instruments used the position of the sun to cast a shadow on a marked and labeled surface, indicating the time of day. They were followed by water and sand clocks, which measured time by the water or sand that trickled out of a tiny hole at one end of the device.

In eleventh-century China, a team of engineers developed a towering forty-foot water clock that used falling water and a unique bucket mechanism; when a bucket reached capacity, a lever was tripped, the bucket moved, and the water started to fill the next bucket, providing a reasonably accurate measurement of time.

A major advancement in clock technology occurred in 1927, when a Canadian engineer named Warren Marrison invented the quartz clock. The quartz clock uses the precise vibrations of a quartz crystal hit with an electrical current to track and measure time and remains the most common type of modern clock, over a hundred years later. The atomic clock is the most recent advancement in clock technology—it uses the vibrations of atoms to measure time. Atomic clocks are so accurate that they won't stray by a single second over ten billion years.

As our ability to measure time advanced, a scientific pull to *understand* time developed. Sir Isaac Newton was the leading proponent of an absolute, universal view on time. He believed that time existed independent of any perceiver, that it was fixed and unchanging across the universe, flowed uniformly, and could only be understood mathematically. Newton's absolute view on time—now known as Newtonian time—was central to his formulation of the laws of motion and universal gravitation and remained largely unchallenged until the early-twentieth-century arrival of a German theoretical physicist named Albert Einstein.

Einstein contested the notion of absolute time and proposed the concept of *space-time*. The idea is that space and time are intimately connected, meaning that time is experienced differently by different observers based on their relative motion and position. His groundbreaking theory of relativity implies that time can move more slowly for a person who is in motion relative to a fixed observer. Put differently, if you were to hop on a galactic spaceship and zip around at close to the speed of light and then return to Earth, you would have aged less than anyone who had stayed put. This theory is vividly brought to life in Christopher Nolan's space epic *Interstellar*, in which Matthew McConaughey's character returns from his space voyage to the jarring reality that he is significantly younger than his daughter.

Our journey from worship to measurement to understanding brings us to the present and our modern desire for control. Humans are living longer than ever before; the average life expectancy around the world has steadily increased for the past two hundred years.[4] We have technology and tools, from machines to computers to AI, that make us more efficient with that time than ever before. But despite all this progress—we have more time and an advanced ability to make productive use of it—the control we seek remains elusive.

To understand this unique modern struggle and to construct a solution, we turn to an unlikely source: one of history's most famous children's fantasy novels.

RUNNING FASTER TO STAY IN PLACE

In *Through the Looking-Glass*—Lewis Carroll's dark and ominous sequel to *Alice in Wonderland*—there is a scene in which Alice is running with the Red Queen that offers an important metaphor for our modern struggle with time:

> All she remembers is, that they were running hand in hand, and the Queen went so fast that it was all she could do to keep up with her: and still the Queen kept crying "Faster! Faster!" . . . The most curious part of the thing was, that the trees and the other things round them never changed their places at all: however fast they went, they never seemed to pass anything.

When Alice questions the Red Queen about their lack of forward progress, which appears to defy the laws of physics, the two have a short yet poignant exchange:

"Well, in *our* country," said Alice, still panting a little, "you'd generally get to somewhere else—if you ran very fast for a long time, as we've been doing."

"A slow sort of country!" said the Queen. "Now, *here,* you see, it takes all the running *you* can do, to keep in the same place. If you want to get somewhere else, you must run at least twice as fast as that!"

The Red Queen Effect says that we must run just to stay in place and that we must run even faster if we ever hope to get ahead. The term was introduced by American biologist Leigh Van Valen in 1973 when he formulated the evolutionary biological hypothesis that a species must evolve if it hopes to survive. If a species fails to evolve faster than its predators, competitors, or environment, it will "fall behind," fail to develop the necessary traits to survive and thrive, and become extinct. While the evolutionary biological application is interesting, the Red Queen Effect's application to our modern lives and careers is certainly more relevant to this book (and your life).

If you're reading this book, chances are you're a victim of the Red Queen's paradox—running faster and faster just to stay in the same place.

Rest assured, you're not alone.

During my research process, I heard hundreds of stories from real people who feel the same:

- A mid-forties investment banker who spends most of his time on planes traveling to win new clients and visit existing ones. The lifestyle that was exciting in his twenties and thirties has taken its toll in his forties. "I don't remember the last time I felt *ahead*—every morning, I wake up and feel like I'm somehow already behind and need to sprint to catch up."
- A mid-thirties marketing manager whose teenage dream was to live in New York City. Now that she's there, she finds the constant mad rush overwhelming. She describes her life as a game of Pong, bouncing from emails to meetings to work dinners, rarely finding time for herself. She always answers

"Busy" when people ask how she's doing, and there's no end in sight, she says: "Even my bosses struggle to find time for life."

- An early-twenties medical student who finds herself over-whelmed by constant exams and residency interviews. "My parents wanted me to be a doctor, and I thought I wanted the same, but if this is a sign of what's to come, I'm having second thoughts."
- An early-forties mother of two who was previously an executive in the magazine-publishing industry but decided to put her career on hold to raise her two young children. While she finds motherhood deeply fulfilling, she also describes it as never-ending: "Between the meals, activities, cleaning, and bedtime, I'm always behind, never ahead."
- A late-thirties personal trainer and aspiring content creator who enjoys helping people but can't see a path to scale up his impact, given the fixed nature of his time and commitments. "I'm just feeling trapped, like my time has me in a straitjacket and I'm sinking in the river, but there's no Houdini magic to break free."

One old story puts it this way: When a gazelle wakes up in the morning, it knows it must outrun the lion or be killed, and when a lion wakes up in the morning, it knows it must outrun the gazelle or starve, so whether you're the gazelle or the lion, when the morning comes, you'd better start running. You're definitely running, but just like Alice and the Red Queen, it's unclear whether you're actually getting anywhere.

In the past month, how many times have you said some variation of "Busy!" when asked how you're doing? I'm willing to bet the number is high—probably much higher than you'd like to admit. The problem: You want to take control, but with an old scoreboard entirely focused on Financial Wealth as the measure of your worth, if you're anything other than "Busy!" you're considered a failure. Society assures you that it's okay to feel time-poor as long as it's a by-product of a chase for more money. *Busy* has become standard fare, equal parts reality and pseudo-dystopian status symbol. The invisible hand is silently increasing the speed on your treadmill.

Ironically, that busyness, and the scattered attention it creates, is the very reason you lack control over your time—it is the *maker* of the modern struggle.

Your attention is more divided than ever. Even as you're reading these words on the importance of attention, you're probably feeling the urge to grab your smartphone. The concept of *attention residue* was first identified by University of Washington business professor Sophie Leroy in 2009. In the original paper, Dr. Leroy defines attention residue as "the persistence of cognitive activity about a Task A even though one stopped working on Task A and currently performs a Task B."[5] In other words, there is a cognitive switching cost to shifting your attention from one task to another. When your attention is shifted, there is a residue of it that remains with the prior task and impairs your cognitive performance on the new task. You may think your attention has fully shifted to the new task, but your brain has a lag. That lag has become even more prominent in the modern digital world, where you carry (and wear) multiple devices and tools that constantly pull on your attention with their notifications, beeps, and alluring lights.

It's easy to find examples of this effect in your own life:

* You have back-to-back meetings and find yourself still thinking about the prior meeting in the current one.
* You rush from one kid's activity to another's but can't remember exactly how you got there.
* An email notification pops up and completely derails your focus on the current task.
* You check your phone under your desk during a lecture and find yourself unable to refocus on the professor's words.
* You're having a conversation with a friend or partner, but your mind is on the work email you just received, not on what the other person is saying.

The research indicates that it doesn't seem to matter whether the task switch is macro (that is, moving from one major task to the next) or micro (that is, pausing one major task for a quick check on some minor task). Stopping to check your email or messages is just as bad as jumping from one major project to another. Bestselling author Cal Newport puts it well when he talks about the cultural propensity to "just check" on phone or email notifications: "If, like most, you rarely go more than 10–15 minutes without a *just check,* you have effectively put yourself in a persistent state of self-imposed cognitive handicap. The flip side, of course, is to imagine the relative cognitive enhancement that would follow by minimizing this effect."[6]

The consequences of the modern struggle—of perpetual busyness, digital alerts, and scattered attention—are dire. In *Time Smart,* Ashley Whillans, a researcher and professor at Harvard Business School, notes the steep costs of time poverty on the individual: "The data I and others have amassed show a correlation between time poverty and misery. People who are time poor are less happy, less productive, and more stressed out. They exercise less, eat fattier food, and have a higher incidence of cardiovascular disease."

In a 2009 survey, 75 percent of British parents said they were too busy to read bedtime stories to their children.[7] According to a 2021 report from the email platform Superhuman, 82 percent of knowledge workers check their email within the first thirty minutes of waking up, and 39 percent check within the first five minutes.[8] Eighty-four percent of U.S. executives have canceled a vacation to work.[9] An astounding 80 percent of professionals say they simply don't have time to do everything they want to do.[10] Where children of prior generations were encouraged to explore their curiosity, children of the current generation are told to fill their résumés with every possible after-school activity and hour of faux community service, all in the hope of running just a tiny bit faster than the others sprinting toward the same end.

You have more time than your ancestors but less control over how you spend it. You have more time, but somehow you have less time for the things that truly matter to you.

It takes all the running we can do to keep in the same place.

You're running faster and for longer, but you're not getting anywhere—at least not anywhere worth going.

But there is a solution.

From a scientific perspective, Albert Einstein's theory that time is relative was revolutionary, but from a philosophical perspective, the notion that *not all time is equal* has been around for thousands of years. The ancient Greeks had two different words for time: *chronos* and *kairos*. *Chronos* refers to sequential, quantitative time—the natural sequence and flow of equal parts of time. *Kairos* refers to a more fluctuating, qualitative time—the idea that certain moments are weightier than others, that not all time is the same. *Kairos* brings to life the notion that time does more than simply pass and flow, that it has substance, texture, and weight, but only if we are perceptive enough to recognize it (and capitalize on it). *Kairos* suggests that specific moments have unique properties—that the right action in the right moment can create outsized results and growth.

Case in point: The charts from the previous chapter show that not all time is equal. There are windows and moments of particular importance—*kairos* time—when energy can be invested with the greatest possible return.

This insight is the foundation for the solution to the modern struggle: Identify those moments of greatest time leverage and direct your attention to them.

You don't have to feel behind. You can get ahead.

It's time to stop running faster and start running *smarter.*

8.

The Three Pillars of Time Wealth

DAVE PROUT IS A seasoned video-game industry executive with over twenty years of experience; he has conceived, designed, developed, and launched some of the world's most popular games, such as Call of Duty, Halo, and Medal of Honor. He was born and raised in Seattle, Washington, but, like many children, he left home at age eighteen and never moved back. He built a life in Austin, Texas, a city he grew to love for its space and relatively low cost of living, which made it possible for him to raise his four children the way he desired.

His parents had stayed in Seattle, and given all of the various life commitments that had accumulated, Dave told me he was seeing them only about twice each year. His mother had been diagnosed with cancer in 2020, but he and the rest of the family assumed she would be fine, with the quality of the care she would receive. By early 2022, the treatments had sent the cancer into remission several times, but in each instance, it came back.

In May 2022, with his mother undergoing another round of treatment in Seattle, Dave was scrolling through Twitter when he came across a post I had written on the platform:

"Call your parents more often—they won't be around forever.

When you're young and arrogant, death is a theoretical construct. Realize the people you love won't be there forever. If your parents are 60 and you visit once a year, you may only see them 20 more times in your life."

Upon reading it, Dave thought to himself, *Man, I wonder what that number would be for me.* Realizing the finite nature of the time he had left with them, particularly given his mother's most recent cancer recurrence, he decided he had to make a change.

"I started to travel to see my parents every six weeks the rest of that year. I got in several visits in 2022 that wouldn't have happened if not for seeing that post."

Unfortunately, in January 2023, a team of doctors informed the family that there was nothing more they could do for his mother. Rather than transition into hospice care, she returned to their childhood home to live out whatever time she had remaining. Dave accelerated the cadence of his visits as the family took turns caring for his mother and supporting his father through the end.

On May 28, 2023, Dave Prout's mother passed away peacefully in her home. Tragically and beautifully, the date was his parents' wedding anniversary. A few hours after she passed, Dave went on a long walk to process his sadness. "I noticed what a beautiful spring day it was. I just felt so much gratitude that she was able to pass on her terms, at her home, her family all there, and with the weather as pretty as it was. It was, in a sense, kind of perfect."

Later that day, sharing the sad news on Twitter, Prout referenced my May 2022 post while reflecting on the time that was *created* with his mother through the increased visit frequency:

"Thanks to this thread, I started visiting my parents more often last year. . . . My mom passed away this morning. Thanks to this I visited my mom and dad at least 2x more often than I would have otherwise. Probably 10 visits total. Because of this, I now have a whole set of memories of my mom, not just the tough ones from the last few weeks as she got weaker."

This story offers a perfect introduction to the three core pillars of Time Wealth:

- AWARENESS: An understanding of the finite, impermanent nature of time
- ATTENTION: The ability to direct your attention and focus on the things that matter (and ignore the rest)
- CONTROL: The freedom to own your time and choose exactly how to spend it

The three pillars of Time Wealth—awareness, attention, and control—are individually important, but are best thought of as a progression: awareness first, attention next, control last. Each pillar builds on and is a by-product of the foundation established by the others. From awareness (developing an understanding of the fleeting time remaining) to attention (narrowing the aperture to focus on the things that truly matter) to control (allocating time according to goals and values), Dave Prout cultivated his Time Wealth—and you can too.

As you measure Time Wealth, the three pillars provide a blueprint for the right action to build it. By developing an understanding of these pillars and the high-leverage systems that affect them, you can begin to create the right outcomes.

AWARENESS: TIME AS YOUR MOST PRECIOUS ASSET

Awareness is characterized by the understanding and appreciation of the impermanent, precious nature of time—of its tangible value and importance as an asset. Graham Duncan, an investor and cofounder of East Rock Capital, coined the term *time billionaire* to refer to someone with over one billion seconds remaining in their life. Referring to the concept on an episode of *The Tim Ferriss Show* podcast in 2019, he said, "We're so obsessed, as a culture, with money. And we deify dollar billionaires in a way. . . . And I was thinking of *time billionaires* that when I see twenty-year-olds—the thought I had was they probably have two billion seconds left. But they aren't relating to themselves as *time billionaires*."

When you're young, you're a time billionaire—literally rich with time. At age twenty, you probably have about two billion seconds left (assuming you live to eighty). By fifty, just one billion seconds remain.

When I asked Duncan what sparked the thinking behind the term, he replied that it came to him through the hundreds of interviews he had conducted with young analysts who applied to his firm over the years. "It struck me how they all had this hidden assumption that if they could just make a billion dollars, then they'd be happy. I used to have that assumption too. But then I had the realization that if you went to Warren Buffett and asked him whether he'd trade a billion dollars for a billion seconds, he'd take the time over the money."

Would you trade lives with Warren Buffett? He has a net worth of approximately $130 billion, access to anyone in the world, and spends his days reading and learning. That all sounds great, and yet I'm willing to bet that very few of you would agree to trade lives with him.

Why not? Warren Buffett is, at the time of this writing, ninety-four years old. It doesn't matter how much money, fame, or access he has—you probably wouldn't agree to trade your remaining time for his. On the flip side, as Graham Duncan pointed out, there is a decent chance that Buffett would trade all of his *billions of dollars* to have *your* time.

This brings a paradox to the surface—one I call the paradox of time: You are subconsciously aware of the immense value of your time, but you regularly and consciously take actions that disregard that value. In his *On the Shortness of Life,* Seneca wrote, "We are not given a short life but we make it short, and we are not ill-supplied but wasteful of it." You know how important your time is, yet you ignore its passage and engage in low-value activities that pull you away from the things that really matter.

The goal is to bring to the surface the awareness of the precious nature of the time you do have. Without this awareness, you will never value time enough until suddenly, at the very end, it will become all that you value.

Conscious awareness is a necessary first step, but awareness without attention is incomplete. If you want to change your life, you must change your attention.

ATTENTION: UNLOCKING ASYMMETRIC OUTPUTS

In 1666, when the bubonic plague was devastating London and its surrounding cities, forcing universities to shut their doors and send students home, a twenty-three-year-old at Trinity College at the University of Cambridge fled to his small village fifty miles away. Just as in the early months of our COVID-19 pandemic, young students were forced by unfortunate circumstances to pause their lives and enter a state of lockdown.

But rather than wallow away while in isolation, this particular bright young man ran with the forced constraint and spent the year in a perpetual state of creative and intellectual flow. Despite the absence of formal educational requirements, he immersed himself in his books, studies, and experiments, pursuing his curiosities with intense focus and fervor.

During the single year of his confinement, the young student made groundbreaking discoveries in fields across science and mathematics, among them:

* Developing the initial principles of calculus
* Formulating the law of universal gravitation
* Defining the three fundamental laws of motion
* Laying the foundation for the understanding of the behavior of light
* Designing a reflecting telescope

The young student was Isaac Newton, and 1666 became known as his annus mirabilis (Latin for "miracle year"), a nod to the breadth and depth of his output over such a short period. In a single year, he had produced the output of several incredible lifetimes.

Attention is defined as the state or act of applying the mind to something. This application of mental energy is how we create progress. Your choice of how and when to deploy your limited attention determines the quality of your outcomes.

The climactic final scene in Pixar's classic animated film *Toy Story* offers a useful analogy to bring this to life.

The two protagonists, Woody and Buzz Lightyear, are attempting to light a small rocket to propel them back to safety, but their match flames out. Woody looks up at the sun and has an idea: He grabs Buzz and angles his glass helmet toward the sky—creating a makeshift magnifying glass—and directs the concentrated beam of the sun's energy onto the fuse of the rocket. It bursts into flame and the two are successfully launched toward a happy ending to the epic adventure.

While the movie might have been intended for children, the underlying insight is important: The focused, concentrated energy of the sun through the helmet magnifying glass was significantly more powerful than its scattered, unconcentrated energy.

The same insight applies to your attention: Focused, concentrated attention is significantly more powerful than scattered, unconcentrated attention.

Outcomes follow attention. Scattered attention leads to random, ordinary outcomes; concentrated attention leads to focused, extraordinary outcomes. We see a perfect example in the story of a young Isaac Newton: Deep, intense, deliberate attention deployed in a short, unique window of time (a distraction-free plague-lockdown environment) created astonishing outcomes.

In an average environment, output is fixed to input: One unit of input creates one unit of output. If you want to create two units of output, you need to generate two units of input. This fixed relationship keeps you busy, scattered, and trapped—you're running faster and faster but never achieving the ten or one hundred units of output that would constitute getting somewhere.

Using our *Toy Story* analogy, the sun can shine for hours on the rocket fuse, but it will never set it alight. The fixed relationship of the unit of input from the sun and the corresponding unit of output of heat on the fuse is insufficient to create the desired end state. The magnifying glass changes the game; it concentrates the energy from the sun so the same single unit of input creates one hundred units of output of heat on the fuse. The fixed relationship is broken to unlock asymmetric output and achieve the desired end state (the lit fuse).

Sir Isaac Newton, Lionel Messi, and Warren Buffett became famous because they directed their attention to a limited number of moments and opportunities to consistently create one-thousand-plus units of output per unit of input.

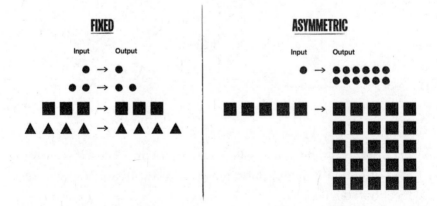

In the context of your life, concentrated attention is the dedicated, deep focus on the high-leverage projects, opportunities, people, and moments that truly matter. Attention is what allows you to get ahead, to stop running faster (more units of input) and start running smarter (higher output per unit of input). It requires appropriate project selection and rejection—saying yes to a few high-leverage things and no to everything else.

Attention needs to be directed, managed, and harnessed.

As attention is deployed efficiently and effectively into the key moments or opportunities of import—the *kairos* time—you break the fixed relationship between inputs and outputs in your life. You put in the same input but generate significantly more output—the same amount of effort yields dramatically improved results. With this fundamental shift, time morphs from a fixed asset that you must *take* to a dynamic asset that you can *make*.

Time enters the realm of your control.

CONTROL: THE ULTIMATE GOAL

Cassie Holmes, a professor of marketing and behavioral decision making at UCLA Anderson School of Management and author of *Happier Hour,* has done extensive research on the impact of free time on happiness. In a 2021 paper in the *Journal of Personality and Social Psychology* that reviewed two large-scale datasets of 35,375 Americans, Dr. Holmes and her coauthors found that the relationship between free time and happiness follows an inverse U-shape—meaning that both too little and too much free time lead to unhappiness.

The lesson: Each of us has a Goldilocks level of free time, the level that is *just right.*

Control places you in the driver's seat to identify this level and live in line with it. Control is the desired end state—the ability to choose what you do and when you do it. You own your time, and you make your own decisions on how to allocate it. Without control, your time is not yours. Other people own it, literally or figuratively. You are a *time taker*—time is given to you along with a specific set of instructions to follow. Control turns you into a *time maker*—you dictate the time you have and how you will allocate it. Awareness and attention create the conditions to shift your stance from *taker* to *maker.*

Consider an example of how this works:

- Previously, to create ten units of output (the necessary output to fulfill your responsibilities), you had to generate ten units of input (a 1:1 ratio).
- With improved awareness and concentrated attention directed to the most important projects, high-leverage opportunities, and moments, let's assume the ten units of output can be created with just five units of input (a 2:1 ratio).
- With this improved ratio, the remaining five units of unused input represent created time that can be freely allocated according to your values and goals. You can use that time to create more professional output or allocate it to a different arena of your choice. You are in control.

The freedom to allocate time according to your preferences—to choose how you spend it, where you spend it, and whom you spend it with—is the ultimate goal. This is the desired end state of true control over your time.

———

With an understanding of these three pillars of Time Wealth, we can move to the Time Wealth Guide, which provides you with the specific tools and systems to build upon these pillars and cultivate a life of abundance.

9.

The Time Wealth Guide

Systems for Success

THE TIME WEALTH GUIDE that follows provides specific, high-leverage systems to build each of the pillars of Time Wealth. The systems are supported by clear research and are battle-tested through my own personal experience, which I share throughout. This isn't one-size-fits-all and you shouldn't feel compelled to read every single one; browse through and select those that feel most relevant and useful to you. Everyone enters at a different starting point, and the guides at the end of each section should allow you to "create your own adventure" as you progress through the book.

As you consider and execute the systems for success provided in the guide, use your responses to each Time Wealth statement from the Wealth Score quiz to narrow your focus to the areas where you need to make the most progress (those where you responded *strongly disagree, disagree,* or *neutral*).

1. I have a deep awareness of the finite, impermanent nature of my time and its importance as my most precious asset.
2. I have a clear understanding of the two to three most important priorities in my personal and professional lives.

3. I am able to consistently direct attention and focus to the important priorities that I have identified.
4. I rarely feel too busy or scattered to spend time on the most important priorities.
5. I am in control of my calendar and priorities.

A few common Time Wealth anti-goals to avoid on your journey:

* Spending too much of my time on low-value, energy-draining activities
* Being so busy that I'm unable to prioritize time with the people who truly matter
* Losing the spontaneity in my life as I pursue my most important priorities

Here are twelve proven systems for building Time Wealth.

The Time Wealth Hard Reset

PILLAR: Awareness

My entire life changed when I confronted the mathematical reality of the amount of time I had remaining with the people I loved most. It was a hard reset for my life—an emotionally challenging yet necessary intervention that sparked new awareness and priorities.

I want you to confront the same reality by completing this simple exercise:

Start by writing down the name of a friend or family member you love deeply but don't see enough. Approximate the number of times per year that you see that person. Write that number down.

Next, write down your age and the other person's age. Subtract the older person's age from eighty.* This is the approximate number of years you have remaining with this person.

Now, do some basic math: Multiply the number of times you see that person per year by the number of years you have remaining with that person. With some terrifyingly simple math, you've determined the number of times you will see your loved one before the end.

Here's an example of the math I confronted in my own hard reset in 2021:

- I saw my father about once a year while we were living three thousand miles apart.
- He was sixty-five years old at the time. Subtracting that from eighty, I got fifteen.
- Multiplying fifteen by the number of times I saw him per year, I concluded that I would see him fifteen more times before he was gone.

* Note: Eighty is a rough approximation for the life expectancy of an adult. If you or the other person is over eighty or if you feel optimistic, use one hundred as the reference number.

TIME WEALTH HARD RESET

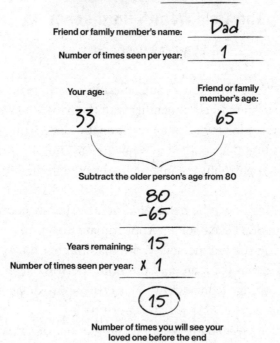

Friend or family member's name: _Dad_

Number of times seen per year: _1_

Your age: **33**

Friend or family member's age: **65**

Subtract the older person's age from 80

$$80$$
$$-65$$

Years remaining: **15**

Number of times seen per year: X **1**

(15)

Number of times you will see your
loved one before the end

It's important to note that not all of these numbers are fixed—
some are within your control. When my wife and I moved across the
country to be closer to our parents after this hard reset, the number
of times I would see my father again before the end expanded from
fifteen into the hundreds.

One action—moving—literally created time with our loved ones.

It was a drastic but necessary move in our lives. The changes you
make may not need to be as significant; some people need to see this
math in order to prioritize regular lunch dates with their friends,
more walks with their siblings, or annual reunions with family. The
point is simple: Once you see this math, you'll be inspired to *create
more time* with those you love most.

Repeat the exercise for as many loved ones as you see fit. It will
serve as your hard reset—the intervention that will spark new awareness and priorities.

How to Establish Your Baseline:
The Energy Calendar
PILLARS: Awareness and Attention

Before you can harness your attention, you need to develop an awareness of how you're spending your time relative to how you should be spending it.

There are two challenging problems here:

1. Establishing a baseline of how you're spending your time
2. Identifying what should be prioritized, delegated, or deleted in a jam-packed schedule

To solve these problems, use the Energy Calendar.

For one week, at the end of every weekday, go through your calendar and color-code each event from the day that just finished:

* GREEN: Energy-creating—these activities left you feeling energized.
* YELLOW: Neutral—these activities left you feeling neutral.
* RED: Energy-draining—these activities left you feeling drained.

Avoid overthinking the color-coding; trust your gut instinct on how you felt after the activity.

At the end of the week, zoom out, look at your calendar, and ask yourself a few questions:

1. What are your common energy-creating (green) activities?
2. What are your common neutral (yellow) activities?
3. What are your common energy-draining (red) activities?

Based on the answers, you can formulate an action plan for your time:

- **ENERGY-CREATING ACTIVITIES SHOULD BE PRIORITIZED AND AMPLIFIED.** How can you spend more time on these activities in future?
- **NEUTRAL ACTIVITIES SHOULD BE MAINTAINED OR DELEGATED.** How can you slowly work to outsource or delegate some of these neutral activities to free up your time for more energy-creating activities?
- **ENERGY-DRAINING ACTIVITIES SHOULD BE DELEGATED, DELETED, OR ADJUSTED.** How can you slowly work to outsource, delegate, or delete some of these energy-draining activities? Are there ways to make subtle adjustments to these energy-draining activities that would move them up to neutral (for example, shifting from an energy-draining video call to a neutral walking call)?

The Energy Calendar is designed to give you a view of your baseline time and energy outlay to spark the necessary questions to improve on the current baseline. The goal is not to eliminate all neutral and energy-draining activities (most likely an impossible pursuit) but to slowly improve on your energy-creating-to-energy-draining ratio (green-to-red ratio).

How to Establish Priorities: The Two-List Exercise

PILLARS: Awareness and Attention

The two-list exercise originated from a fabled conversation between Warren Buffett and his personal pilot Mike Flint. One day, Flint was bemoaning his lack of clarity around his personal and professional aspirations and goals, and Buffett asked him to go through a three-step process that would help.

First, Buffett told Flint to write down twenty-five career goals, all the things he wanted to focus on and accomplish in the months and years ahead. Next, he asked Flint to circle the top-five goals from the list. This required some effort to narrow down, as Flint cared about all of them. Eventually, Flint was able to circle his top five. Finally, Buffett told Flint to separate it into two lists. He asked Flint what he would do with the non-circled items. Flint replied that he would work on those whenever he had free time. Buffett shook his head and replied that everything Flint hadn't circled should become his Avoid at All Costs List. These items should get no attention until success was achieved with the top five.

The point: The most important items had been highlighted; everything else was simply a distraction threatening to derail Flint's progress.

Every successful person will give you some variation of the same advice: Focus on the most important things. But how do you identify what those things are? How do you identify the projects, opportunities, and goals you should be focusing your attention on? What are the two to three areas that have the potential to drive the asymmetric rewards in your personal and professional spheres?

Use the two-list strategy to identify the most important things and harness your attention:

1. MAKE A LIST: Create a comprehensive list of your top professional priorities. Repeat this for your top personal priorities.

2. NARROW THE LIST: Go through the professional priority list and circle the top three to five items. These should be the absolute top priorities in your professional life, the items that will have the greatest impact on your trajectory—the long-term value drivers. These are the items that truly matter. Repeat this process for your personal priority list.

3. SPLIT THE LISTS: On a fresh sheet of paper, write down the circled three to five priorities on the left side and all the remaining priorities on the right side. Label the left side of the sheet *Priorities* and the right side of the sheet *Avoid at All Costs*. Repeat this process for your personal list.

To bring this practice to life, here is a visual example of the process:

MAKE A LIST

PROFESSIONAL PRIORITIES

1. Revamp corporate website and social platforms.
2. Learn a new language to expand opportunities.
3. Identify software to increase efficiency.
4. Pursue further education, e.g. master's degree.
5. Seek mentorship to learn from experienced professionals.
6. Serve on boards or committees to bolster my résumé.
7. Become an expert in the M&A process.
8. Establish a mentorship program in our organization.
9. Launch a groundbreaking product or service.
10. Develop public-speaking skills to increase self-confidence.
11. Create a flexible work schedule to accommodate personal life.
12. Enroll in conflict-resolution training.
13. Design a robust employee-evaluation program.
14. Establish beneficial partnerships with other businesses.
15. Contribute to retirement accounts regularly.
16. Secure a position with more international responsibilities.
17. Increase annual income or salary by upwards of 40 percent.
18. Implement remote work options for my team.

19. **Enhance negotiation skills for business deals.**

20. **Increase the strength of my network.**

NARROW THE LIST

PROFESSIONAL PRIORITIES

1. Revamp corporate website and social platforms.

2. Learn a new language to expand opportunities.

3. Identify software to increase efficiency.

4. Pursue further education, e.g. master's degree.

5. **Seek mentorship to learn from experienced professionals.**

6. Serve on boards or committees to bolster my résumé.

7. Become an expert in the M&A process.

8. Establish a mentorship program in our organization.

9. **Launch a groundbreaking product or service.**

10. **Develop public-speaking skills to increase self-confidence.**

11. **Create a flexible work schedule to accommodate personal life.**

12. Enroll in conflict-resolution training.

13. Design a robust employee-evaluation program.

14. Establish beneficial partnerships with other businesses.

15. Contribute to retirement accounts regularly.

16. Secure a position with more international responsibilities.

17. Increase annual income or salary by upwards of 40 percent.

18. Implement remote work options for my team.

19. Enhance negotiation skills for business deals.

20. **Increase the strength of my network.**

SPLIT THE LISTS

PRIORITIES

1. **Seek mentorship to learn from experienced professionals.**

2. **Launch a groundbreaking product or service.**

3. **Develop public-speaking skills to increase self-confidence.**

4. **Create a flexible work schedule to accommodate personal life.**

5. **Increase the strength of my network.**

AVOID AT ALL COSTS

1. Revamp corporate website and social platforms.

2. Learn a new language to expand opportunities.

3. Identify software to increase efficiency.

4. Pursue further education, e.g. master's degree.

5. ~~Seek mentorship to learn from experienced professionals.~~

6. Serve on boards or committees to bolster my résumé.

7. Become an expert in the M&A process.

8. Establish a mentorship program in our organization.

9. ~~Launch a groundbreaking product or service.~~

10. ~~Develop public-speaking skills to increase self-confidence.~~

11. ~~Create a flexible work schedule to accommodate personal life.~~

12. Enroll in conflict-resolution training.

13. Design a robust employee-evaluation program.

14. Establish beneficial partnerships with other businesses.

15. Contribute to retirement accounts regularly.

16. Secure a position with more international responsibilities.

17. Increase annual income or salary by upwards of 40 percent.

18. Implement remote work options for my team.

19. Enhance negotiation skills for business deals.

20. ~~Increase the strength of my network.~~

By separating the lists into *Priorities* and *Avoid at All Costs*, we create a very clear line that separates what we will focus on from what we will delegate or delete.

Consider this your first line of defense: When new opportunities arise, refer to your two-list exercise and make a quick assessment of whether it falls into the category of one of your priorities or if it should be avoided at all costs.

Use the two-list exercise to harness your attention and begin to break the fixed relationship between inputs and outputs.

How to Manage Priorities: The Eisenhower Matrix

PILLARS: Awareness and Attention

President Dwight D. Eisenhower was an American military officer and politician born in Denison, Texas, in 1890.

His list of accomplishments is long:

* A West Point graduate, he rose through the ranks of the military to become a five-star general in the U.S. Army.
* During World War II, he served as supreme commander of the Allied Expeditionary Force in Europe and orchestrated the famed invasion of Normandy on D-Day.
* Eisenhower served as president of Columbia University and as the first supreme commander of NATO before being elected as the thirty-fourth president of the United States, a position he occupied from 1953 to 1961.

As his military and civilian accomplishments indicate, Eisenhower was a highly effective leader and executive. He became known for his prolific, almost superhuman productivity. His secret: He never confused the urgent with the important, as evidenced by a quote that is widely attributed to him: "What is important is seldom urgent and what is urgent is seldom important."

We can define the *urgent* and *important* as follows:

* Urgent: A task that requires prompt attention
* Important: A task that advances your long-term values or goals

The Eisenhower Matrix is a productivity tool formulated by author Stephen Covey in his bestselling book *The 7 Habits of Highly Effective People* that forces you to differentiate between the urgent and the important to prioritize and manage your time more effectively. While the two-list exercise helps you narrow your attention on a macro level, the Eisenhower Matrix is designed to harness your attention on a micro, daily level.

EISENHOWER MATRIX

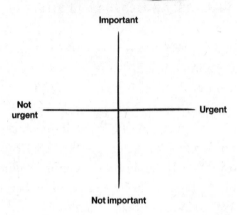

The two-by-two matrix requires you to categorize your tasks into one of four quadrants:

- **IMPORTANT AND URGENT:** These are tasks that require immediate, focused attention but also contribute to your long-term mission or goals. These are *Do now!* tasks. Goal: In the short term, you want to handle these immediately, but in the long term, you want to manage the important tasks so that they rarely become urgent.
- **IMPORTANT AND NOT URGENT:** These tasks are your compounders—they build long-term value in your life. These are the projects and opportunities that you want to dedicate focused attention toward. Goal: Spend more time on these tasks—plan the time to do deep work here. In the long term, this is where you should try to spend most of your time and energy.
- **NOT IMPORTANT AND URGENT:** These tasks are the *Beware* category—they can drain time and energy without contributing to your long-term goals or vision. These are Delegate tasks. Goal: Spend less time here and slowly try to build sys-

tems that allow you to delegate these tasks to people for whom they will be important.

- NOT IMPORTANT AND NOT URGENT: These are the time-wasting tasks and activities that drain your energy and sap your productivity. These are *Delete* tasks. Goal: Spend less time here.

EISENHOWER MATRIX

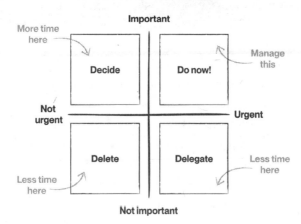

The Eisenhower Matrix creates a visual awareness of the types of tasks on which you are spending your time. This awareness allows you to adjust course as necessary in order to spend most of your time on the important, long-term projects and opportunities.

To summarize the three key Eisenhower Matrix goals:

1. Manage the top right.
2. Spend most of your time in the top left.
3. Spend less time in the bottom half.

I have never found a single productivity tool that is more useful than the Eisenhower Matrix when it comes to creating time awareness and directing my attention. I find myself turning to it regularly, especially when I have a lot on my plate and need to reset my focus.

How to Simplify Your To-Do System:
The Index Card

PILLAR: Attention

You can test every fancy productivity system in the world, or you can use the simple strategy that works for junior analysts and billionaires alike: an index card.

Marc Andreessen, the successful technology founder and investor, is a proponent of this simple strategy. In an essay on his personal productivity, he wrote, "Each night before you go to bed, prepare a 3 x 5 index card with a short list of 3 to 5 things that you will do the next day."[11] Ideally, this is a list of important tasks that directly contribute to your long-term values or goals (items identified in the top half of the Eisenhower Matrix). Avoid writing down all the miscellaneous urgent and unimportant to-do items.

TODAY   **3/21**

- ① ~~Finish 3 Pillars~~
- ① Purpose Dharma
- ① Audio Recordings
- ① Financial Bio Q
- ① _____
- ① _____
- ① _____
- ① _____
- ① _____
- ① _____

In the morning, start at the top of the list and work your way down, crossing off the important items as you get through them. Your goal is to cross each item off the list by the end of the day. If that is all you accomplish, the day was a win, because these were the three to five truly important tasks that furthered your values or long-term goals.

We tend to overestimate what we can accomplish in a day, so be intentionally conservative in the number of items you list. As a rule of thumb, it should be three unless there is a very specific reason for it to be more.

The fanciest productivity systems often require a lot of thinking and maintenance. If you're spending time thinking about your productivity system, you're focusing on movement over progress. The simple index card strategy harnesses the core principles of focus and momentum to allow you to get more of what matters done.

Always remember: Simple is beautiful.

How to Eliminate Time Waste: Parkinson's Law

PILLAR: Attention

Parkinson's law is the idea that work expands to fill the time allotted for its completion. It was formulated by British author Cyril Northcote Parkinson in a satirical essay in *The Economist* in 1955. While his piece was intended as a humorous critique of bureaucratic inefficiency, the principle is applicable to a range of situations, from personal time management to large-scale projects.

The generalized insight rings true:

- Have all day to process email and you end up emailing for the entire day. Have thirty minutes to process email and you crank through your entire inbox in a flash.
- Have months to complete an assignment and you procrastinate enough for the assignment to take months. Have two days to complete an assignment and you work efficiently and get it done.

Open time frames lead to a lot of movement and very little progress—the rocking-horse phenomenon of busywork culture. We tend to be more efficient and productive when constraints come into play. We also tend to focus on the *important* when pressed for time.

You can leverage Parkinson's law to be more efficient and effective in your professional and personal life:

- Establish time blocks that are shorter than you're comfortable with for low-importance but necessary tasks. Use this artificial pressure to avoid procrastination and free up time for important, high-value tasks.
- Batch-process email in one to three short, time-constrained windows. If you allow yourself to check your email throughout the day, you'll be plagued by attention residue and never get

through your work. Condense the processing into short windows to become more efficient and avoid the negative cognitive impact of task-switching.

- Shorten standard meetings to twenty-five minutes. The tighter window makes participants more efficient (avoids "How about the weather" small talk) and gives you a five-minute break to reset in between meetings.
- Work on big projects in one- to three-hour focus blocks. Get a simple focus app on your computer or phone and set the timer. Start at sixty minutes and work your way up. The time constraint will make you more efficient, and the breaks in between will reset your mental energy.
- Batch dreaded personal tasks (tidying up, laundry, dishes, et cetera) into short, dedicated windows. Focusing on those tasks in sprints is more effective than lingering on them for extended jogs.

I leverage Parkinson's law in the structure of my calendar to concentrate in short sprints of energy on my priority projects. The first three hours of my day—from five A.M. to eight A.M.—are always dedicated to my most important creative project (right now, this book!). The forced constraint of time-bound blocks generates an intensity that meaningfully improves my output quantity and quality.

When you establish long fixed hours to do your work, you find unproductive ways to fill it—you work longer but get less done. The better way, to paraphrase entrepreneur Naval Ravikant, is to work like a lion: Sprint, rest, repeat.

Leverage Parkinson's law to become a more efficient, focused, and healthy professional.

How to Stop Procrastinating:
The Anti-Procrastination System

PILLAR: Attention

Procrastination is defined as the action of postponing or delaying something. Ancient Greek philosophers called it *akrasia*—acting against your better judgment. You procrastinate when it's easier to delegate a task to your future self. The proclivity to procrastinate is literally hardwired into our DNA. We value immediate pleasure even if we know that it isn't what's best for us in the long term. Unfortunately, procrastination is a growth limiter—it holds you back from your potential—so you need a system to fight against it.

The anti-procrastination system involves three core steps:

1. Deconstruction
2. Plan and stake creation
3. Action

STEP 1: DECONSTRUCTION
Procrastination is often a direct by-product of intimidation. In a TED Talk that has been viewed over seventy million times, author Tim Urban used the example of a senior thesis to illustrate this point. If you define the project as "write my one-hundred-page thesis," you're already pre-wired for procrastination.

To the procrastinator, large, long-term projects are a big, scary black box. Your imagination fills that box with endless complexity and horrors. The whole is too intimidating, so you push it out to your future self.

Deconstruct the big and scary project into small and individually manageable tasks.

In the example of the senior thesis, the tasks might be:

- Construct a note-taking system.
- Gather important pieces of research.
- Annotate key pieces of research.
- Craft the thesis outline.
- Draft the thesis.
- Edit and complete the thesis.

The goal here is a simple mental conversion from big and intimidating to small and manageable.

STEP 2: PLAN AND STAKE CREATION

Next, you need to develop a plan of attack to check off the deconstructed-task list.

The plan for each micro task should be

- SPECIFIC: Exactly what you'll do
- TIME-BOUND: When you'll do it

When setting time bounds, lean toward being less ambitious on the micro scale. Give yourself easy wins early on with achievable time bounds.

Create a project document:

- Write down the specific tasks under each major deconstructed pillar of the project.
- Write down your timeline for each task.

Create stakes to drive better outcomes:

- PUBLIC DECLARATION: State your process intentions publicly. Put it on social media, post it on LinkedIn, tell a bunch of friends at a dinner. No one wants to break their word.
- SOCIAL PRESSURE: Make a plan to meet a friend somewhere to do the initial work. Schedule a time and place to meet and

decide exactly what work you're going to be tackling while you
are there.

- **REWARD:** Plan a reward if you do what you're supposed to.
  Allow yourself to have a nice walk, a coffee break, or dinner
  with friends.
- **PENALTY:** Plan a penalty if you don't do what you're supposed to.

Use stakes to gamify big projects. It can be very effective.

STEP 3: ACTION

Action is often the hardest part. Specifically, the first action—the
first motion. To create initial movement, you can try the following:

- **PLAN A SYNC SESSION:** Similar to the social-pressure stake
  above, meet a friend for the initial movement.
- **REWARD INITIAL MOVEMENT:** Attach a small reward to completing the initial movement (for example, a walk outside).
- **USE THE LION TECHNIQUE:** Commit to a single short (thirty-
  minute) sprint followed by luxurious rest.

The hardest part is getting started. Give yourself a quick win. Big
wins are simply the result of consistent small wins.

PUTTING IT ALL TOGETHER

The three steps of the anti-procrastination system:

1. **DECONSTRUCTION:** Deconstruct the big, scary project into
   small, manageable tasks.
2. **PLAN AND STAKE CREATION:** Create a project document with
   specific, time-bound tasks. Create stakes to gamify their completion.
3. **ACTION:** A body in motion tends to stay in motion. Create systems that spark initial movement. Engineer small wins (they
   become big wins over time).

This is the exact system that I used to break through my own struggles with procrastination in writing this book. I deconstructed the project into sections and then further into chapters, which reduced the up-front intimidation and made the undertaking feel more manageable. I created a project document with deadlines and established micro-rewards (usually allowing myself to buy something if I hit each deadline). Finally, I took daily action, writing every single morning immediately after waking up. The movement on the big project to start the day engineered a small daily win that built momentum as the days, weeks, and months progressed.

The entire anti-procrastination system is intended to be dynamic and iterative. As you work through your big projects, be sure to constantly assess and tweak your plan and process. Find new ways to raise the stakes and get moving. It's not perfect, but this system will help you burst through the walls of procrastination. The pages you're currently reading are a case in point!

How to Concentrate Attention:
The Flow State Boot-Up Sequence

PILLAR: Attention

In his bestselling book *Deep Work,* Cal Newport pushes the importance of focused, uninterrupted, undistracted work on the most important priorities as the only way to grow and thrive in the modern economy. In Newport's words, "The Deep Work Hypothesis: The ability to perform deep work is becoming increasingly rare at exactly the same time it is becoming increasingly valuable in our economy. As a consequence, the few who cultivate this skill, and then make it the core of their working life, will thrive."

The ability to concentrate your attention and engage this deep focus—a flow state—is essential to Time Wealth, as it enables you to break the fixed relationship between inputs and outputs. Deep-focused blocks of work won't be easy to execute at first. You're forcibly overriding a lot of the natural dopamine-reward response that all these apps, digital tools, and social platforms were built on.

You'll build your focus muscle progressively:

- Start with thirty minutes, once per day.
- Work your way up to one hour two to three times per day by the end of the first month.
- From there, extend the periods to two hours (my personal maximum) or four hours (an ambitious target) as your focus muscle strengthens.

Once your flow windows are planned, you need an approach for entering the deep-focused state necessary for high-quality work. When you power up a computer and stare impatiently at the screen, the computer is doing something very important: It's running a boot-up sequence. The boot-up sequence is simply a fixed set of operations that the computer performs when it is switched on to initiate and prepare the operating system for use. This sequence ensures that the operating system is engaged appropriately and ready for the onslaught of task processing that the user will put it through during the upcoming session. You are no different than this computer—to flow optimally as you process important tasks, you need to prime and prepare your operating system.

You need a personal boot-up sequence.

The personal boot-up sequence is a fixed set of actions and environmental cues that mentally and physically mark the start of a focus-block session. While it can technically be used for any work session, I find it particularly valuable in priming for a focus block. The sequence becomes a doorway to the flow that you need to enter. An effective, repeatable sequence will allow you to enter your flow state and execute deep, focused work on your most important projects quickly and consistently.

The sequence can be built around the five core senses:

1. TOUCH: What movement/body action you engaged in prior to start
2. TASTE: What you're drinking, chewing, or snacking on
3. SIGHT: What you see in your environment
4. SOUND: What you hear in your environment
5. SMELL: What you smell in your environment

Using this simple framing, I built a personal boot-up sequence that looks like this:

1. TOUCH: Prior to sitting down for a deep work session, I either go for a five-minute walk outside or take a three-minute cold plunge. Both actions unlock my creative energy and prime my system.
2. TASTE: I always have a black cold-brew coffee that I sip on prior to the start of the session and keep next to me during the session. The caffeine helps, but it's mostly psychological, as I rarely finish the drink.

3. SIGHT: My writing desk faces a window with dark walls on either side, some plants, and neutral art.
4. SOUND: I listen to a Spotify playlist called Classical Essentials.
5. SMELL: I love the smell of wood, so my writing nook has cedarwood/sandalwood candles or oils.

I typically go through this sequence twice each day, once first thing in the morning (around 5 A.M.) when I start my first deep creative session and once in the afternoon after lunch (around 12:30 P.M.) when I start my second deep work session. Going through this sequence has become an incredibly effective routine that gets me into the appropriate state to enter my flow.

To build your sequence, sit down and walk through each of the five senses. For each sense, think about a time when you were truly in flow. How was that sense engaged during (or before) that session? Write down the different ways these senses were engaged in prior periods of flow to give you an idea of the range of options at your disposal. Select the option for each sense that is most actionable and repeatable. If you were in a flow state while sitting at a café overlooking the Mediterranean in Positano, Italy, and sipping a twenty-euro espresso, that's probably not repeatable (if it is, please trade lives with me!). If you were in a flow state while sitting at your local coffee shop and listening to your favorite house track, that's probably quite repeatable.

Once you've established your actionable, repeatable options for each of the five senses, write down your full personal boot-up sequence. Until it becomes a habit, check the items off the list as you boot up for a deep-work session.

How to Create Time Leverage:
Effective Delegation

PILLARS: Attention and Control

The Eisenhower Matrix encourages you to delegate specific tasks to people for whom they will be important. But effective delegation is not a subject on any standard school curriculum, so most people have no idea how to do it. Use this guide to get started on your delegation journey.

There are three core principles of effective delegation:

1. APPROPRIATE TASK PROFILING: Profile tasks for delegation according to their risk and reversibility. Delegate low-risk, high-reversibility tasks that require minimal oversight, and delegate high-risk, low-reversibility tasks that need significant oversight. For example, calendar management is generally low risk and reversible, so it can be delegated with minimal oversight, while key customer communication is high risk and not reversible, so it should be delegated with significant oversight. Clear task profiling prior to delegation is essential for effective expectation setting and feedback.

2. CLEAR EXPECTATIONS: Establish clear expectations for every task's completion, including deliverables, timeline, anticipated feedback loops, and risk profile. For example, asking someone to "do the customer report" is significantly less effective than asking someone to "create the customer report by Tuesday afternoon for the executive team to review before presenting the highlights in a meeting with the board of directors on Wednesday." The former is vague and ambiguous; the latter provides the clarity of timeline, importance, and use that makes the likelihood of a quality output much higher. Always ask the person to whom you delegate the task to repeat back

the expectations in their own words to confirm mutual understanding prior to proceeding.

3. INFINITE FEEDBACK LOOPS: The most effective delegation involves constant, iterative feedback loops such that the participants get smarter and better as information is gathered. The
   participants collaborate on what went well, what was missing,
   and how the entire process can be improved. Establish a clear
   cadence for oversight, feedback, and adjustments, be it a daily,
   weekly, or monthly check-in, depending on the task.

By leveraging the three core principles, you can work your way up
from a base level to a top level of delegation. The three levels may
appear as follows:

- BASE LEVEL: Direct delegation system in which participants
  are given exact instructions for task completion, monitored
  closely, given feedback on set schedules, and iterate accordingly.
- MIDDLE LEVEL: Semiautonomous delegation system in which
  participants are given up-front instructions for task completion but then manage and iterate on the process independently with only modest oversight or intervention required.
- TOP LEVEL: Autonomous delegation system in which participants are fully aware of the required tasks and operate independently with minimal oversight or intervention required.

HIERARCHY OF DELEGATION

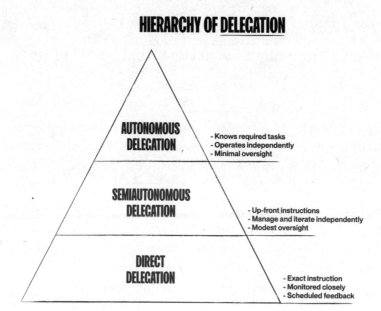

The idea is to progress from the base, direct system, to the top, autonomous system, over a period. Leverage the three core principles of an effective delegation model to build a system that unlocks new time in your life.

How to Streamline Commitments: The Art of No

PILLAR: Control

In *Happier Hour,* author Cassie Holmes references a phenomenon psychologists refer to as the Yes-Damn Effect. The idea, first proposed by Gal Zauberman of the University of North Carolina and John Lynch of Duke, is that humans systematically overestimate the amount of free time they will have in the future, so they say yes to future things, assuming they will have time for them, but when that future date arrives, they find they're wrong. In other words, you say, "Yes," and then the future date arrives, and you say, "Damn!"

If you want to take control of your time, you need to learn the Art of No.

Two shortcuts to use:

For personal commitments, use the Right Now test:

- When deciding whether to take something on, ask yourself, *Would I do this right now?* Functionally, you can think of *right now* as today or tomorrow. The aim is to eliminate the future time distortions observed by psychologists; by pulling the event into the present, you make a more clear, rational decision.
- If the answer to *Would I do this right now?* is no, say no.
- If the answer is yes, take it on.

THE RIGHT NOW TEST

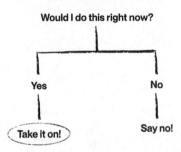

Would I do this right now?

Yes   No

Take it on!   Say no!

For professional commitments, use the New Opportunity test:

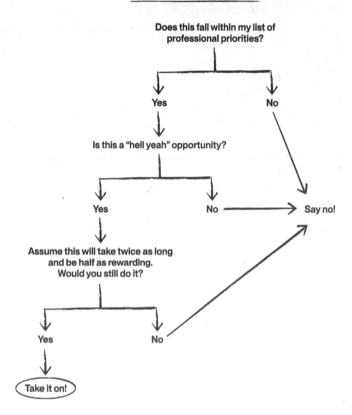

NEW OPPORTUNITY TEST

Does this fall within my list of professional priorities?

Yes → Is this a "hell yeah" opportunity?

No → Say no!

Is this a "hell yeah" opportunity?

Yes → **Assume this will take twice as long and be half as rewarding. Would you still do it?**

No → Say no!

Assume this will take twice as long and be half as rewarding. Would you still do it?

Yes → Take it on!

No → Say no!

STEP 1: Reference your two lists from the earlier exercise. Does the opportunity fall within your priority professional items? If not, say no. If so, proceed to step 2.

STEP 2: Is this a "Hell yeah!" opportunity? Writer Derek Sivers proposed this simple rule: If something isn't a "Hell yeah!" then it's a no. If it is a "Hell yeah!" opportunity, proceed to step 3.

STEP 3: Assume this opportunity takes twice as long and is half as rewarding as you expect it to be—would you still want to do it? Humans tend to be overly optimistic when taking on something new. Force a degree of rationality into the decision by lowering your expectations. If the answer now is no, say no. If the answer is yes, take it on.

Using these two shortcuts—the Right Now test and the New Opportunity test—you can master the Art of No and begin to take control of your time.

How to Manage Your Time: Time-Blocking and the Four Types of Professional Time

PILLAR: Control

There is a lot we can apply to the future by studying the past. In his autobiography, Benjamin Franklin shared a breakdown of his daily calendar and routine. Franklin's routine, reproduced below, uses time-blocking, a simple time-management and calendar strategy that blocks out discrete windows of time for specific activities.

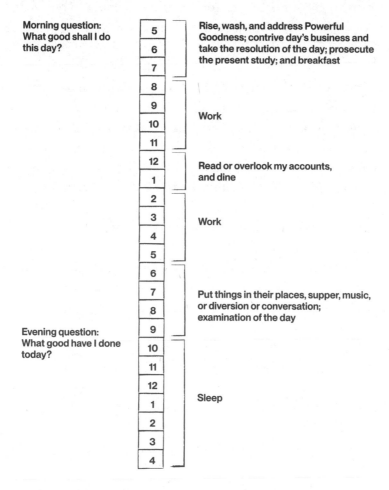

Morning question:
What good shall I do
this day?

Time	Activity
5, 6, 7	Rise, wash, and address Powerful Goodness; contrive day's business and take the resolution of the day; prosecute the present study; and breakfast
8, 9, 10, 11	Work
12, 1	Read or overlook my accounts, and dine
2, 3, 4, 5	Work
6, 7, 8, 9	Put things in their places, supper, music, or diversion or conversation; examination of the day
10, 11, 12, 1, 2, 3, 4	Sleep

Evening question:
What good have I done
today?

His entire day is batched into six blocks of time:

5:00 to 8:00 A.M.: Rise, wash, and address Powerful Goodness;
   contrive day's business and take the resolution of the day;
   prosecute the present study; and breakfast
8:00 A.M. to 12:00 P.M.: Work
12:00 to 2:00 P.M.: Read or overlook my accounts, and dine
2:00 to 6:00 P.M.: Work
6:00 to 10:00 P.M.: Put things in their places, supper, music, or
   diversion, or conversation; examination of the day
10:00 P.M. to 5:00 A.M.: Sleep

While Franklin's routine was clearly missing some of the life re-
alities that many of us encounter (childcare, home responsibilities,
and so on), we can adopt its overarching structure to improve the
way we manage our days.

The concept of time-blocking is simple: Windows of time are
blocked to work on distinct, specific tasks. Rather than manage your
life through a to-do list, you manage your life through your calendar.
Time-blocking leverages the well-established psychological principle
that setting an intention for your time is critical for driving progress.
Planning your day in this manner will allow you to focus deeply on
the specific task at hand, limit the negative impact of distractions, and
give you a degree of control over what you do and when you do it.

In my version, I use time-blocking for my professional responsibilities but leave my personal time open (I prefer not to feel like I'm
scheduling time for things like family, workouts, and relaxation). For
time-blocking professional time, I use a model I developed that
splits professional time across four areas.

THE FOUR TYPES OF PROFESSIONAL TIME
There are four types of professional time:

1. Management
2. Creation

3. Consumption
4. Ideation

Let's walk through each type to understand it more clearly.

TYPE 1: MANAGEMENT

Management Time is what most of us spend the majority of our professional lives in. It is a staple of large organizations.

Typical activities of Management Time include:

* Meetings
* Calls
* Presentations
* Email processing
* Team and people management

It can be highly productive and efficient, but it can also create a focus on movement rather than progress.

TYPE 2: CREATION

Creation Time is the second most common type of professional time. It's what most of us scramble to get done in the gaps between Management Time blocks.

Typical activities of Creation Time include:

* Writing
* Coding
* Building
* Preparing

Creation is where new progress is found. Thriving organizations have a focus on Creation Time and ensure that Management Time doesn't infringe on it.

TYPE 3: CONSUMPTION

Consumption Time is one of the two forgotten types of professional time. It is where new ideas for creation and growth are planted.

Typical activities of Consumption Time include:

* Reading
* Listening
* Studying

To paraphrase *Atomic Habits* author James Clear, everything you create is downstream from something you consume.[12] Consumption Time focuses on quality upstream to ensure quality downstream.

TYPE 4: IDEATION

Ideation Time is the second of the two forgotten types of professional time. It is where new ideas for creation and growth are cultivated and grown.

Typical activities of Ideation Time include:

* Brainstorming
* Journaling
* Walking
* Self-reflecting

Most of us have zero time for stillness and thought in our day-to-day professional lives, so we make linear progress and miss out on the asymmetric opportunities that require creative, nonlinear thinking. Ideation Time is focused on this stillness and thought.

Before you can make improvements to your balance of time, you need to understand your starting point. I began with a simple calendar exercise to identify my own current balance across the four types of time.

Starting on a Monday, at the end of each weekday, color-code the events from that day according to this key:

- Red: Management
- Green: Creation
- Blue: Consumption
- Yellow: Ideation

At the end of the week, look at the overall mix of colors on the calendar. Focus on identifying the trends.

- What color dominates the calendar?
- Are there distinct windows for Creation Time?
- Are the colors organized or randomly scattered?

This simple exercise should give you a clear picture of what your current mix of professional time looks like. From that baseline, you can work toward a more optimal balance.

THREE TIPS FOR AN OPTIMAL BALANCE

	Monday	Tuesday	Wednesday	Thursday	Friday
7 8 9	**CREATE** 1. Content writing 2. Filming	**MANAGE** 1. Emails 2. Work meetings 3. Team direction 4. Finances	**IDEATE** 1. New ideas	**CREATE** 1. Content writing 2. Filming	**CONSUME** 1. Learning 2. Reading 3. Listening 4. Watching
10 11	**MANAGE** 1. Emails		**MANAGE** 1. Team direction 2. Finances	**CONSUME** 1. Reading	
12 1 2	**CONSUME** 1. Learning 2. Reading 3. Listening	**CREATE** 1. Filming	**CONSUME** 1. Learning 2. Reading 3. Listening 4. Watching	**MANAGE** 1. Emails 2. Work meetings 3. Team direction	**IDEATE** 1. Creative thinking
3		**IDEATE** 1. Free flow 2. Creative thinking			**MANAGE** 1. Work meetings 2. Team direction
4 5 6	**IDEATE** 1. New ideas 2. Free flow 3. Creative thinking	**CONSUME** 1. Learning 2. Reading 3. Listening	**CREATE** 1. Content writing 2. Filming	**IDEATE** 1. Free flow 2. Creative 3. Challenges 4. Opportunities	**CONSUME** 1. Learning 2. Reading 3. Listening
7 8					

TIP 1: BATCH MANAGEMENT TIME

Management Time is necessary for most of us, but it can bleed out and dominate our days if we let it. Calls, meetings, presentations, and email tend to fill every moment of the day, making us feel like we're constantly busy, running faster and faster but never getting anywhere.

Leverage Parkinson's law and work toward a batched schedule:

- Create discrete blocks of time each day when you will handle major Management Time activities.
- Have one to three email-processing blocks per day.
- Have one to three call and meeting blocks per day.

The goal here is to avoid a schedule where the red bleeds out across every single day. We are trying to keep the Management Time windows as discrete as possible to create space for the other types of time.

Note: Your ability to do this will rise with your career progress. If you're just starting out, then tiny, incremental batching improvements will be a win. If you're further along in your career, you may be able to make more aggressive batching improvements.

TIP 2: INCREASE CREATION TIME

Creation is what propels us forward with more interesting projects and opportunities. We all need more Creation Time in our days.

As you batch Management Time, carve out distinct windows for Creation Time. Block them on your calendar. Don't check your email or messages during them. Focus on creation during your Creation Time.

TIP 3: CREATE SPACE FOR CONSUMPTION AND IDEATION

Consumption and Ideation are the forgotten types of time because we rarely create space for them, but they are critical to long-term, compounding progress. History's most successful people have all made a practice of creating space for reading, listening, learning, and thinking. We can draw a lesson from this.

To start, schedule one short block per week for Consumption and one short block per week for Ideation. Stay true to the purpose of the block. Own that before increasing the presence of these types of time in your schedule.

With these three tips in mind, you're well on your way to finding a more optimal balance across the four types of professional time. Give them a shot and experience the benefits immediately.

How to Fill Your Newly Created Time:
The Energy Creators

PILLAR: Control

Through improved awareness and more concentrated attention, the simple, actionable systems in this Time Wealth Guide have enabled you to *create new time.*

The key question then becomes this: What should you do with this newly created time?

- What activities should you take on?
- What pursuits are calling you?
- Whom should you spend more time with?

This is the power of taking control over your time: You have the freedom to choose exactly how to spend it.

As a simple exercise to ground your thinking as you begin the upcoming sections, consider this, a longer-term, zoomed-out expansion on the Energy Calendar:

Review your calendar from the previous year. What were the Energy Creators in your personal and professional life?

- What activities outside of work felt life-giving and joyful?
- Who made you feel energized?
- What new learning or mental pursuits sparked your interest to go deeper?
- What rituals created more peace, calm, and mental clarity?
- What physical pursuits did you enjoy?
- What professional or financial pursuits felt effortless (or even fun)?

Answering these questions is all about determining what fills your cup. It is about determining what brings life into your world so you can take your newly created time and put it toward more of those activities, people, and pursuits.

The four sections that follow—on Social Wealth, Mental Wealth, Physical Wealth, and Financial Wealth—will provide a deeper dive into each area to which you may want to allocate some of that newly created time.

The journey is just beginning—and the best is yet to come.

10.

Summary: Time Wealth

TIME WEALTH OVERVIEW

THE BIG QUESTION: How many moments do you have remaining with your loved ones?

THE THREE PILLARS OF TIME WEALTH:
* AWARENESS: An understanding of the finite, impermanent nature of time
* ATTENTION: The ability to direct your attention and focus on the things that matter (and ignore the rest)
* CONTROL: The freedom to own your time and choose exactly how to spend it

The Time Wealth Score: For each statement below, respond with 0 (strongly disagree), 1 (disagree), 2 (neutral), 3 (agree), or 4 (strongly agree).

1. I have a deep awareness of the finite, impermanent nature of my time and its importance as my most precious asset.
2. I have a clear understanding of the two to three most important priorities in my personal and professional lives.

3. I am able to consistently direct attention and focus to the important priorities that I have identified.
4. I rarely feel too busy or scattered to spend time on the most important priorities.
5. I am in control of my calendar and priorities.

Your baseline score (0 to 20): _____

Goals, Anti-Goals, and Systems

Use the goal-setting framework to calibrate your Time Wealth compass:

* GOALS: What Time Wealth Score do you want to achieve within one year? What are the two to three checkpoints that you will need to hit on your path to achieve this score?
* ANTI-GOALS: What are the two to three outcomes that you want to avoid on your journey?
* HIGH-LEVERAGE SYSTEMS: What are the two to three systems from the Time Wealth Guide that you will implement to make tangible, compounding progress toward your goal score?

YOUR ONE-WEEK JUMP START

Use the Energy Calendar technique for one week to develop an awareness of your current time usage and identify trends in activities that are creating or draining your energy.

On a sheet of paper, write your energy-creating activities on the left side and your energy-draining activities on the right side. Below your energy-creating list, write down ways that you can spend more time on these activities in the future. Below your energy-draining list, write down ways that you can spend less time on these activities in the future.

More attention on energy-creating activities and less attention on energy-draining activities will build a wealthier life.

Social
Wealth

11.

The Big Question

Who Will Be Sitting in the Front Row at Your Funeral?

IN JANUARY 2023, ERIK Newton was living a rather typical life for a man in his forties. He and his wife, Aubrie, had welcomed their first child, a daughter they named Romy, two years earlier. She had filled their world with a joy they had never experienced, a sensation that her arrival had completed their lives. In his daughter's first years of life, Erik was head down, working crazy hours as chief operating officer at a Silicon Valley start-up. In February 2023, he decided it was time to start something for himself and left the company to figure out what he should do next.

But tragically, fate had other plans.

After months of feeling exhausted and having her symptoms shrugged off by doctors who told her it was just part of being a new mother, Aubrie had finally gotten extensive blood work done. One evening after the two had put Romy to bed and were sitting down to watch a movie, Aubrie's phone rang.

"Doctors don't just call you at nine P.M.; we knew something was wrong," Erik recalled of their reaction when they saw the doctor's office number on the caller ID.

"You need to go to the ER right now," they told her.

The next twenty-four hours were a blur of tests and fluorescent-lit hospital rooms. At the end of it, a group of ashen-faced doctors came in and drew the curtain. Erik felt the life drain out of him as they delivered the news: Aubrie had a blood cancer—a very rare form—and the prognosis wasn't good. Erik and Aubrie stared at the scans together in disbelief. "Her whole body was covered in tumors—her lungs, spleen, stomach, neck. I mean, it was everywhere," Erik recalled.

With tears in his eyes, he told me the next eight months were a roller coaster. "We would bounce from hopeful with a new treatment, to thinking she had days to live, and then back to hopeful. We got very good at saying goodbye to each other before she went into the operating room for whatever procedure she had to endure."

By mid-fall, it was clear that Aubrie did not have long to live. On November 2, 2023, Aubrie Newton passed away peacefully, surrounded by love. In the days and weeks after she left this world, Erik struggled mightily under the weight of his grief and the responsibility to stay strong for his two-and-a-half-year-old daughter, who frequently asked, "Where's Mama?" as she processed the loss in her own way.

When Erik and I spoke in December 2023, he was still in the throes of grief, but he had begun to reflect on the indescribable beauty of their love and what her final days had taught him.

"Aubrie and I fell in love early and fast, but we fell more in love during the time she was convalescing than I thought was possible. Facing death every day allowed us to set aside the silly things and focus on what matters. Our new depth made her death all the more painful, but of course, I wouldn't trade it for the world, not for anything. The privilege of knowing and loving her so deeply outpaces every other experience I've had. It's the one thing that matters."

Erik said that Aubrie seemed to shift to a new level when the end grew near. "Her one regret was that she hadn't spent more time deepening relationships with the people she cared about. Looked at from the other direction, her regret became an insight. The only thing that matters at all is the quality of the relationships with the people we love."

As we spoke about our common bond as new fathers and about

how he had been immersed in his job prior to Aubrie's diagnosis, Erik reflected on the tension between work and fatherhood. "We all have obligations in life that need our attention, and those things pull us away from contemplating love with one hundred percent of our awareness. But we must remember what's behind our desire to do those things in the first place; we must remember our *center*. And it's not the money."

Close your eyes and take three deep breaths. Imagine you're dead. You're at your funeral. People are walking in, crying, hugging each other. Everyone sits down. Who is sitting in the front row? Imagine their faces. These people—your Front-Row People—are the ones who truly matter.

Open your eyes and think about them.

* What are you doing to cherish the people who hold those special seats in your world?
* How are you letting those people know what they mean to you?
* Are you prioritizing time with them or letting it float by and disappear?

The answers to these questions underlie your Social Wealth—the depth of connection to those few important, irreplaceable people in your world. These deep, meaningful, healthy relationships with a few select individuals will always provide a stable basis of support and love; they are the people with whom you can celebrate life's sweetness and mourn life's bitterness. Whether you're an extrovert or an introvert, a social butterfly or a hermit crab, you can and should build this foundation, as the ability to call upon people for support during hard times becomes increasingly important with age.

Social Wealth is built upon this foundation of **depth**—upon the strength of your ties to these few, cherished relationships. It is expanded through **breadth**—connection to extended circles of friends, communities, and cultures. Finally, it is secured through **earned status**, a durable form of social positioning that cannot be bought.

To be sure, there are dark forces conspiring against your building this type of wealth. Over the past thirty years, technologies designed to bring us together have made us lonelier than ever before:

- How many times have you walked down a crowded street so focused on your phone that you failed to look a single other human in the eye?
- How many times have you been physically surrounded by family or friends but still somehow distant, lost in thought about complete strangers on the latest app?
- How many times has an urgent text, email, or work notification pulled your mind away from the people sitting right in front of you?

Technological innovation has increased your connectedness to the world around you. You have *more connectedness,* but you feel *less connected.*

You need to fight back. Human connection is ultimately what provides the lasting texture and meaning in life. Without Social Wealth, achievement across any other arena will feel unfulfilling, even bland. Do you really picture yourself alone on that plane or yacht? What good is the big house if there is no love to fill it?

The desire to build a life of Social Wealth was what led my wife and me to move three thousand miles across the country—we wanted to be closer to our parents. It was what led one of my readers, a woman in her mid-sixties named Vicki Landis, to uproot her life and move to North Carolina to be near her three sons. Explaining the decision, she wrote, "The one thing I've read of yours that absolutely has changed my life is the example of how often do you see your parents—how many visits are left, then? Made a huge impact, and as a result, I'm moving to where my sons are." And it was what led Erik and Aubrie Newton, struck by a devastating blow of fate, to center their lives on love.

Conventional wisdom says one should focus on the journey, not the destination.

I disagree.

Focus on the *people.* When you surround yourself with inspiring people, the journeys become more beautiful, and the destinations become more brilliant. It's impossible to sit where you are and plan the perfect journey. Focus on the company—the people you want to travel with—and the journey will reveal itself in due time. Nothing bad has ever come from surrounding oneself with inspiring, genuine, kind, positive-sum individuals.

Find your Front-Row People. Cherish them. Be one to someone else.

12.

The Uniquely Social Species

AMERICAN ANTHROPOLOGIST MARGARET MEAD was once asked what she considered to be the first sign of civilized human society. The student who asked the question anticipated a response about tools, cave paintings, or other ancient artifacts, but Mead took the question in an interesting direction. She answered that the first sign of human civilization was a healed broken femur.

Why did the anthropologist hold this ancient skeletal finding in such high regard?

The femur—the thigh bone—is the longest bone in the human body, and it was particularly important for our ancestors' survival in the wild, given its involvement in all core movements. A broken femur requires a notoriously long time to heal, sometimes up to ten weeks. Mead reasoned that in pre-civilized societies, a broken femur was a death sentence; the clan's immediate survival would have taken precedence over the individual's needs, and the unfortunate victim would have been left behind. But a *healed* femur indicated that the individual had been cared for, which implied a change from the usual immediate-survival thinking. This, she believed, was the first sign of a civilized society—a willingness to care for one another in times of need.

The veracity of this anecdote has been questioned over the years, but its lesson is clear: The human desire and need for connection, love, cooperation, and support is what allowed our species to survive and thrive.

Human history overflows with examples of how social connection is intertwined with progress, culture, and happiness. Our earliest human ancestors with similar-size brains walked the earth about seven hundred thousand years ago.[1] They developed divisions of labor, had communal gathering spaces, and may even have buried their dead. Hunter-gatherers relied on communication and collective effort to hunt big game; the specific coordination of movement and force required to take down a ten-thousand-pound woolly mammoth is quite hard to fathom.

Ancient human cities often included elaborate gathering places where people would come together for political, social, and cultural activities. From the agora in ancient Greece to the forum in ancient Rome, from the open public spaces in Mohenjo Daro to the ceremonial plazas of the ancient Incans, and from the mystical Stonehenge to the Pueblo Bonito ceremonial site of the Puebloans, it's fair to say that social connection has long been a driving force behind the design of human lives. Spoken and written language developed as a means to disseminate information and knowledge to other humans across space and time.

Social connection began as a simple means of survival—the sharing of resources and support—but it slowly developed beyond that into a strategic resource, with language enabling the rise of broader human networks and coordination (for good and bad). Countless wars have been waged and millions of lives lost on the basis of belonging to one social network (regional, national, religious, and so on) or another. Humans are a complex species; the same social connection that enabled survival and love also enabled war, murder, sadness, and loss.

Anthropologist Robin Dunbar is most famous for his research-based determination of the number of stable social relationships a single person can maintain (the aptly named Dunbar's number is 150). He also found that the strongest predictor of brain size across species is the size of the typical social group. The human brain is uniquely large relative to body size, which Dunbar attributes to the fact that our species is highly social.

Put simply: You are social because you are human, and you are human because you are social.

"RELATIONSHIPS, RELATIONSHIPS, RELATIONSHIPS"

In 1938, two unrelated research teams in Boston, Massachusetts, began tracking the lives of two very different groups of young men. The teams could not have known it at the time, but what they began in 1938 would become the most important study of human development on record and would change the way scientists think about human connection forever.

One research team was led by a Harvard physician, Arlie Bock, who wanted to escape the tendency in medicine to focus on the sick and instead study the attributes of the normal and successful. Dr. Bock hoped that such a study could distill the recipe for general happiness, health, and success, a result he believed would be more powerful than anything he might achieve through a more traditional course of research. With the financial support of Boston-based department store magnate W. T. Grant, he got to work. The Grant Study had an initial participant pool of 268 Harvard College undergraduate men.

The other research team was led by Sheldon Glueck and his wife, Eleanor, both on the faculty at Harvard Law School and both of whom studied juvenile delinquency and criminal behavior. The Gluecks focused their research on 456 boys from Boston's most troubled families and neighborhoods in an effort to determine the factors that contributed to delinquent behavior.

For over thirty years, the two longitudinal studies ran in parallel but as something of a mirror image, one studying the lives of society's most privileged and the other studying the lives of some of its least privileged. In 1972, George Vaillant, a Harvard psychiatrist and researcher, took over as director of the Grant Study and made the historically important contribution of integrating the Gluecks' study into the research. The integration dramatically increased the breadth of the socioeconomic profile of the participant base and unlocked a range of potential study insights.

Longitudinal studies typically experience funding challenges when interest wanes or original benefactors move on (or die!), but Dr. Vaillant's leadership and storytelling enabled the study to thrive. Remarkably, as of this writing, the Grant Study (now formally known as the Harvard Study of Adult Development) is still running, over eighty-five years later. Researchers gather data from the participants every two years via a survey consisting of thousands of questions on life satisfaction, health, mood, and more; they also conduct a comprehensive set of physiological tests every five years. The study has tracked and measured the lives of a combined 724 original male participants and more than 1,300 of their male and female descendants. It is widely considered to be the longest longitudinal study on the health and happiness of individuals.

While the study's findings are broad and far-reaching, its most important takeaway is simple: Relationships are, quite literally, everything.

Dr. Vaillant put it bluntly. "The key to healthy aging is relationships, relationships, relationships."[2]

The study has found that strong, healthy relationships are the best predictor of life satisfaction, far outpacing other hypothesized predictors, such as social class, wealth, fame, IQ, and genetics. Perhaps even more important, the study found that relationship satisfaction had a direct positive impact on physical health. The study's current director, Robert Waldinger, highlighted the findings in a TED Talk that has been viewed more than fifty million times. "It wasn't their cholesterol levels that predicted how they were going to grow old," he said. "It was how satisfied they were in their relationships. The people who were the most satisfied in their relationships at age fifty were the healthiest at age eighty."

To reiterate that critical point: *The single greatest predictor of physical health at age eighty was relationship satisfaction at age fifty.*

On the flip side, loneliness was found to be worse for one's health than regular use of tobacco or alcohol. Dr. Waldinger summarized, "Taking care of your body is important, but tending to your relationships is a form of self-care too. That, I think, is the revelation."

Researchers from the Harvard Study of Adult Development always ask participants this question: Who could you call in the middle of the night if you were sick or scared? The responses ranged from a long list of names to "nobody" and served as a simple measure of an important metric: loneliness. Dr. Waldinger, commenting on those who had answered "nobody," said, "That's real loneliness—this sense that nobody in the world has my back. The costs of that are huge. It makes us feel unloved and unsafe, and eventually breaks down our health."

THE LONELINESS PANDEMIC

My maternal grandmother, Vimala Pawar Reddy, was a strong and proud woman, born and raised in India. She was a magnetic human, a storyteller at heart, a deeply social being who thrived in a crowd from early childhood into her adult years. I vividly recall countless days and nights spent seated on the floor as she regaled me and her other grandchildren with stories from her youth—mischief, adventures, and near-death experiences. She was the type of woman who was never far from a friend or loved one. In fact, when my grandfather built a house for them in their later adult years, he decided to do it on a small cul-de-sac near their three closest friend couples, mostly to ensure that his extroverted wife would always have companionship, even after he was gone. When my grandfather passed away in 2006, she remained surrounded by love, both metaphorically and literally. One by one, the men in those four homes on the tiny street passed away, but their wives lived on; the proximity to friendship and love proved life-giving during good times and bad.

My grandmother continued to thrive; at her ninetieth birthday celebration in 2019, she took the mic, gave a sweet, childlike smile, and thanked everyone for attending. But like most of the world, she was wildly unprepared for the chaos that struck soon after. She seemed to age twenty years in the span of two during the on-and-off lockdowns that gripped India from March 2020 through mid-2022. Her busy social schedule, which had previously included a weekly Scrabble club, daily lunches, and regular visits from family and friends, came to a standstill. She never contracted COVID-19, but as the research highlights, the deterioration in her health and cognitive faculties might have been due purely to the lack of human connection. When I was finally able to visit her again, in January 2023, she appeared nearly catatonic on the evening of our arrival. By the second day of our visit, she was up and about, chatting actively and even managing to playfully dominate my Harvard professor father and myself in a game of Scrabble (while consoling us with the assertion that she was "just getting very good letters"). The social connection, warmth, and love served as the best medicine for her various maladies.

In 2023, U.S. surgeon general Vivek Murthy released "Our Epidemic of Loneliness and Isolation,"[3] a comprehensive report that added scientific rigor to my anecdotal observation. The report noted that connectedness was at an all-time high, with 96 to 99 percent of teens and adults under age sixty-five using the internet, and the average American using it for six hours per day. Approximately one in three U.S. adults said they were connected "almost constantly." Social media use increased from 5 percent in 2005 to 80 percent in 2019, and 95 percent of teens reported using social media in 2022.

This is a big deal, because constant technological connectedness pulls us away from in-person human interactions—a dangerous zero-sum battle being fought for our attention. When social media and technology consistently win that battle, feelings of loneliness and social isolation rise. The amount of time Americans spend alone has increased steadily in the social media age, from 285 minutes per day in 2003 to 309 minutes per day in 2019 (and 333 minutes per day during the COVID pandemic, according to the 2020 survey).[4]

The result is what many are calling a "friendship recession." According to a study[5] cited in the surgeon general's report, loneliness among young adults increased every year from 1976 to 2019. Teenagers and young adults are spending 70 percent less time with their friends in person than they did two decades ago.[6] The trend appears particularly dire for men, with 15 percent of men reporting that they have zero close friendships (a fivefold increase from 1990); the number of men who say they have at least six close friendships was cut in half over the same period.[7] A 2022 Gallup study found that only 39 percent of U.S. adults felt very connected to others.[8] While the COVID-19 pandemic may have amplified perceptions of loneliness, it is clear that they have been accelerating under the surface for a long time.

Sadly, my grandmother passed away in October 2023. In my mind, she was yet another victim of this new and pervasive global challenge: the loneliness pandemic. The technologies that we have created and adopted are conspiring against us. Perhaps not in the dystopian, attack-of-the-robots manner of our favorite science-fiction thrillers, but in a silent, Trojan Horse manner that is terrifyingly effective. What's more, in a culture where financial optimization has become the celebrated norm, many of us are taking actions that exacerbate the loneliness problem.

THE OPTIMIZATION TRAP

In a 2021 survey of Americans who had recently moved, about one-third expressed some regret over the decision, with the most common regret being leaving friends and family.[9] The so-called Great Resignation of 2021, in which the United States experienced an unprecedented labor-market churn, is now being cheekily referred to as the Great Regret; a recent survey showed that about 80 percent of those who hopped from one job to another now regret the move. According to an article in *Fortune* citing the survey, "The most common reason job-hoppers gave for wanting a return to their former employers was that they missed their old colleagues, with almost a third of respondents saying they missed their former teams."[10] The loss of familiar, stable relationships outweighed the benefits in pay, geography, or flexibility.

When you fail to measure and value your Social Wealth, you fail to consider it in your decisions.

This raises an important point, particularly in the context of the popular narratives around geographic arbitrage, digital nomadic culture, tax optimization, and the like:

- What's the point of all that financial optimization if you're alone?
- How many people have sold their homes and moved to areas with lower taxes to save money only to realize that without their families and friends, they don't feel at home?
- How many people have jetted around the world and seen incredible sights only to realize that seeing them alone isn't quite as meaningful?
- How many people have taken high-paying jobs in new locations only to find themselves deeply unhappy without their support networks, friends, and family?

A dear friend in his early thirties had a thriving social life in New York City but decided to move an hour away to avoid the significant city tax that would hit his earnings when his employer was acquired or publicly listed. After just six months, he began to see his miscalculation: "I was saving hundreds of thousands [of dollars] on paper, but I had failed to place any value on the relationships and social life that were so central to who I was as a person." After twelve months, he moved back to New York City and paid the full tax burden— a wise choice, if you ask me.

The loneliness and social isolation that often follows a financially motivated move abroad is a common theme on the popular r/expats page on Reddit. In a recent post, one user noted, "I like my job and my colleagues, [but] I suffer from depression and anxiety and I've been finding living alone to be really hard. I've been calling my parents every night for the last two weeks. . . . It's taken such a strain on me that I'm taking a few weeks off work so I can go home and be with my family."

The research, stories, and insights all align around one fundamental reality: You can ignore the importance of Social Wealth, but you do so at the risk of your own long-term happiness and fulfillment.

Speaking from my own experience: Nothing improved our quality of life more than living within driving distance of our family and closest friends. Proximity to people you love is worth more than any job will ever pay you.

You may need food, water, and shelter to survive, but it is human connection that allows you to thrive.

13.

The Days Are Long but the Years Are Short

Parents, Kids, and Lost Time

GREG SLOAN WAS ON the fast track.

Just into his early thirties, he had risen to become a vice president at Goldman Sachs, one of the most prestigious financial institutions in the world, and he served as a trusted financial adviser to a long list of well-known corporate executives. His expertise and guidance were valuable, a fact that was reflected in his steadily rising salary and bonus compensation at the firm.

Sloan was achieving everything he had set out to achieve—the money, the trust, the client list, the respect: All of it was there. The path forward was clear and well lit until one day, a simple interaction with his five-year-old son changed everything.

His son's preschool was set to have a Doughnuts with Dad event, where the dads joined the students for a morning of doughnuts and fun activities. Unfortunately, Greg would be on an important business trip at the time, so he would have to miss it. When his wife told his son the news, he reacted with a shrug and said, "That's okay, Dad's never around anyway."

The words felt like acid when his wife repeated them to Greg that evening. This, he decided, was the final straw.

"I quit my job at Goldman Sachs later that year. My son is twenty-four years old now. No regrets."

THE MAGIC YEARS

For ten years, you are your child's favorite person in the entire world.

After that, children have other favorite people—best friends, girl-friends, boyfriends, partners, and, eventually, their own children. But during those ten years, you are everything to them. You occupy a unique place in their world. It is during this period that the foundation for the parent-child relationship—so central to many people's Social Wealth—is built. It might be a strong foundation that is likely to last for decades or a flimsy one that's likely to crumble in years, but there is one terrifying truth: By the time your children are eighteen, you've already used up the vast majority of the time you'll have with them. Unfortunately, we live in a society where children's early years coincide with their parents' peak working hours, travel, and other professional responsibilities. For many of us, these special years come and go in the blink of an eye—a blur of late nights in the office, meetings about meetings, emails at the dinner table, and weekend calls.

In a viral Reddit post from May 2023, a user wrote, "20 years from now, the only people who will remember that you worked late are your kids." Commenters responded with emotion-filled posts, such as "The graveyard is full of 'irreplaceable' and 'important' people" and "I've missed so many birthdays, plays, and events for work, and I can't even tell you why. I don't remember what I was working on, I can't tell you why it was important. But I can tell you how my not being there made my kids feel."

I am of two minds on this:

1. Being present and spending time with those you love is the most important thing in the end.
2. Having the people you love see you work hard on things you care about is a principle they'll remember for the rest of their lives.

The importance and value of the second point often gets lost in the narrative around work-life balance. Understanding, navigating, and balancing the tension of these two beliefs is how you truly "win" the game. Put differently, the goal is not to sacrifice your career progression, fail to live up to your professional potential, or stop learning or growing in an effort to be constantly present with your kids.

The goal is to have the clarity to choose—to define your balance and live by design rather than by default.

The goal is to ask the question and craft your own answer, not to blindly accept the "right" answer someone else wants to sell you. The goal is to understand that these ten short years are different— that they may not be the right time to lean into that promotion or new role at work. At the very least, you need to recognize and internalize the trade-offs you are making if you do.

Greg Sloan made his choice. When his colleagues "drank the Kool-Aid that financial success would solve our work-life balance issues," he opted for a different path. Reflecting on his decision years later, Greg smiled and said, "Leaving [Goldman Sachs] allowed me to coach [my son's] baseball teams and be heavily involved in his sports passion. He is now twenty-four years old and we have a special bond." He even credits the bold choice with saving his marriage: "I believe there is a high likelihood that Katherine and I would have gotten divorced if I had stayed. The travel lifestyle and high stress was simply not healthy for our marriage. We'll celebrate thirty-one years of marriage in June."

The ability to choose is a privilege in and of itself, as it requires a certain level of baseline comfort. For those who have the ability to choose, it's important not to squander it by falling into the default path. It's important to ask questions, think clearly, and wrestle with the trade-offs this book urges you to consider.

My own approach is informed by my experience with my father. His ability to balance the two worldviews is something I will always remember. He would come home for dinner, play catch with me outside, then work late once I went to bed. Much of my own discipline and work ethic came from seeing him work hard on things that lit him up intellectually but that he never allowed to get in the way of what was most important to him—his family. I vividly recall going with him on one of his international work trips when I was ten. While I watched movies and enjoyed the snacks on the long flight, he stayed up for twelve straight hours working on his presentation. When I asked—almost incredulously—how he had not watched a single movie on the entire flight, he smiled and replied, "This is what is necessary—to deliver up to my expectations for myself and to be able to bring you along for the trip."

I always felt connected to his work because he took the time to explain the *why*—why he was working hard on things and what he hoped to achieve with them. Involving your loved ones in your journey this way is a beautiful thing. They will understand why you're working hard, the value it creates for them and you, and feel connected to your growth and achievement. An absence due to work becomes better understood and more appreciated with the benefit of context.

The magic years should be a call to arms: wrestle with this tension, be there and appreciate that brutally short window of time you have with your kids. Stop living the deferred-happiness plan, saying, "Well, I'm just going to work really hard now so that I can be happy and spend time with my kids when I'm sixty."

Because when you're sixty, they're not going to be three years old anymore.

The magic years will fade away and disappear if you let them. Reject the defaults, ask the questions, embrace the tension, and design the balance that fits your world.

Always remember: The days are long, but the years are short.

14.

The Three Pillars of Social Wealth

IN EARLY 2022, A message from a twenty-eight-year-old subscriber to my newsletter caught my attention.

Rohan Venkatesh was, in a sense, a slightly younger version of me. The eldest son of two Indian immigrants, he had grown up in a small town outside Boston, Massachusetts, where he excelled academically at the public high school. He went to Northeastern University in Boston, graduated magna cum laude, and began his career in finance, accepting a prestigious, demanding role as an analyst at an investment bank. A few years of strong performance later, he joined an investment fund and saw his responsibilities grow. Just as I had, he put his head down and did the work with the deep-rooted belief that the best was yet to come.

Things certainly seemed that way until one August morning in 2021 when everything changed.

On that morning, Rohan woke up ready to take on the world. He had just accepted a new job that would catapult him to an office in the heart of New York City. The morning began like any other: a little bit of work followed by a run with his mother, something that had become a bit of a ritual. While on the run, Rohan felt an odd sensation in one of his legs. Assuming he was fatigued from workouts or lack of sleep, he simply walked home and jumped on his next work call. In the middle of the call, he noticed that he couldn't move his left arm. He called for help. A few minutes later, his condition had worsened to the point that he required a wheelchair to enter the hospital. Within twenty-four hours, a team of doctors walked into his room and delivered the stunning news: Rohan Venkatesh had an inoperable brain tumor.

In the span of one day, his future went "from wonderfully infinite to terrifyingly finite."

The week he had excitedly marked on his calendar as the start of his new job became the week he started his radiation treatment. The months that followed were a blur of hospital rooms, tests, and treatments. He endured six weeks of radiation that threatened to drain the life out of him. He endured the period that followed as he awaited news on whether the treatment had halted the tumor's growth. He endured the months of rehabilitation as he worked to regain his mental and physical strength, a process that continues today.

When Rohan reached out to me and shared his story, he had just entered what might best be described as a "holding pattern" with the tumor—it hadn't disappeared, but it had stopped growing. I was taken with his infectious, almost inexplicable optimism for a fresh lease on life. Over the year that followed, I had a chance to spend time with him, and we developed a friendship. We spoke about the light of life found in the darkness of death, the beauty of a life devoid of the false pretenses that perceived permanence instills in you. Apple founder Steve Jobs put it well: "Almost everything—all external expectations, all pride, all fear of embarrassment or failure—these things just fall away in the face of death, leaving only what is truly important. Remembering that you are going to die is the best way I know to avoid the trap of thinking you have something to lose. You are already naked."[11]

Rohan Venkatesh was already naked—and in the face of the darkness, he found his light:

"I had the power to choose."

An old Buddhist parable echoes this sentiment. The Buddha asks his student, "If a person is struck by an arrow, is it painful?" The student nods yes. The Buddha asks, "If a person is struck by a second arrow, is that even more painful?" The student again nods yes. The Buddha then explains, "In life, we cannot always control the first arrow—the bad thing that happens. However, the second arrow is our reaction to the bad thing, and that second arrow is *optional.*" The first arrow is the negative event that hits you—the chaos, pain, challenges, and complexity that threaten to derail you, to take you out of the game. It hits and it hurts. But the second arrow is your response to the first, and as the parable teaches us, you can avoid being struck by the second arrow; it is entirely within your control.

Rohan Venkatesh was determined to avoid being hit by that second arrow, even in the face of dire circumstances. "I had lost a lot. I had this (literal and figurative) Sword of Damocles* hanging over my head. But every morning, I got to choose what to focus on. I could choose to focus on things outside my control. I could choose to sit alone in my misery. I could choose to scroll on social media and see people doing the things I could no longer do. Or I could choose to focus on things within my control. I could choose to spend time with people who lift me up, who inspire me to grow. I could choose to be the type of person who they would want to be around."

Life is so very fragile, but no matter how fragile it is, each day we have a choice of how to live it. Each day is a fresh start, a fresh choice to make. Rohan's words on choosing his people are particularly poignant. You have many choices over the course of your life, but one stands out as the most important choice you will ever make: Who will you choose to join you on this wild, crazy journey? Who will you choose to gift your energy, love, and respect to? Who will you choose to spend your *terrifyingly finite* time with?

You need connection to survive and thrive, for your health, happiness, and fulfillment. You need to build a life of Social Wealth.

Your Social Wealth is built across three core pillars:

---

* The Sword of Damocles is a reference to an ancient Greek story of a courtier named Damocles who is allowed by King Dionysius to sit on the throne for a day, but the entire time, a sword hangs above his head by a single thread of horsehair. The Sword of Damocles represents the constant anxiety of waiting for imminent doom.

- **DEPTH:** Connection to a small circle of people with deep, meaningful bonds
- **BREADTH:** Connection to a larger circle of people for support and belonging beyond the self, either through individual relationships or through community, religious, spiritual, or cultural infrastructure
- **EARNED STATUS:** The lasting respect, admiration, and trust of your peers that you receive on the basis of earned, not acquired, status symbols

This does not require any special starting place, family situation, or financial means. It does, however, require a sense of urgency: The time horizon of our investment in Social Wealth matters. In *The Good Life,* the *New York Times* bestselling book by Marc Schulz and Harvard Study of Adult Development director Robert Waldinger, the authors point out, "Like muscles, neglected relationships atrophy." If we incorrectly assume an infinite time horizon for our relationships—meaning that an investment in the future is effectively the same as an investment now—we may find that many of these relationships have atrophied to the point of no return by that later date.

If you skip those family trips in your twenties and thirties, you might not have the chance in your forties and fifties. If you fail to check in on your friends in your thirties and forties, they might not be around when you're in your fifties and sixties. If you don't join that local community group in your forties and fifties, you won't have those connections in your sixties and seventies. If you don't show up for your loved ones during their times of need, they won't show up for you during yours.

Investing in your Social Wealth now through daily, deliberate actions to improve your social fitness is the clearest path to developing a life rich in connections, from depth to breadth and beyond.

As you measure Social Wealth as part of your new scoreboard, the three pillars—depth, breadth, and earned status—provide a blueprint for the right action to build it. By developing an understanding of these pillars and the high-leverage systems that affect them, you can begin to create the right outcomes.

DEPTH: THE FRONT-ROW PEOPLE

Depth is the connection to a small inner circle of people with deep, meaningful, durable bonds. It forms the foundation of your Social Wealth—the small group that you can rely on for love, connection, and support during your highest highs and your lowest lows. You know depth when you feel it. It is the people you can call at 3:00 A.M. when everything is going wrong. It is your Front-Row People.

Depth is built through three primary actions, behaviors, and attitudes:

* **HONESTY:** Sharing your inner truth and weakness, listening to theirs
* **SUPPORT:** Sitting in the darkness during their struggle
* **SHARED EXPERIENCE:** Encountering positive and negative experiences together

You cultivate depth over long periods—it is forged during and across the ups and downs of life. Like a muscle, depth is built when relationships are forced to endure struggle, pain, and tension. Just as the muscle becomes stronger after being tested, so will your most durable relationships.

While this circle may include family members, there is no requirement that depth be found through familial relationships. Depth of connection is personal—*where* you find it in your life is not important; what is important is *that* you find it.

One example comes from Okinawa, a Japanese island with one of the highest densities of centenarians in the world. The residents of Okinawa have a notoriously lively and structured social life. The term *moai*—which roughly translates to "meeting for a common purpose"[12]—refers to the friend groups that residents form during their youth (sometimes when they're as young as five years old) and maintain throughout their lives. These friend groups are for fun as well as for social support as the inevitable challenges of life arise. The friends regularly meet, converse, gossip, laugh, and love, a system that has stood the test of time and appears to contribute to their long, healthy lives.

Further, your circle of depth is not a constant—it has a living, fluctuating nature. Relationships, like your life, have seasons. You can build depth in new relationships in new places or grow it in old relationships that are finally ready to thrive.

It may take many years for a relationship to blossom to the full extent of its depth. My sister is about three years my senior. For most of our childhood, I viewed her as the golden child, the one who could do no wrong. She got better grades, got into the best schools, and always seemed to excel in the areas my family valued. My immaturity created an environment of competition with my sister rather than one of joyful support and love. At times, I resented her success, wishing I were accomplishing all the things she was. Unfortunately, that immature, competitive mindset harmed the depth of our relationship through our young adulthood. But in the past few years, something amazing happened that changed everything: We both had children. Suddenly, that thin veil of competition that had clouded our relationship was torn away, and what remained was an understanding, a recognition that for the first time, we were in the same phase of life. On the same journey, in the same mud.

Thirty years into our relationship, we met for the first time. We could see each other with beautiful clarity; we knew each other. I have seen my relationship with my sister blossom into one of true depth—with the knowledge that there are years of unvarnished love and support ahead.

The lesson: You will have a deep, loving, supportive relationship with someone you haven't even met yet.

Depth is the foundational pillar of Social Wealth. It is built through daily actions and behaviors—honesty, support, and shared experience—embraced consistently over long periods. Without depth, you cannot live a happy, fulfilling life. With depth, anything is possible.

BREADTH: BELONGING TO SOMETHING BIGGER

From the foundation of depth with a small circle, you can build to breadth with a larger one.

Breadth is the connection to a larger circle for support and belonging. In his book *Friends: Understanding the Power of Our Most Important Relationships,* Robin Dunbar proposes the concept of *circles of friendship* to visualize an individual's relationships. The innermost circle—about fifteen of your closest relationships—is the foundation of depth that we have discussed. As the circles extend outward to good friends, friends, acquaintances, and beyond, we move into the realm of breadth. These relationships are important, as they can provide varied support such as networks for career opportunities, enjoyment, warm connections to new romantic partners, and more.

This breadth can be built through incremental individual connections as well as through community. Community can take many forms—cultural, spiritual, local, regional, national, and more—but in its broadest sense, it is built around the connection to something bigger than the self. Participation in a community creates leverage in your Social Wealth ecosystem—it connects you to individuals you haven't physically met. That connection instills a feeling of belonging that is a source of lasting fulfillment in life. A recent WSJ-NORC poll[13] found that the percentage of U.S. respondents who indicated community involvement, religion, and patriotism were very important to them has fallen sharply since 1998. The only core value that rose in importance: money. In the same poll, the percentage of people who reported being "not too happy" sharply increased—a fact that is hard to write off as coincidence, if you ask me.

Breadth is built through behaviors that expose you to new people and environments:

- Join a local club or community around an area of interest. It could be a book club if you love reading, an art club if you love creating, or a gym if you love fitness. Be a child again, participating in new activities to meet friends.

- Attend a weekly spiritual gathering if you are a faith-driven individual.
- Participate in digital meetups for causes that you care about.
- Coordinate regular walks or hikes with others in your area.
- Go to the networking event you've been shying away from.

All of these create the potential for many new nodes of connection through a single action.

Breadth requires you to try new things, to open yourself up to the world around you. If you give generously with no expectation of return, you will build a new breadth of connection that will create lasting Social Wealth.

EARNED STATUS: SOCIAL CURRENCY THAT LASTS

You are a status-seeking animal—and there's nothing wrong with that.

Status can be defined as the standing or positioning of one person in relation to another person or group. The desire to be respected and admired by your fellow humans is natural (and evolutionarily helpful). Cecilia Ridgeway, an American sociologist and the Lucie Stern Professor in the Social Sciences at Stanford University, refers to status as "the esteem that other people have for us, how we are seen by others, how we're evaluated, the worth they attribute to us in the situation."[14] Status is a basic form of social currency—it dictates our interactions with those around us.

While it may carry something of a negative connotation, status is a very natural (and important!) human phenomenon. In *The Status Game,* author Will Storr remarked, "Back in the Stone Age, increased status meant greater influence, access to a wider choice of mates and more security and resources for ourselves and our children. It still does today." In *Spent: Sex, Evolution, and Consumer Behavior,* author Geoffrey Miller noted, "Humans evolved in small social groups in which image and status were all-important, not only for survival, but for attracting mates, impressing friends, and rearing children." Ridgeway referred to status as a "brilliant social technology," as it enabled humans to coordinate and organize.

Winning the status game, it turns out, is good for your health. In a study published in 2014 in the journal *Evolution, Medicine, and Public Health*, a group of researchers found that among the Tsimane, a small, pre-industrial, politically egalitarian society in Amazonian Bolivia, the higher-status individuals exhibited lower levels of stress and better health.[15] Other studies have similarly shown the health benefits of sitting closer to the top of the social-status hierarchy, even when controlling for variables such as financial wealth.[16]

For our ancient ancestors, status was typically signaled through displays of physical prowess, size, or association with the most attractive mates. In today's world, where overt demonstrations of physical fortitude are (generally) frowned upon, it's not altogether surprising that humans choose to signal their relative position in society largely through the acquisition and display of materials. That Rolex, Range Rover, and Gucci bag—the status symbols of the present world—are the modern-day equivalents of our ancestors' chest pounding.

The problem: The durable, lasting status you seek—the true respect and admiration of your peers—cannot be bought. What's more, the incessant pursuit of it has led many men and women down a dark, winding road to nowhere.

You've undoubtedly seen others walking down this road (or done so yourself):

- You splurge on the new wardrobe but are disappointed when it goes unnoticed, overshadowed by your colleague's new watch and shoes.
- You get the fancy new car but forget about it the second you see the newer model in your neighbor's driveway.
- You join the new club but are quickly dissatisfied when the most recognizable members leave to join the even newer one across town.

- You buy the new home but become frustrated when you hear whispers that it isn't in the "right" part of town.

The allure of these symbols is not that you respect and admire the people who have them; it is that you imagine the respect and admiration that *you* will receive once you have them. As author Morgan Housel noted in his bestselling book *The Psychology of Money,* "When you see someone driving a nice car, you rarely think, 'Wow, the guy driving that car is cool.' Instead, you think, 'Wow, if I had that car people would think I'm cool.'"

To avoid falling into this trap, you have to identify the people you truly respect and admire and then determine what specific assets or traits elicit that respect and admiration. I'm willing to bet they do not include the alluring symbols you find yourself chasing. Those are fleeting; they may impress on the surface, but respect and admiration come from depth.

Entrepreneur and investor Naval Ravikant once said, "A fit body, a calm mind, and a house full of love. These things cannot be bought—they must be earned." The most universally treasured, valuable, and durable things in life cannot be acquired with money. The things that earn the deep respect and admiration of your peers are not for sale.

This leads to an important distinction. There are two types of status—bought and earned.

Bought status is the improved social positioning garnered through acquired status symbols:

- The club membership that makes you a part of the scene
- The expensive car, watch, handbag, or jewelry acquired for the sole purpose of showing others your financial wealth
- The private-plane flight or boat trip taken more for the Instagram photo than for the utility

Earned status, however, is the real respect, admiration, and trust received through hard-won treasures:

- The freedom to choose how to spend your time (and whom to spend it with)
- The healthy, loving family relationships made possible by years of present energy
- The purpose-imbued work and mastery within a domain, built through years of effort
- The sought-after wisdom accumulated through decades of lived experience
- The adaptable mind capable of navigating stressful encounters shaped through a steady mindfulness practice and thoughtful introspection
- The strong, fit physique built through hours of movement and disciplined eating
- The professional promotion or company sale achieved after an extended period of hard work in the dark

As you will note, earned status is a natural by-product of the pursuit of a life grounded in the concepts in *The 5 Types of Wealth*. These status symbols may not be showy, but they convey a depth to those around you that is impossible to acquire through financial means.

Status games are a part of life and critical for establishing your position in the relative hierarchies that govern your personal and professional worlds. You will never escape them—you simply need to play the right ones.

Bought status is fleeting. It may improve your relative position, but only until the next level is unlocked and you're right back at the bottom. It will keep you trying to enter what author C. S. Lewis famously referred to as "the inner ring": "As long as you are governed by that desire you will never get what you want. You are trying to peel an onion; if you succeed there will be nothing left."

Earned status is lasting. It will elicit the durable respect, admiration, and trust that you seek from the people who matter to you, those whose opinions you value and cherish.

To live a life of abundant Social Wealth, focus on what must be earned, not what can be bought.

Importantly, while the pillars of Social Wealth remain the same, their application will be different for everyone, as the level of social connection people need to feel happy, healthy, and fulfilled varies from person to person. A natural extrovert might need significant breadth and depth of connection to keep loneliness at bay, while a natural introvert may need only a few close relationships to do the same. Accordingly, the systems and exercises in the Social Wealth Guide that follows are intended to be dynamic and applied in the context of your own personal needs. They are universal in their foundation but not in their application.

With an established understanding of the three pillars, we can move to the Social Wealth Guide, which provides the specific tools and systems to build upon these pillars and cultivate a life of Social Wealth.

15.

The Social Wealth Guide

Systems for Success

THE SOCIAL WEALTH GUIDE that follows provides specific, high-leverage systems to build each of the pillars of a life of Social Wealth. This isn't one-size-fits-all and you shouldn't feel compelled to read every single one; browse through and select those that feel most relevant and useful to you.

As you consider and execute the systems for success provided in the Social Wealth Guide, use your responses to each Social Wealth statement from the Wealth Score quiz to narrow your focus to the areas where you need to make the most progress (those where you responded *strongly disagree, disagree,* or *neutral*).

1. I have a core set of deep, loving, supportive relationships.
2. I am consistently able to be the partner, parent, family member, and friend that I would want to have.
3. I have a network of loose relationships I can learn from and build on.
4. I have a deep feeling of connection to a community (local, regional, national, spiritual, and so on) or to something bigger than myself.

5. I do not attempt to achieve status, respect, or admiration through material purchases.

A few common Social Wealth anti-goals to avoid on your journey:

- Allowing my pursuit of financial success to hurt my deepest relationships
- Losing my connection to my local networks and community
- Chasing status symbols to improve my social position

Here are ten proven systems for building Social Wealth.

Social Wealth Hacks I Wish
I Knew at Twenty-Two

A collaboration with Arthur C. Brooks, social scientist, Harvard Business School professor, and number one *New York Times* bestselling author of *From Strength to Strength* and *Build the Life You Want*.

1. Happiness is not a destination but a direction; how you travel through life and whom you travel with is what counts.
2. People are made for love—we all crave it, and we can find something lovable in just about everyone we meet. We don't always give it or accept it, because we make a lot of mistakes, but love is what all our hearts desire.
3. People who disagree on politics can still enjoy close relationships.
4. Happy people love people, use things, and worship the divine; unhappy people use people, love things, and worship themselves.
5. It's a bad trade to be special rather than happy. That's what people are doing when they choose the fourteenth hour of work before the first hour with their children.
6. Approach disagreements with your partner not as a "me" but as a "we." The most harmonious couples are the ones who learn to play on the same team. Their predominant mode of interaction is collaborative, not competitive.
7. Happiness does not depend on a certain net worth, family configuration, or set of ideological views. It requires that you be generous in love and allow yourself to be loved.
8. Talk to people unlike you. The social path of least resistance is to stay in your traditional friend group, where interactions are familiar and easy. The social path of greatest benefit is to stray from that traditional group and expose yourself to new beliefs, mindsets, and views.

9. Treat fighting like exercise. It will be painful, sure, but you shouldn't be unhappy about doing it regularly, because it makes you stronger—especially if you do it in a spirit of growth, not contempt.

10. Focus on your relationships; don't leave their quality and intensity to chance. Treat them with the kind of seriousness that people usually reserve for their money or career.

11. When it comes to love, expand your time horizon. Thinking short term leads to bad relationships.

12. True entrepreneurs risk their hearts by falling in love, even when it is risky.

13. Say exactly what you mean. No one—not even your family—can read your mind.

14. Don't treat your family like emotional ATMs. When people treat their family as a one-way valve of help and advice—usually, it's parents giving and children receiving—relationships suffer.

15. Make friendship an end in itself, not a stepping-stone to something else.

16. Feelings are contagious—don't spread the virus of misery.

17. Put on your own oxygen mask first. Work on your own happiness before trying to help others. Forgoing your own joy for the sake of another person might seem like the more virtuous path, but that is a lose-lose strategy.

18. Don't focus on looks and status in others. Good teeth and a high-paying job don't predict faithfulness and kindness. Seek out evidence of the two latter traits.

19. When you think something nice about someone, let them know.

20. Tell your partner one thing you appreciate about them every single day.

21. If you're trying to make conversation with people who intimidate you, ask what they're currently working on that they're most excited about. Ask follow-ups and listen intently.

22. When someone is going through hell, saying, "I'm with you," is the most powerful thing you can do. Be the "darkest-hour friend" to those you love.

23. Record a video interview with your parents. Ask them questions and have them tell stories about their childhoods, adventures, hopes, dreams, and fears. Our time with them is finite, but we often fail to recognize that until it's too late. These recordings will last forever.

24. If you're torn on what gift to send someone, send a book you love.

25. Carry a pocket notebook and pen with you everywhere you go. If someone says something interesting, take it out and write it down.

26. Never keep score in life. When you're with friends, pick up the check now and then—it all evens out if they're real friends. Quid pro quo is a terrible way to live.

27. If you have too many *deal friends*, you won't have enough *real friends*.

28. If you're about to take an emotion-induced action, wait twenty-four hours. Many relationships have been broken by actions taken in the heat of the moment. Don't fall into that trap.

29. Give a stranger a compliment every single day. Say you like someone's shirt or shoes, compliment the person's haircut, whatever. Don't use it as a conversation starter—say it and continue on.

30. Stop trying to be interesting and focus on being interested. Interested people give their deep attention to something to learn more about it. They open up to the world; they ask great questions and observe. Being interested is how you become interesting.

31. In your twenties and thirties, do a few things that you'll be excited to tell your kids about someday. Go on an adventure, train for some wild event, get your hands dirty on a crazy project, whatever. Create a few stories worth telling.

How to Assess Your Baseline:
The Relationship Map

PILLARS: Depth and Breadth

The relationship map is a simple exercise to assess your current social baseline and areas for focus and improvement. It is an adaptation of an exercise proposed in *The Good Life* by coauthors Robert Waldinger and Marc Schulz.

The relationship-map exercise involves three steps:

STEP 1: LIST CORE RELATIONSHIPS

The first step is to create a list of the core social relationships that occupy your life. These can include family, friends, partner, or coworker relationships. For most people, there will be about ten to fifteen relationships on this list, but others may have up to twenty-five.

STEP 2: ASSESS CORE RELATIONSHIPS

For each core relationship, ask these two assessment questions:

1. Is the relationship supportive, ambivalent, or demeaning?
2. Is the relationship interaction frequent or infrequent?

To define the key terms associated with the first assessment:

* A *supportive relationship* is one where there is a mutual understanding of care, love, respect, and comfort.
* A *demeaning relationship* is characterized by the absence of the qualities of a supportive relationship and typically involves specific behavior that undermines one's self-worth.
* An *ambivalent relationship* has elements of both supportive and demeaning relationships at different times—it is inconsistent.

Surprisingly, while you might expect demeaning relationships to be the most damaging to your life, research has shown that ambivalent relationships create the most trouble for your physical and mental well-being. For example, one study[17] found that participants experienced higher blood pressure after an interaction with someone who inspired mixed feelings than with someone who inspired purely negative feelings. The inconsistency of the interactions is damaging.

You have likely experienced a relationship like this in your own life, a person who provides love and support at some times but criticism and contempt at others. The love and support cause you to open up, let the person in, which makes the future criticism and contempt all the more painful. As bestselling author Adam Grant wrote in a *New York Times* opinion piece on the topic, "The most toxic relationships aren't the purely negative ones. They're the ones that are a mix of positive and negative."[18]

STEP 3: MAP THE CORE RELATIONSHIPS

After you have assessed your core relationships, place them on a relationship map, a simple two-by-two grid with *Relationship Health* on the x-axis (from demeaning to supportive) and *Relationship Frequency* on the y-axis (from rare to daily).

RELATIONSHIP MAP

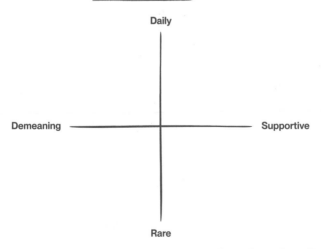

Once the core relationships are placed on the relationship map, consider the relevant zones and the implications for each:

- GREEN ZONE: Highly supportive and frequent. These relationships should be prioritized and focused on to maintain their position and strength.
- OPPORTUNITY ZONE: Highly supportive and infrequent. These relationships should be focused on to increase frequency of interactions.
- DANGER ZONE: Ambivalent and frequent. These relationships should be managed to reduce the frequency of impact or to improve the supportiveness of the interactions.
- RED ZONE: Demeaning and frequent. These relationships should be managed or removed to reduce frequency of impact.

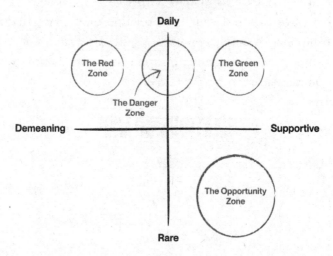

RELATIONSHIP MAP

To bring this to life, here are the findings from my first experience with the exercise:

- GREEN ZONE: Fortunately, there were several relationships that I identified as being both frequent and supportive. I will continue to prioritize these relationships and make sure I am letting these people know how much they mean to me.

- OPPORTUNITY ZONE: I identified over ten relationships that were infrequent but very supportive, some with old friends and colleagues and a few with family members. I deliberately increased the frequency of interactions with this group in various ways, including through group trips and more casual check-ins (texts, calls).
- DANGER ZONE: There were three relationships that I flagged as being frequent and ambivalent (inconsistent, both supportive and demeaning). In one case, I communicated directly with the individual (a family member) to explain how certain behaviors felt demeaning. The open communication led to improved interactions, and this relationship is now pushing into the Green Zone. In the other two cases, I reduced the frequency of my interactions with the individuals, which has pushed them out of the Danger Zone.
- RED ZONE: There was one professional relationship—a partner in one of my businesses—that I identified as being both frequent and demeaning. With the nature of the relationship identified, I made the decision to communicate a staged exit from my involvement with the business. It took six months, but once it was completed, the frequency of the demeaning interactions was significantly reduced.

With a completed relationship map in hand, you are well equipped to focus on the relationships that create the most energy, value, and emotional prosperity in your life.

The relationship map is not static; it's highly dynamic. Relationships will shift on the map, and you will undoubtedly add and remove people across the various seasons of your life, so it's worth revisiting the exercise regularly.

How to Navigate Romantic Relationships:
Two Rules for Growing in Love

PILLAR: Depth

Whom you choose to partner with in life is the single most important decision you will ever make.

Recall the graphs from the Time Wealth section of whom you spend your time with. Your partner is the only person with whom you spend more and more time up until the end.

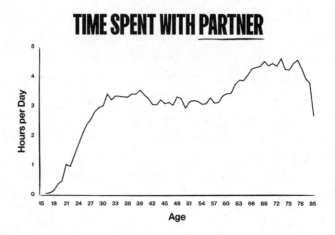

TIME SPENT WITH PARTNER

I have been extremely fortunate in my own experience and observation of love. At the time of this writing, my wife and I have been married for seven years and together for over seventeen, since we met and started dating in high school. My parents have been married for forty-two years, my wife's parents for over thirty, and all our grandparents were married up until the end.

I learned a tremendous amount from being surrounded by these relationships. Most important, I learned about what it means to *grow* in love.

Falling in love is easy. *Growing* in love is hard. Falling is what you see on social media. Growing is what you don't see. Growing in love is about developing and deepening a bond through discomfort, painful periods, darkness, hard conversations, and challenges. Growing in love happens over long periods, across seasons of life, in waves that come and go. Growing in love is what creates the depth of a lifelong bond.

There are two rules that I have observed couples who successfully grow in love follow, both of which have been particularly valuable in my wife's and my relationship.

RULE 1: UNDERSTAND LOVE LANGUAGES

In 1992, a Baptist pastor named Gary Chapman published a book called *The Five Love Languages: How to Express Heartfelt Commitment to Your Mate.* Chapman suggested that there are five love languages that govern the way romantic partners give, receive, and experience love:

1. WORDS OF AFFIRMATION: Verbal expressions of love and affection. People who use this love language feel most loved when they hear compliments, words of encouragement, and expressions of appreciation.
2. QUALITY TIME: Time and present, dedicated energy. People who use this love language feel loved when their partners give them undivided attention and spend quality time with them. They are present in the moment, engage in meaningful conversations, and create shared experiences together.
3. GIFTS: People who use this love language value the thought and effort behind gifts. They feel loved when receiving thoughtful and meaningful gifts.
4. ACTS OF SERVICE: People who use this love language value actions over words. They feel loved when their partners perform acts of service to make their lives easier or more comfortable (doing household chores, running errands, or taking on tasks to lighten their load).
5. PHYSICAL TOUCH: People who use this love language find that physical, human connection is what makes them feel most

loved—hugs, kisses, holding hands, cuddling, and other forms of physical contact. Nonsexual touch is just as important as sexual intimacy for them.

The awareness and recognition of your and your partner's love language is essential for a thriving relationship because it allows each of you to show up in the way that is most effective for the other person.

For example, I know that my wife's love language is physical touch. When she's upset or stressed, a hug or back rub is more effective than any other actions I can possibly take. When she's feeling great, a hand-hold and kiss on the cheek creates a powerful, lasting feeling of connection. For years, I struggled to meet her where she needed me to be, simply because I was not aware that this physical connection was all that she required from me at difficult moments.

To put the five love languages into practice, make it into a game with your partner. Sit down together and take a free quiz at 5lovelan guages.com/quizzes/love-language. Guess each other's love language before starting and see if you were right. After you've determined the correct answers, consider how you can incorporate the understanding of each other's love languages into your day-to-day interactions and expressions of love. Your relationship will benefit from the consideration.

RULE 2: AVOID THE TRAPS

Earlier in the book, I mentioned a quip from the late Charlie Munger: "All I want to know is where I'm going to die so I'll never go there." Consider the importance of this line in the context of your romantic relationships: Know where your relationship is going to die so you'll never go there.

Fortunately, psychologist John Gottman has done the hard work of finding where that place is. His research predicts who will eventually get divorced, and in one such experiment was shown to be correct a stunning 94 percent of the time.

In a seminal 1992 study, Dr. Gottman and his team interviewed fifty-two married couples. They asked them a variety of questions about how they met, why they decided to get married, and what changes their relationships had been through and observed them as they took part in a fifteen-minute discussion about a current area of relationship conflict. Based on the short interviews and observations, Dr. Gottman and his team were able to predict with 94 percent accuracy which couples would stay together and which would separate within three years of the study.

Dr. Gottman described the four communication styles that consistently appeared in relationships that went on to fail (he called them "the Four Horsemen," a nod to the Four Horsemen of the Apocalypse).

I consider these the places where your relationship will go to die:

1. CRITICISM: While articulating a complaint is fair game and necessary for a healthy relationship, Dr. Gottman defined *criticism* as an ad hominem attack on the other person.
2. DEFENSIVENESS: In response to criticism, most people will try to protect themselves through defensive strategies with excuses. When we are defensive, we fail to be accountable for our failures and actions.
3. CONTEMPT: Treating the partner with disrespect, attacking the person's character and core. Dr. Gottman's research revealed contempt to be the single greatest predictor of divorce.
4. STONEWALLING: In response to contempt, one or both partners may simply shut down, preferring to entirely evade engagement on the issue.

With an awareness of where your relationship will go to die, you can focus on never going there. If you notice these communication styles cropping up in your relationship, Dr. Gottman and his team developed a set of "antidotes" that are effective in fighting back:

1. CRITICISM ANTIDOTE (THE GENTLE START-UP): Focus on a complaint without blame by avoiding the word *you* and focusing on the word *I*. This reframe avoids blame and focuses instead on what you feel or need from your partner.

2. **DEFENSIVENESS ANTIDOTE (TAKE RESPONSIBILITY):** Acknowledge and accept your partner's perspective and offer an apology for actions or behaviors that created the perspective.

3. **CONTEMPT ANTIDOTE (BUILD A CULTURE OF APPRECIATION):** Create a regular reminder of your partner's positive traits, actions, or behaviors and ground yourself in gratitude for those features.

4. **STONEWALLING ANTIDOTE (PHYSIOLOGICAL SELF-SOOTHING):** Pause and take a break. Spend that time engaged in a soothing, distracting, or relaxing activity, like walking, breathing mindfully, or sitting with your eyes closed.

Developing an understanding of the common traps on the journey and learning how to avoid them has been a huge positive for my wife's and my relationship. I'm certain it will be one for yours as well.

FIVE HUNDRED YEARS OF RELATIONSHIP ADVICE

For my wife's and my seventh wedding anniversary on December 17, 2023, I asked couples who had been married forty, fifty, or even sixty years a simple question:

What relationship advice would you give to your younger selves?

The participants ranged from a mid-sixties couple who had just celebrated their fortieth anniversary to a ninety-nine-year-old who had just celebrated sixty-six years of happiness with his bride. In total, the advice captured more than five hundred years of earned wisdom from these beautiful relationships.

Here are ten pieces of relationship advice that everyone needs to hear:

1. Never keep score in love. Scoreboards are for sports games, not marriages.
2. Maintain interests and passions separate from your partner's. Marriage should not be the end of individuality.
3. It can't always be fifty-fifty. Sometimes it will be ninety-ten; sometimes it will be ten-ninety. All that matters is that it adds up to one hundred.

4. One man said, "Never stop dating. I'm ninety-nine and still courting my wife!" Marriages don't get boring; you stop trying.

5. No one has ever argued their way to a happy marriage. When facing a challenge, face it together.

6. You cannot take care of your partner if you aren't taking care of yourself. Make a list of your daily needs to feel good and have your partner do the same. Make sure you and your partner are able to do the things on that list.

7. Never involve nonprofessional third parties (parents, friends, siblings, coworkers) in disagreements. You'll forget about it, but they won't.

8. Your spouse should always take priority over your birth family. Remember that when the two feel in conflict.

9. Complementarity is just as important as compatibility. Allow each other the space to lead within different domains in your relationship.

10. Your love is yours. Forget the approval of others. You won't be able to make everyone happy. Accept that and embrace each other.

I'll close by repeating the beautiful line from the ninety-four-year-old woman who took part in the birthday exercise I mentioned in the beginning of the book:

"When in doubt, love. The world can always use more love."

The Life Dinner: Creating a Monthly Relationship Ritual

PILLAR: Depth

The Life Dinner is a powerful monthly relationship ritual originated by entrepreneur Brad Feld.

The problem: Over time, your life becomes increasingly hectic. It is easy to allow your relationship with your partner to sit on the back burner while you deal with the more pressing fires of day-to-day life. While this may seem okay in the short term, it can lead to problems in the long term.

The solution: A fixed monthly date to sit down for a meal with your partner to reflect on personal, professional, and relationship progress, challenges, and goals. The Life Dinner is a thoughtful way to keep your relationship thriving despite the time constraints and stresses of daily life.

A few specifics for conducting your Life Dinner ritual:

- Set a recurring monthly date.
- Pick a favorite spot, explore a new place, or cook a meal at home.
- If you don't have time for a full meal, do it over a coffee or a drink.

The point is to make it a sacred monthly ritual.
Three areas to cover in the discussion:

- Personal
- Professional
- Relationship

Within each area, each person should have the floor to reflect on the prior month's progress and challenges and discuss forward-looking goals. After both of you have had your time, you can discuss key items as a team. The goal is to give each of you time to speak freely before the joint discussion.

My wife and I love the Life Dinner because it creates a structure through which we can grow together. Since we had our son, in May 2022, it's been a critical part of our system for ensuring we continue to grow together despite having a newborn in the house.

If you're in a relationship but find it difficult to slow down in the face of life's chaos, I'd encourage you to give the Life Dinner a shot. At worst, you'll get a nice meal together—but I'm willing to bet you'll get much more out of it than that!

How to Improve Relationship Communication: Helped, Heard, or Hugged

PILLAR: Depth

I'm a fixer: When people come to me with problems, my bias is to try to fix them. This is (mostly) good in a professional context, but when I bring this bias into my relationships, the results can be decidedly mixed. Over the years, my fix-it mentality led to a lot of tense moments with my wife, family, and friends. They'd come to me with a problem, and I would immediately start deconstructing the situation and offering potential solutions. I found it puzzling that the other person often rejected my solutions and withdrew (or even became angry with me for offering them).

What I came to realize (after far too long) was this: Sometimes people don't want you to fix it. They just want you to be there with them.

The "helped, heard, or hugged" method is used by therapists, teachers, and counselors, but it is also immensely helpful in improving your handling of these everyday relationship situations; it allows you to give other people what they need.[19]

When someone you love comes to you with a problem, ask, "Do you want to be helped, heard, or hugged?"

- HELPED: Deconstruct the problem and identify potential solutions. The fix-it mentality can come out to play.
- HEARD: Listen intently and allow the other person to express (and vent) as needed.
- HUGGED: Provide comforting physical touch. Touch is a powerful love language for many (including my wife). Sometimes people just want to feel your presence with them.

The idea is to ask the question to create a two-way awareness of what is needed in the situation. This awareness snapped me out of my fixer default setting. Rather than showing up for loved ones in the way that was convenient and natural *for me*, I was forced to meet others in the way that was best suited *for them*.

PS: Specifically asking "Do you want to be helped, heard, or hugged?" can be helpful at first, but after a while, a recognizable pattern should emerge.

If you're anything like me and have struggled to appropriately identify what your partner, friend, or family member needed in a situation, give the "helped, heard, or hugged" method a shot.

How to Make Conversation: The Four Principles
of a Master Conversationalist

PILLAR: Breadth

The skilled conversationalist can take many different forms:

- Extrovert or introvert
- Theatrical storyteller or prudent fact deliverer
- Giver or taker

The point is that your natural predisposition does not make or break your ability to become a skilled conversationalist. The extrovert who constantly runs away with conversations and doesn't let the other person get a word in is just as challenged as the introvert who refuses to create forward momentum with active listening or progressions. The goal is to make the most of our natural skill sets and become the best conversationalists we can be.

Here are four core principles of the master conversationalist that anyone, regardless of natural disposition, can use:

PRINCIPLE 1: CREATE DOORKNOBS

An improvisation artist once referred to the concept of "doorknobs" in conversations. Most questions are like stop signs: They invite an answer that naturally ends the conversation. Doorknobs are questions or statements that invite the other person to open them and walk through. They invite the other person to start telling a story.

An example:

- Stop-sign question: Where did you get married?
- Doorknob question: How did you decide on the wedding venue?

The stop-sign version likely leads to a conversational stop when the person responds with a location. The doorknob version likely leads to a story.

Every story offers new opportunities for you, the listener, to further the connection and discourse. Doorknobs create stories—you should create the doorknobs.

Here is a set of great doorknobs that I like to use in conversations. Choose a few to incorporate in your tool kit and use them the next time you're in an unfamiliar social or professional situation. I'd recommend thinking about your own response to these topics, as you will likely encounter situations where the person flips them on you to get the conversation moving.

CONVERSATION STARTERS:
- What are you most excited about right now, personally or professionally?
- What was your favorite (or least favorite) thing about your hometown?
- What's the origin of your name? Why did your parents give you that name?
- What is the most interesting thing you've read or learned recently?
- What is the best movie or show you've seen recently? What made it so compelling to you?
- What's been making you smile recently?
- If you had an entire day to yourself with zero responsibilities, how would you spend it?

CONVERSATION DEVELOPERS:
- What do you remember as some of the more formative moments of your life? What made them so formative?
- What have you changed your mind about recently?
- If you could have dinner with three to five people from any point in history, who would you choose and why?

- What is something you've purchased for a little money that has made a big difference in your life?
- How do you escape or unwind?
- What is the kindest thing anyone has ever done for you?

These are in no particular order, but they've all been effective and led to deep connections with new and old friends in my life.

PRINCIPLE 2: BE A LOUD LISTENER

In his *New York Times* bestselling book *How to Know a Person,* David Brooks referred to the idea of loud listening. Loud listening can take many forms, but generally, the listeners act to let the speakers know that they are being heard and felt.

A few examples of loud listening:

- SOUNDS: Saying "Yes" or "Uh-huh" or "Hmm" to signal listening and encourage continued energy from the speaker
- FACIAL EXPRESSIONS: Changing facial expressions to react to the story being told
- BODY LANGUAGE: A forward-leaning posture toward the speaker signals engagement and positive energy. Never turn away or turn sideways, as it signals you are trying to leave a conversation and immediately hurts the energy of a moment.

We've all been in conversations where it becomes very clear the other person is uninterested in who we are or what we have to say. We know that feeling. Don't create it for others.

PRINCIPLE 3: REPEAT AND FOLLOW

Active listening leads directly to the "repeat and follow" method: Repeat key points back to the speaker in your own words and follow that with an additional insight, story, or doorknob question. This is an opportunity to relay the things you agree or disagree with and shows engaged listening. It builds conversational momentum and cements connection.

PRINCIPLE 4: MAKE SITUATIONAL EYE CONTACT

Eye contact is nuanced—too little and you look shifty; too much and you look psychotic.

I like situational eye contact:

* Deep and connected while the other person speaks
* Organic while you speak. It's okay to gaze off while you think, but use eye contact to emphasize key points and moments in a story.

If you focus on those four core principles, you'll immediately improve your overall ability as a conversationalist. Whether you're an introvert or an extrovert, a storyteller or a fact deliverer, you have the potential to be a great conversationalist. Mastering the art and science of conversation will pay off professionally but, more important, personally, as it leads to the meaningful connections that provide new texture and richness to life.

Use the four core principles to get started on your journey to becoming a master conversationalist.

How to Build New Relationships:
The Anti-Networking Guide

PILLAR: Breadth

Harsh truth: Networking is dead . . . at least in the traditional sense of the word *networking*.

You don't get anywhere by accumulating thousands of transactional personal and professional connections. You get somewhere by building genuine relationships:

* Giving with no intention of receiving in return
* Acting in the service of others
* Creating value for those around you

Those who invest in building relationships rather than networking will reap the most valuable long-term rewards—health, wealth, and happiness.

Here's a confession: I'm not a natural relationship builder. In fact, I am a bit introverted and socially anxious, particularly in large group settings like conferences, cocktail parties, and crowded events. And yet I've built a depth and breadth of connections that has brought me great joy and value over the years.

Whether you're moving to a new area, starting a new job, progressing in your current career, going to a professional event, or just want to make new friends, this guide will help.

Here are four core anti-networking principles that anyone can use:

PRINCIPLE 1: FIND VALUE-ALIGNED ROOMS
The best advice I've ever received when it comes to building new relationships: Put yourself into rooms with a high density of value-aligned individuals.

What this means: Think about your core values, hobbies, and professional and personal interests, then consider what "rooms" are likely to filter for people with a similar set of values and interests. An example: If you're a dog owner and love being outside, local dog parks, outdoor beer gardens, or walking trails would likely have a high density of others with similar interests.

The point here is that you can increase your odds of meeting people with whom you will connect by putting yourself in the rooms where several levels of filtering have already occurred before you even arrive.

- If you're passionate about fitness and health, frequent the local farmers' market, the gym in the early morning, and local hiking trails.
- If you're focused on your career in marketing, look up any local marketing mixers or events and attend any social media or creator conferences.
- If you're into books and art, find a local book club, go to art-gallery openings, and join the local museum community.

In professional tracks, the rooms are usually easier to find, as your business or company will have specific conferences, events, parties, and dinners you'll be encouraged to attend. In your personal life, you will need to do a bit more work to find these rooms.

Place yourself in the right rooms and you'll already be well positioned to build new relationships.

PRINCIPLE 2: ASK ENGAGING QUESTIONS

Once you're in the rooms, strike up conversations with new people. A warm hello and a smile is generally a great place to start, as it tends to be disarming and cut the tension in any situation.

From there, I have a few go-to questions that I have found create reliably engaging discourse:

- What's your connection to [insert current place or event]?
- What are you most excited about currently?

- What's lighting you up *outside* of work?
- What's your favorite book you've read recently?

Note: Always avoid "What do you do?" as a question. It's generic and generally gets you a cookie-cutter, automated response or an uncomfortable one if people don't feel proud of their work. "What are you most excited about right now?" leads to more personal, interesting replies and increased conversational momentum.

If you're socially anxious, much of your nervousness in these situations arises from a self-induced pressure to be "interesting" to other people. Flip it around—focus on being *interested*. Ask engaging questions. It's much easier (and more effective).

Principle 3: Become a Level 2 and Level 3 Listener
There is a concept that there are three levels of listening:

Level 1. "Me" listening: You're having a conversation, but your internal voice is relating everything you hear to something in your own life. Your internal voice runs off on tangents; you're thinking about your own life while the other person is talking. You're waiting to speak, not listening to learn. This is the default mode of listening for everyone.

Level 2. "You" listening: You're having a conversation, and you are deeply focused on what the other person is saying. You're not waiting to speak; you're listening to learn.

Level 3. "Us" listening: You're building a map of the other person, understanding how all the new information being shared fits into that broader map of the person's life and world. You're listening to understand, considering the layers beneath what the other person is saying.

Most people default to Level 1 listening, but charismatic people have a practiced intention around Level 2 and Level 3 listening. If you want to build new, genuine relationships, you have to live in Level 2 and Level 3.

Be a loud listener. After you ask questions, lean in and show your focus and presence with body language, facial expressions, and sounds.

As you listen, make mental notes of a few pertinent facts about the person's interests or anything else that jumps out to you. These will become relevant alongside Principle 4.

PRINCIPLE 4: USE CREATIVE FOLLOW-UPS

When a conversation has run its course, don't feel pressured to keep it going. Exit gracefully. I've always found "It was so great meeting you, I look forward to seeing you again soon!" works well in any personal or professional setting. If it makes sense, you can offer to share contact information for the future.

Following the conversation, log the mental notes you made in your phone or a notebook and create a plan to follow up in the days ahead.

As an example, I used to talk about my favorite books with new people. If I was speaking to a new professional contact and it struck me as a relationship I hoped to deepen, I would send a copy of the book with a handwritten note to the person's office. I've built many great mentor relationships with that as the start.

A few ideas for thoughtful, creative follow-ups:

* Share an article or podcast that you think the person will like for a specific reason.
* Provide value in the form of a new idea related to one of the points of professional tension that was uncovered in the conversation.
* Offer to connect the person with a friend who has a shared interest.

The aim is to show that you were listening intently and that you took the initiative to follow up. Playing hard to get is childish. Invest energy in building new, genuine relationships and you will be rewarded.

Note: If you and the other person didn't share contact information, you may need to use a bit of research and finesse to get a physical of-

fice address or an email address. For instance, if you didn't get an email address at the event, guess it:

- *[first name] @ [company] . com*
- *[first initial] [last name] @ [company] . com*
- *[first name] . [last name] @ [company] . com*
- *[last name] @ [company] . com*

Email address data shows those syntax structures cover over 80 percent of emails. A little bit of hustle goes a long way!

Remember: Relationship satisfaction affects health! Relationships are, quite literally, everything. So stop networking. Use these four principles of anti-networking and start building genuine relationships—they will pay dividends in all areas of your life for many years to come.

How to Build a Personal Board of Advisers: The Brain Trust

PILLAR: Breadth

Pixar Animation Studios is widely regarded as one of the most creative studios of all time; its films have earned over twenty Academy Awards and countless other recognitions. Throughout its thirty-plus-year history, the studio has created and fostered beloved films, including *Toy Story, Finding Nemo, A Bug's Life, Monsters, Inc., The Incredibles, Wall-E, Coco, Inside Out,* and more. If you are a parent or if you grew up in the 1990s or 2000s, odds are that you've fallen in love with a Pixar storyline and character.

But this kind of prolific creative output doesn't happen by chance. As Pixar cofounder Ed Catmull revealed in his bestselling book *Creativity, Inc.,* systems and processes were deliberately put in place to ensure the absolute highest quality and consistency of the product across the decades.[20]

One such system—referred to at Pixar as the Braintrust—is particularly relevant as a model that can be applied to our own lives.

Pixar's Braintrust is a group of individuals who meet every few months to discuss in-process movies. The group includes the primary directors of the movies being discussed as well as a collection of others who are not directly involved in the films but who are part of the company and have a vested interest in their success. As Catmull explained, "Our decision making is better when we draw on the collective knowledge and unvarnished opinions of the group . . . we rely on [the Braintrust] to push us toward excellence and to root out mediocrity. It is our primary delivery system for straight talk."

We can apply the general model of a brain trust—a group of individuals with different perspectives and lenses asking questions and pressure-testing assumptions to improve the quality of the final product—to our own lives for our own personal and professional pursuits.

Traditionally, people have turned to mentorship to navigate the uncharted waters they encounter at new stages in life. But the term *mentorship* feels very formal. It connotes a fixed cadence and time commitment. From the mentor's perspective, it may feel like a big commitment, which dilutes the quality of the relationship, experience, and results. Furthermore, having one formal mentor often falls short of what someone needs. Your single mentor may not have encountered the challenge you're facing—that person may not have a map that you can leverage to navigate the terrain.

Rather than finding a single mentor, you can leverage Pixar's creation to form your own brain trust—a personal board of advisers for your life. Just as Pixar used this group to improve the quality of its creative decisions, you can use your brain trust to improve the quality of your personal and professional decisions.

Your brain trust is a group of five to ten individuals.

A few key features of the group:

1. Unbiased (ideally not family)
2. Diverse experiences, perspectives, lenses
3. Willing to provide candid, raw feedback
4. Vested interest in your success (that is, they want to see you win)

As you construct your brain trust, it may be helpful to think about each member as fitting a particular archetype:

* Senior executive (navigating hierarchies and senior ranks)
* Inspirational leader (leadership principles and people management)
* Intellectual sparring partner (very willing to pressure-test your thinking)
* Contrarian thinker (willing to play devil's advocate)
* Connector (deep relationships and network)
* Peer (at a similar personal or professional stage)

It's not about the most *impressive-sounding* brain trust. You want people who are genuinely interested in seeing you succeed. Over time, you can add and subtract from your group—add the new and deep relationships, subtract the people whose value has diminished as you or they have changed or progressed.

Unlike Pixar, you won't need to host formal meetings of your brain trust (this avoids the formality challenge of mentorship in general), so the members don't need to know one another or that they are part of your brain trust. As you encounter challenges, key decisions, or inflection points in your personal and professional life, you can reliably turn to the members of your brain trust for grounded perspectives, candor, feedback, and advice.

Our time and energy are finite, so the fact that these people are using a portion of their time to support you is no small thing. Always let them know they are appreciated. Buy them books. Send them handwritten thank-you notes for spending time with you. Tiny gestures of gratitude go a long way.

How to Build Authority:
The Public Speaking Guide

PILLARS: Breadth and Earned Status

Confession: I used to be a nervous public speaker.

I know I'm not alone—in fact, several surveys have found that people rank public speaking ahead of death on a list of their greatest fears. But confident public speaking is a critical skill for many people's careers and lives; it expands potential relationship circles and builds authority and expertise that are markers of earned status. It has the potential to accelerate personal and professional endeavors meaningfully. You can't just hide from it—you need a set of strategies to increase your confidence and perform as the best version of yourself.

Here are the strategies I've used to build a powerful public-speaking muscle—strategies you can start using immediately.

PRE-EVENT PREPARATION
CREATE CLEAR STRUCTURE
The best public speakers don't deliver a speech—they tell a story. They take the audience on a journey. Create a clear structure that is familiar and easy to follow. It's helpful to be clear and explicit about that structure up front, whether in the presentation materials or in your early delivery.

BUILD YOUR LEGO BLOCKS
When you're nervous about a speech, toast, presentation, or talk, your natural bias is to memorize the content word for word. The memorization is intended to serve as a protective wall that shields you from your fears. You can recite something and semi-disassociate from the act itself.

Unfortunately, I have found (and observed) that memorization often has the opposite effect.

When you memorize material, one tiny slip-up can throw you off. You know the material only in one fixed linear trajectory, so you're unable to adapt. All it takes is one glitch in the slides, an off-track question from the audience, or a slight stumble in your opener, and your preparation goes out the window.

My recommendations:

* Build Lego blocks by practicing the key moments, such as the opening, transitions, and punch lines. Perfect these Lego blocks.
* Practice the speech in segments rather than sequentially. This may seem counterintuitive, but it will make you more dynamic if things don't go perfectly according to plan.

One other *weird* trick for a big speech: Practice once while briskly walking or lightly jogging. I have found that it effectively simulates the heart rate increase you might experience when you take the stage.

OPTIONAL PRE-WORK: STUDY THE BEST

If you want to improve at anything, study the best practitioners of it. We live in an incredible era with access to the best speaking coaches in the world at the click of a button. Identify three to five speakers you admire. They can be politicians, business leaders, comedians, motivational coaches, whatever. Go on YouTube and find videos of each one delivering a speech. Slow down the playback speed and take notes.

Pay attention to the following:

* How are they structuring their talks?
* What is the pacing of their words? When are they pausing and when are they accelerating?
* When are they raising their voices? When are they lowering them?
* Note their movements on the stage. How are they gesturing?
* How are they engaging with the audience?

By studying the best, we naturally move to embody the traits we've identified.

PRE-STAGE PREPARATION
ADDRESS THE SPOTLIGHT

The spotlight effect is a common psychological phenomenon in which people overestimate the degree to which other people are noticing or observing their actions, behaviors, appearance, or results. Public speaking is one of the moments when the spotlight effect is most pronounced (and potentially crippling).

To dim the spotlight, try the "So what?" approach:

- Confront your worst fears about what could go wrong.
- Imagine the worst fear becoming reality. Now ask yourself, "So what?" So what if you forget your remarks or you don't deliver them perfectly? You'll stumble through, but it won't kill you. Your family will still love you when you get home and life will move on.

Usually the answer to "So what?" isn't nearly as bad as we think. As Seneca famously wrote, "We suffer more in imagination than in reality."

GET INTO CHARACTER

Character invention is a technique in which you create a character that can show up and perform in situations that induce in you fear or self-doubt.

The general strategy: Create a character in your mind who can nail the speech, then "flip the switch" to become this character before stepping into the spotlight.

Envision the public-speaking character that you would like to embody:

- What traits do they possess?
- How do they interact with their surroundings?

- How do they physically appear to others?
- What is their mentality?

Turn on your character and take on the moment with new energy as the best version of yourself.

Eliminate Stress

The physiological sigh is a remarkably effective, science-backed technique to quickly eliminate stress.

It's a breath pattern marked by a long inhale, a short inhale, and a long exhale. People do it naturally when levels of carbon dioxide in the bloodstream get too high. It creates a relaxing sensation by releasing a lot of carbon dioxide very fast.

If you feel your nerves rising before the event, try it:

- Inhale through your nose twice, once slowly, then once quickly.
- Long exhale through your mouth.
- Repeat two to three times.

Immediate positive impact.

Delivery
Cut the Tension

A few minutes before I gave a keynote speech in June 2023, the organizers asked me what song I wanted to enter to. They probably assumed I'd pick some upbeat pump-up music. I told them "Girl on Fire" by Alicia Keys. They thought I was joking, but I was dead serious. Why? Doing something unexpected and funny early in a talk immediately cuts the anxiety and tension in the room. When I entered to that song, I had a built-in joke!

"You're probably wondering why I just entered to 'Girl on Fire' . . . well, it's my one-year-old son's favorite song, and I figured he'd be more excited to watch the replay if his dad entered to his favorite jam."

My anxiety disappeared when I saw the smiling and laughing faces in the crowd.

Lesson: Find a simple way to cut the tension early and get people on your side.

PLAY THE LAVA GAME

You may remember playing a childhood game where parts of the floor are lava that you can't touch. During a speech, I try to play a similar game. I think of my pockets and torso as lava—I can't touch them.

This simple framing forces you to get your arms away from your body, gesture broadly, and express confidence.

Pro tip: Use big, bold, body-opening gestures early in the talk. I have found that doing so builds confidence and momentum (consider this my hat tip to Amy Cuddy's much-debated power-pose research).

MOVE PURPOSEFULLY

Pacing around like you're on the phone with your childhood crush isn't helpful. It just makes you more nervous.

Take slow, methodical, purposeful steps. Move with gravitas. Use your movements to add dramatic pauses to your words as you navigate the room.

There are people who move to move, and then there are people who move with intention, who are going places. Always be the latter.

PUTTING IT ALL TOGETHER

These nine strategies will work wonders for your public speaking:

1. STUDY THE BEST: Use YouTube to study speakers you admire.
2. CREATE CLEAR STRUCTURE: Be deliberate about the storytelling arc.
3. BUILD YOUR LEGO BLOCKS: Relentlessly practice the opening, transitions, and key lines, but avoid rote memorization.
4. ADDRESS THE SPOTLIGHT: Ask "So what?" about your worst fears and stop suffering in your imagination.

5. GET INTO CHARACTER: Turn your ideal character on prior to the start.
6. ELIMINATE STRESS: Use the physiological sigh to eliminate stress.
7. CUT THE TENSION: Find a way to cut the tension early with a joke or self-deprecating remark to get the audience on your side.
8. PLAY THE LAVA GAME: Use big, confident gestures and avoid touching your pockets or torso.
9. MOVE PURPOSEFULLY: Take slow, methodical, purposeful steps.

Public speaking is a muscle that we can all work to build. By leveraging these strategies, you'll be well on your way.

How to Play the Right Games: The Status Tests

PILLAR: Earned Status

Denis Diderot was an eighteenth-century philosopher and writer who had a reputation as a deep thinker in intellectual circles. His work did not lead to any level of financial riches, a fact that did not seem to trouble Diderot, but when he was unable to provide a dowry for his daughter, his lack of financial means was thrust to the forefront of his mind. Fortunately, his work had won him many fans, including Catherine the Great, the empress of Russia; hearing of his financial struggle, she offered to buy his library and retain his services as her personal librarian, for which she would pay him handsomely.

Shortly after this good financial fortune, Denis Diderot came to own a fancy new scarlet robe. Diderot liked the status that the fancy robe conferred on him but felt the remainder of his possessions could not compare to the beauty and prestige of this new one.

How could he be expected to dress in such a robe but sit in such a shabby chair, walk in such tattered shoes, or write at such a spartan desk? In quick succession, he purchased a new leather chair, new shoes, and an elaborate wooden desk, all of which seemed a suitable match for his scarlet robe—or, perhaps more important, a suitable match for the type of person who wore such a fancy scarlet robe.

The new robe had created a new identity, one that Denis Diderot became attached to and that he wanted to continue signaling to the world. In an essay later in life, which he titled, appropriately, "Regrets for My Old Dressing Gown," Diderot lamented, "I was the absolute master of my old robe. I have become the slave of the new one."

Denis Diderot had fallen victim to the perils of bought status—the slow, creeping thirst for more, for the next thing that would confer upon him a level of external affirmation.

Identifying and avoiding these bought-status games and playing earned-status games instead is important for building a life of Social Wealth.

Here are two simple tests you can use to assess the games you are playing:

THE BOUGHT-STATUS TEST
Would I buy this thing if I could not show it to anyone or tell anyone about it?

Bought status is the fleeting improved social position garnered through acquired status symbols. Asking this question cuts through the noise to determine if the item itself provides happiness or utility or if its sole purpose is to signal your success or achievement to others.

For example:

* Are you buying the fancy watch because you love the intricacies of watch engineering and details or because you want people to see that you have a fancy watch?
* Are you buying the fast car because you are obsessed with cars and dream about driving on mountain roads on your days off or because you want people to see you in the car and think you've made it?
* Are you paying for the table at the charity event because you believe in the mission of the charity and would donate the money anonymously or because you want to be seen at the event as someone who purchased a full table?

It is unlikely that you will ever eliminate bought-status games from your life, but asking these questions about your underlying motivations for a given purchase will create new awareness and encourage you to focus your time and energy on earned-status games instead.

THE EARNED-STATUS TEST
Could the richest person in the world acquire the thing I want by tomorrow?

Earned status is the great equalizer. It is the real respect, admiration, and trust received through hard-won treasures:

- Free time
- Loving relationships
- Purposeful work, expertise, and wisdom
- Healthy mind and body
- Hard-won financial success

The richest people in the world cannot acquire these things in a day. If you don't make a clear effort to create the space and prioritize effectively, each of these markers will prove elusive. The world's richest people cannot build a loving relationship any faster than you. They cannot forge a healthy mind and body any faster than you. None of them can buy their way to expertise, wisdom, or purpose. Money may improve the odds of acquiring some of them—free time, for instance—but the effort is unavoidable. As the saying goes, "Rome wasn't built in a day."

Entrepreneur Naval Ravikant once quipped, "Play stupid games, win stupid prizes."

Denis Diderot played a stupid game and won a stupid prize. Don't fall into the same trap: Avoid bought-status games and focus on playing earned-status games, because the prizes are much more fulfilling.

16.

Summary: Social Wealth

SOCIAL WEALTH OVERVIEW

THE BIG QUESTION: WHO will be sitting in the front row at your funeral?

THE THREE PILLARS OF SOCIAL WEALTH:
* DEPTH: Connection to a small circle of people with deep, meaningful bonds
* BREADTH: Connection to a larger circle of people for support and belonging beyond the self, either through individual relationships or through community, religious, spiritual, or cultural infrastructure
* EARNED STATUS: The lasting respect, admiration, and trust of your peers that you receive on the basis of earned, not acquired, status symbols

The Social Wealth Score: For each statement below, respond with 0 (strongly disagree), 1 (disagree), 2 (neutral), 3 (agree), or 4 (strongly agree).

1. I have a core set of deep, loving, supportive relationships.
2. I am consistently able to be the partner, parent, family member, and friend that I would want to have.

3. I have a network of loose relationships I can learn from and build on.
4. I have a deep feeling of connection to a community (local, regional, national, spiritual, and so on) or to something bigger than myself.
5. I do not attempt to achieve status, respect, or admiration through material purchases.

Your baseline score (0 to 20):

Goals, Anti-Goals, and Systems

Use the goal-setting framework to calibrate your Social Wealth compass:

- GOALS: What Social Wealth Score do you want to achieve within one year? What are the two to three checkpoints that you will need to hit on your path to achieve this score?
- ANTI-GOALS: What are the two to three outcomes that you want to avoid on your journey?
- HIGH-LEVERAGE SYSTEMS: What are the two to three systems from the Social Wealth Guide that you will implement to make tangible, compounding progress toward your goal score?

YOUR ONE-WEEK JUMP START
Use the Relationship Map to develop an awareness of your current relationships and identify opportunities for depth and breadth.

Start by listing all the core relationships that occupy your life. Assess each core relationship according to whether the relationship is supportive, ambivalent, or demeaning and the frequency of interaction in the relationship. Using this information, create a map of your core relationships on a two-by-two grid with *Relationship Health* on the x-axis (from demeaning to supportive) and *Relationship Frequency* on the y-axis (from rare to daily).

Consider how you can prioritize the relationships in the green zone (healthy, frequent) and spend more time with the relationships in the opportunity zone (healthy, infrequent).

Mental
Wealth

17.

The Big Question

What Would Your Ten-Year-Old Self Say to You Today?

THE NINETY-YEAR-OLD MAN SAT down in the front row of the college lecture hall and took out his notebook.

When class started, he listened intently and jotted down notes on the big bang, the solar system, and the eventual fate of the sun. When class ended, he smiled, gathered his things, and walked out, *almost* blending in with the sea of eighteen-year-old Harvard College freshmen exiting the introductory astronomy class.

The man's name was Hank Behar, and when people ask me what I want to be when I grow up, I tell them I want to be like Hank.

Hank Behar lived in the same community as my parents when I was young. He is, in some ways, quite ordinary—he isn't particularly rich, famous, or powerful—but the sum of his *ordinary* starts to look rather *extraordinary*. Hank spent most of his career as a Hollywood screenwriter and director and has a keen, clever wit to show for it. He's been married for more than fifty years to the same woman, Phyllis, a glamorous former soap opera star whom he met on a set and, as he described it, somehow convinced to go on a date with him. Hank and Phyllis have three children, four grandchildren, and two great-grandchildren. Hank has a sweet, loving personality that shines through, and he is always quick with a self-deprecating joke. He remains active despite his age, and he and Phyllis have been known to hop on a plane or take a cruise for a new adventure on a whim.

In 2014, Phyllis asked Hank what he wanted for his ninetieth birthday. Both of them were in good health, and she assumed he would ask for a nice vacation, weekend getaway, or perhaps just a special dinner.

His response surprised her:

"I've always wanted to see what those geniuses were up to at Harvard. I'd like to spend a day there."

Never ones to be deterred by a challenge, they contacted my father, a longtime professor at the school. He and a handful of professors arranged for Hank to attend classes for a day—his birthday wish was in motion. A few weeks later, Hank woke up early, put on a nice pair of slacks, a shirt, and a sweater, and made the pilgrimage to Cambridge, Massachusetts, to spend the day at Harvard University.

So it was that this ninety-year-old man found himself in the front row of an introductory astronomy class among some of the world's brightest eighteen-year-olds. He was a model student; he arrived early, took notes, and even asked questions when he didn't understand something.

The visual alone is enough to bring a smile to anyone's face. But Hank's day at Harvard is much more than just a heartwarming story. It carries a deeper set of insights and lessons with science-backed implications for how you can live a healthier, more fulfilling life well into your sunset years.

THE REAL FOUNTAIN OF YOUTH

Curiosity is the foundation of a life of Mental Wealth.

It is also part of your manufacturer's default setting: You are literally born with it. If you have children or have spent time around children you've seen firsthand what true, uninhibited curiosity looks like. Children pursue everything with a wide-eyed, completely unfiltered awe. The newness sparks a wonder about the world that seems impossible to contain. Curiosity is how you learn about the world and how you stay alive.

The science supports this idea. Curiosity, it turns out, is very, very good for you. It is the real Fountain of Youth.

A 2018 study found that the brain systems that are engaged by curiosity contribute to maintaining cognitive function, mental health, and physical health with age.[1] Furthermore, curiosity has been connected to higher levels of life satisfaction and positive emotions and lower levels of anxiety.[2] Curiosity keeps us happier, healthier, and more fulfilled. If curiosity were a pill, all the world's pharmaceutical companies would call it a super-drug and clamor to sell it.

Mental Wealth is about building on the foundation of curiosity that encourages you to search, explore, question, and learn. It is through curiosity that you go on the journey to uncover and live by your **purpose**, unlock new insights and lifelong **growth**, and seek out the **space** necessary to think, reset, wrestle with questions, and recharge.

It's difficult to determine how, but when you pursue life with genuine, inspired, childlike curiosity, good things tend to happen, both personally and professionally.

You can find examples of the power of curiosity all around you:

- The aspiring entrepreneurs who find their "big ideas" by deeply exploring new markets and business models that pique their interest
- The retirees who keep their minds working by learning new languages that intrigue them
- The people who meet their life partners by going to events that spark their excitement
- The CEOs who credit their long-term successes to a regular "Think Day" (a day off to freely contemplate the biggest challenges facing the business)

One fact is clear: Fortune favors the curious.

Unfortunately, that raw childhood curiosity you're born with slowly atrophies throughout your adult life. Reality sets in—the need to provide, the "busyness" of life, the urgency of just about everything—and curiosity takes a permanent back seat.

This is far from conjecture. Studies have shown that intellectual curiosity[3] and degree of openness to new experiences[4] appear to decline with age, beginning in late adolescence and continuing throughout adulthood. One group of researchers has argued that the decline is driven by a lower perception of *future time,* meaning that as you age, you see less value in acting on curiosity, as it will mainly benefit you in a future time window that is quickly closing.

I would propose that the age-related curiosity decline is a clever, albeit outdated, evolutionary survival trait. Curiosity serves you in your early years as you learn about the world; a rapid ascent up the learning curve is what allows you to survive to reproductive age in the wild. But once you've figured out how your world works, that same curiosity is more likely to kill you in your later years if it pushes you to explore beyond the safety of your core routines. Unfortunately, in a modern world where few need to concern themselves with the risk of being eaten by a lion should they get curious about a sound in the brush, I would argue that our diminishing curiosity does more harm than good.

A life without curiosity is a life devoid of the desire to search, explore, and learn and lacks the texture created by this desire. A life without curiosity is an empty life, a life of stasis, a life without wonder.

Paraphrasing a friend on the topic, inside every eighty-year-old is a ten-year-old wondering, *What the f*ck just happened?*

But the seeds of that sentiment are sown many years earlier. They are sown in your twenties and thirties when you stop pursuing any interests or hobbies outside your job. They are sown in your forties and fifties when you stop trying to understand the world and start saying, "That's just the way it is." They are sown in your sixties and seventies when you stop learning new things because you don't see any utility in it anymore.

Most people have lost touch with their inner ten-year-olds—*but it's not too late to reconnect.*

Mental time travel is a neat trick for self-reflection. In its simplest form, it involves separating from one's present self and entering a past or future version of the self. It's a useful tool for creating gratitude—imagine how amazed your younger self would be at what you've accomplished. And it gives you perspective—imagine how much your older self would long to be where you are today. In this instance, mental time travel can provide a clear lens through which we can evaluate our Mental Wealth.

So what would your ten-year-old, hyper-curious, mischievous self say to you today?

- Would that ten-year-old express excitement at your vigor for the journey or resentment that you settled for something less than what you deserve?
- Would that ten-year-old be impressed by your joy for contin-ued growth, development, and learning?
- Would that ten-year-old shudder at the absence of space, still-ness, and silence in your life?

Your ten-year-old self would remind you to stay interested in the world and have some fun along the way. When life pulls you toward the sameness of incurious, static adulthood, you must fight to main-tain your wonder for the universe.

Hank Behar will turn one hundred before this book hits shelves. On his ninety-ninth birthday, one of his grandsons made a short doc-umentary in which he followed Hank for a day and asked about his secrets to a long life. Breakfast is decaf coffee with milk; herring; Cheerios with skim milk, blueberries, and a banana; two crackers with jam; and exactly ten grapes; and after his wife, Phyllis, helps him peel the banana, she departs with a kiss on the cheek. Hank looks at the camera and says, "How do you make it to ninety-nine? You marry a good woman." His loving, mischievous nature shines through. After breakfast, Hank is shown in his recliner, newspaper in hand, where he happily says, "I read the paper every day. I like to know what's going on, of course—who, what, when, and where!"

I hope he has many years of learning ahead of him, and I hope that his story inspires each of you to reconnect with your inner child. I suppose there are many reasons I tell people I want to be like Hank when I grow up, but one stands above the rest:

Hank has built a life of abundant Mental Wealth.

18.

A Tale as Old as Time

Some people die at twenty-five and aren't buried until seventy-five.

—Unknown

A YOUNG PRINCE RAISED in a world of luxury ventures out of the palace and encounters the reality of suffering that exists outside its walls. He sees an old man, frail as he nears the end; a sick person feeling the pain of illness; a corpse lost to this world; and an ascetic who has renounced worldly life. Suddenly exposed to the truth that his royal upbringing has masked, he decides to embark on a journey to confront and overcome suffering and to achieve a higher understanding of existence. He removes the robes and ornaments that signify his princely status and crosses the river to seek out his higher-order purpose.

The young prince, Siddhartha Gautama, faces a long, arduous path of trials that culminate in his stillness underneath a bodhi tree. Here he attains enlightenment, becoming the Buddha, and commits to sharing his learnings on how to overcome suffering. Today, over five hundred million people around the world follow his teachings.

Throughout history, the quest for a life of purpose, growth, and reflection has been a core part of the human experience. This quest appears in different forms across a variety of ancient cultures.

In ancient Hindu traditions, the concept of *dharma* refers to one's sacred duty—the life purpose that allows one to navigate the unknown with bravery and courage. Your dharma does not have to be grand or impressive; it must simply be *yours*. In the opening scene of the Bhagavad Gita, a Hindu text that is part of the epic Mahabharata, the protagonist, Arjuna, stands before a battlefield at the outset of a great war with his rivals. Wrestling with the inner turmoil of a battle that will see him fight family members, Arjuna consults his charioteer, Krishna, a mortal incarnation of the god Vishnu, for guidance. Krishna encourages him to center his actions on his purpose, saying, "One's own dharma performed imperfectly is better than another's dharma well performed . . . It is better to strive in one's own dharma than to succeed in the dharma of another. Nothing is ever lost in following one's own dharma. But competition in another's dharma breeds fear and insecurity."

In ancient Greece, the concept of *arete* was used to capture the idea of living up to one's full potential and purpose. Arete was, in some sense, the earliest known incarnation of the modern self-improvement movement, encouraging the people to strive for continuous growth and excellence across a range of life areas, including relationships, intellectual pursuits, moral conduct, and more. The concept connects closely to *eudaemonia*, a state of flourishing happiness and fulfillment that is achieved only through seeking growth, meaning, purpose, and authenticity. The ancient Greek philosophers believed that through the pursuit of arete, the intentional life of growth and purpose, one can achieve a state of eudaemonic happiness.

In the Buddhist teachings of the young, enlightened prince, the Noble Eightfold Path outlines the key practices to achieve enlightenment. The eight elements are split into three categories: wisdom (right view, right resolve, right speech), ethical conduct (right action, right livelihood, right effort), and mental discipline (right mindfulness, right concentration). The Noble Eightfold Path is a lifelong journey that provides seekers with a clear purpose and direction for their daily practice. It is often referred to as the Middle Way—a life path that exists between a life of pure self-indulgence and a life of pure self-mortification and offers a promise of balance and practicality on the way to liberation from suffering.

The vision quest was a common spiritual practice in various indigenous cultures across the Americas. The seeker would embark on a personal journey that typically included solitude, meditation, and fasting. It was a journey undertaken to understand oneself and one's role in family, community, and universe.

The legendary centenarians of Okinawa, Japan, refer to *ikigai*—a combination of the Japanese word *iki*, meaning "life," and *gai*, meaning "effect" or "worth." Together, they connote "a reason for life"—a driver of their daily vigor. *Ikigai* can be visualized as four overlapping circles: (1) what you love, (2) what you are good at, (3) what the world needs, and (4) what you can be paid for. The area where the four circles overlap represents your *ikigai*.

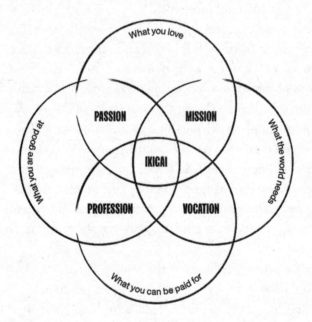

While the Westernized version of the concept has largely focused on purpose through work or professional success, the original, and indeed the version from the centenarian Okinawans, is meant to transcend one's career. While your purpose can certainly involve your professional career and economic considerations, it need not be defined by them. For this reason, my own interpretation of *ikigai* removes the fourth circle from the visual. *What the world needs* can be broadly interpreted to include or exclude professional constructs based on your personal situation.

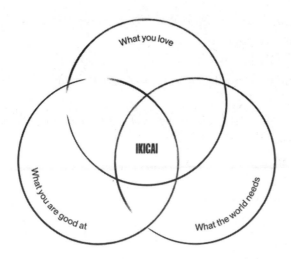

The narrative arc of the hero's journey—an individual in search of a defining purpose navigates the painful trials of life, grows through them, and finds the true self in the process—is irresistible to the human brain because it is exactly the path most people find themselves on. We are all searching for our purpose. It is a tale as old as time, observed, written about, and passed down through the stories and myths of every culture, religion, and society. Siddhartha Gautama's path from sheltered prince to enlightened teacher is a classic example of the hero's journey—a boy escapes the confines of the fate that was written for him and creates his own destiny.

You are on your own hero's journey, a journey to uncover and live through your purpose, to grow through it, and find yourself along the way. Unfortunately, the forces conspiring against you in the modern era are robust. These forces threaten to knock you off your path, to confine you to a life lived by default.

Only you can be the hero of your story—it's time you start acting like it.

THE MOST IMPORTANT FIGHT OF YOUR LIFE

Harsh truth: The world wants you to consent to a life of stasis. The world wants you to settle.

In his final shareholder letter prior to stepping down as CEO, Amazon founder Jeff Bezos quoted a passage from Richard Dawkins's book *The Blind Watchmaker:*

"Staving off death is a thing that you have to work at. Left to itself—and that is what it is when it dies—the body tends to revert to a state of equilibrium with its environment. . . . If living things didn't work actively to prevent it, they would eventually merge into their surroundings, and cease to exist as autonomous beings. That is what happens when they die."

Equilibrium with your surroundings—this state of normalcy—is your natural state. It's easy to live in this natural state, to conform to the path laid out for you, to believe in your limits, to accept the default settings of meaning and purpose bestowed upon you, to allow life to rapidly pass you by.

Reflecting on the passage, Bezos wrote, "In what ways does the world pull at you in an attempt to make you normal? How much work does it take to maintain your distinctiveness? . . . What I'm really asking you to do is to embrace and be realistic about how much energy it takes to maintain that distinctiveness. The world wants you to be typical—in a thousand ways, it pulls at you. Don't let it happen. You have to pay a price for your distinctiveness, and it's worth it."

You must fight to maintain your distinctiveness—consistently, relentlessly.

Distinctiveness is about choosing to live out *your* story, not someone else's:

* The mother who defines her current season of life around a desire to be present with her young children rather than continuing to climb the corporate ladder

- The entrepreneur who pursues the crazy idea everyone laughs at
- The recent graduate who pursues a creative path instead of the obvious one that his classmates defaulted to
- The recent retiree who learns a new language rather than sitting on the beach
- The middle manager who takes on an eccentric hobby because it gives her energy
- The ninety-year-old man who spends his birthday in a Harvard astronomy class rather than watching television

The fight against normalcy is the most important fight of your life. To maintain your uniqueness, to live on your terms in a world that pulls you to blend in, is the only way to realize your full potential and live a fulfilled, texture-rich existence.

Ultimately, this is what it means to build a life of Mental Wealth: to live according to your own purpose, to believe in your own ability to grow, change, learn, and develop, and to find your definition of peace, calm, and solitude in a fast-moving world.

A life of Mental Wealth is a life of victory in the fight against equilibrium; it is a life that pays the price for its distinctiveness from its surroundings and reaps the immense rewards held therein.

19.

The Three Pillars of Mental Wealth

ON A WARM, SUNNY day in June 2005, Apple founder and CEO Steve Jobs walked to the podium at Stanford Stadium in Palo Alto, California.

At the time, Jobs, widely regarded as one of the history's great entrepreneurs—he had founded Apple, Pixar, and computer upstart NeXT—was reeling from a battle waged on unfamiliar terrain, outside his favored design studios, offices, and boardrooms. In 2003, he was diagnosed with a rare form of pancreatic cancer; it required treatment and, eventually, surgery, after which he returned to his life's work at Apple. It was against this backdrop that Steve Jobs took the stage to deliver the commencement address at Stanford University to the graduating class of 2005.

While the entire address is powerful, it ends on a particularly striking note:

Your time is limited, so don't waste it living someone else's life. Don't be trapped by dogma—which is living with the results of other people's thinking. Don't let the noise of others' opinions drown out your own inner voice. And most important, have the courage to follow your heart and intuition. They somehow already know what you truly want to become. Everything else is secondary. . . . Stay hungry. Stay foolish.

Steve Jobs's words offer a fitting introduction to the three core pillars of Mental Wealth:

* PURPOSE: The clarity of defining your unique vision and focus that creates meaning and aligns short- and long-term decision making; the unwillingness to live someone else's life
* GROWTH: The hunger to progress and change, driven by an understanding of the dynamic potential of your intelligence, ability, and character
* SPACE: The creation of stillness and solitude to think, reset, wrestle with questions, and recharge; the ability and willingness to listen to your inner voice

As you measure Mental Wealth as part of your new scoreboard, the three pillars—purpose, growth, and space—provide a blueprint for the right actions to build it. By developing an understanding of these pillars and the high-leverage systems to affect them, you can begin to create the right outcomes.

PURPOSE: LIVING *YOUR* LIFE

In November 2005, *National Geographic* ran a cover story that took the world by storm.

The article—"The Secrets of Long Life"—was based on the findings of Dan Buettner, an intrepid record-holding transcontinental cyclist, Emmy Award–winning producer, and entrepreneur who had spent years exploring and studying the lives of centenarians around the world. Buettner had originally encountered these longevity hot spots on his travels as a cyclist— among them a 15,536-mile ride from Prudhoe Bay, Alaska, to Tierra del Fuego, Argentina, and an 11,885-mile ride from Bizerte, Tunisia, to Cape Agulhas, South Africa—but he began to study them more diligently as he built an education company focused on global, student-directed exploration. Following the sale of his company and his departure from operational duties, Buettner kicked off a formal quest to reverse-engineer the principles of longevity by studying those societies that seemed to have cracked its code. He partnered with Michel Poulain and Giovanni Pes—two longevity researchers who had coined the term *blue zone* to refer to a geographic area characterized by extraordinary human longevity—and set off to identify and decode all such blue zones around the world.

Three years later, after expanding the body of research, Buettner released a book on the topic entitled *The Blue Zones: Lessons for Living Longer from the People Who've Lived the Longest*, which explored the habits of the ageless populations of these locales. One particularly interesting common habit of the world's longest-lived people: They all find their life's purpose.

This purpose provides daily meaning. It creates an identity, an understanding of who you are, what you stand for, and where you're going. It defines how you connect with the world around you.

For example, my purpose is simple: to create positive ripples in the world through my writing and content, businesses I start or invest in, and relationships. This unique (and somewhat abstract) purpose provides clarity around my actions. When I write, I focus on how the words and theme may create chain reactions in the world—how readers may be sparked into actions that will have a positive impact on their lives. When I build or invest, I focus on how the company may create value in the lives of the various stakeholders. When I love, I focus on how I can lift others to new heights, give them a new view on the world, and unlock their full potential. The way I engage with my purpose changes from day to day, but it is always unique to me—it is a part of who I am.

Your purpose is your sword in the fight for distinctiveness, a fight that is won when you extend well beyond the self and manifest that purpose in the world.

Living a purpose-imbued life means regularly connecting to something bigger than you—something outside yourself that defines your identity and guides your daily actions. It might be to build a company that influences millions of lives, to provide for your loved ones, to bring joy to a group that rarely feels it, or to be a useful member of your local community. Your purpose need not be impressive or grand to anyone else—it is personal; it is yours.

Importantly, as the blue-zones research and various scientific studies have found, this is associated with a longer, happier, more fulfilled life. Robert Butler, a legendary gerontologist considered one of the pioneers of healthy-aging research, led an eleven-year study to evaluate the role that purpose plays in longevity.[5] It found that those who expressed a clear purpose in life lived about seven years longer and had a higher quality of life than those who did not. A more recent 2019 study in *The Journal of the American Medical Association* looked at seven thousand Americans and linked a strong sense of purpose with a lower risk of all-cause mortality after age fifty.[6]

Your purpose does not need to be related to your career. In fact, among the over one hundred readers I surveyed who self-identified as having strong clarity of purpose, less than 20 percent said that the work they were doing for primary employment was their purpose.

With this group, purpose was, in essence, like a snowflake, never appearing the same way twice:

* A mid-forties married male had a passion project mentoring local at-risk youth. The opportunity to be the positive force that he felt was missing from his childhood was a powerful driver.
* A mid-fifties mother of three grown children said that her close involvement with her local church had breathed new life into her world since her children had left the house.
* An early-thirties mother identified raising happy, loving children as the purpose of this season of her life. She had been a high-powered creative director in the prior season but felt more intrinsic motivation around this new, non-work purpose than she ever had for anything before.
* A late-twenties single woman focused on climate and political activism. The chance to inspire others to spark change was exhilarating.

- An early-forties married woman pointed to her love for her coworkers and the shared vision within the company to improve the quality of storytelling of the brands they work with.
- An early-seventies retiree said his purpose was to dote on his wife in their golden years after all the sacrifices she had made for their family in the preceding fifty.
- A fifty-year-old husband and father of four was entirely focused on providing for his children. He called it a "sacred duty" and said it made him feel more connected to his job.
- A late-thirties single man identified his defining purpose as building his fledgling start-up to eventually influence a billion lives.

If you are someone who feels a deep purpose and meaning through your primary employment, that is great—but if you don't, remember that you are far from alone, and you can still live a purpose-imbued life by connecting with your purpose outside of work.

Remember the lesson from the Bhagavad Gita: "One's own dharma performed imperfectly is better than another's dharma well performed." Your purpose doesn't have to be grand or important to anyone else—it must simply be *yours*.

GROWTH: CHASING YOUR LIMITLESS POTENTIAL

Hank Behar's wife, Phyllis, is ten years his junior. At eighty-eight years old, she has a smile and youthful glow about her that my friends in their mid-thirties would kill for. When I spoke to her to hear her perspectives on her husband's birthday visit to Harvard and gather any old photos she had from the day, she casually mentioned a new source of joy in her life: "I am convinced that painting is life-giving for me. At eighty-eight, I am in two painting classes, which are wonderful sources of inspiration and companionship."

An eighty-eight-year-old learning and finding joy in the pursuit of new skills that have no utility beyond the sheer enjoyment she gets from the experience and personal growth. The active, continuous pursuit of new interests and curiosities, irrespective of their direct utility, is, as Phyllis Behar noted, *life-giving.*

Growth is how you stay ahead of the forces of nature that conspire against you. The pursuit of improvement is a courageous act in a world where most people avoid friction at all costs. Why learn a new language when you can use Google Translate? Why take up a new hobby when you can sit on the couch and watch the latest show? Why push to master a new professional skill when you can get by with your current competency?

Why do any of that? Because you are capable of so much more than you realize—and chasing that full potential, while difficult, is a worthy lifelong pursuit that keeps you sharp and proves you can change, develop, and adapt.

Interestingly, the pursuit of growth as a means with no desired end does, quite often, produce the most compelling ends. History is littered with examples of lifelong learners who have achieved extraordinary outcomes.

Benjamin Franklin would have had an impressive LinkedIn profile. During his life, Franklin built a media empire, helped craft the earliest founding documents of the United States, and invented the lightning rod, bifocal glasses, and much more. The depth of his experience in any one domain was admirable, but the breadth of his experience across varied domains was something to behold. In his daily schedule, he dedicated an hour every single morning to learning. As it turns out, this practice is a common thread among the world's highest achievers. From Elon Musk and Bill Gates to Oprah Winfrey and Warren Buffett, the most professionally successful people all appear to dedicate daily time to learning and growth.

Fortunately, the science shows that the pursuit of improvement—the ability and willingness to chase your limitless potential—is driven by a mindset rather than an intrinsic aptitude. In other words, this is not reserved for the gifted—anyone can embrace it.

In 1998, Carol Dweck, then a professor of psychology at Columbia University (and now a professor at Stanford University), published several studies related to her research on the impact of mindset and praise on motivation and outcomes. In one, Dweck and her colleagues administered a series of puzzle tests to four hundred young children. The children who were praised for their *intelligence* after completing the first puzzle were less likely to choose a challenging puzzle for the next test than their peers who were praised for their *effort*. In a related study of adolescents, Dweck and her colleagues administered a nonverbal IQ test to a group and again praised the students for either their intelligence ("You must be smart!") or their effort ("You must have worked really hard!"). The intelligence-praised children performed worse when given a harder set of problems, while the effort-praised children performed better on the second set. Further, those praised for their intelligence subsequently avoided challenging new tasks and even lied about their performance on tasks, while those praised for their effort sought out the challenging tasks as new learning opportunities.

In her international bestseller *Mindset: The New Psychology of Success,* Dr. Dweck drew upon her extensive body of research to build a generalized model for how our beliefs about ourselves—in particular the belief in our ability to grow, improve, and change—affect every area of our lives. Dweck summarized, "For twenty years, my research has shown that the view you adopt for yourself profoundly affects the way you lead your life. It can determine whether you become the person you want to be and whether you accomplish the things you value."

According to her research, there are two core mindsets:

1. The fixed mindset, which assumes ability, intelligence, and character are static
2. The growth mindset, which assumes ability, intelligence, and character are dynamic

The fixed mindset is grounded in the central belief that everything about who you are as an individual is immutable—set in stone. As Dr. Dweck showed through her research, this belief has wide-ranging implications for how you work, live, and even love. The fixed mindset creates a hunger for external affirmation, rewards, and approval, a deep fear of failure and rejection, and a flawed conclusion that if things aren't good now, they never will be.

The growth mindset, however, is grounded in the central belief that everything about who you are as an individual is malleable—that sincere effort can cultivate change, growth, and continuous improvement. The growth mindset creates a focus on intrinsic motivation, inputs, and process, an embrace of failure as learning, and a fundamental belief that starting circumstances do not determine final outcomes.

Those who adopt a growth mindset are prepared to face life's inevitable challenges with a positive, optimistic, and resilient outlook. They avoid the pitfalls of tying their identity too closely to a single set of outcomes, instead preferring to ground their identity broadly across their efforts and energy for improvement. They are able to work at things, personally and professionally, because they understand that good things are not immaculately conceived; they are earned through effort. In a world of beautiful imperfection where *perfect* is reserved for fairy tales, those who believe in their ability to change, who focus on inputs, process, and daily improvement, will always find a way to thrive.

Mental Wealth is built on this fundamental belief—in the ability to grow, learn, and change—but the belief is just the start. Like Hank Behar attending astronomy classes at Harvard and Phyllis Behar taking painting classes at the local community center, the mentally wealthy act on it every single day.

As Mahatma Gandhi famously said, "Live as if you were to die tomorrow. Learn as if you were to live forever."

SPACE: FINDING YOUR GARDEN

The middle-aged monk sat calmly as hundreds of electrical sensors and wires were attached to his face and bald head, his traditional Buddhist red-and-gold robes accentuating the bleached medical whiteness of the 256 sensors.

Matthieu Ricard earned a PhD in cellular genetics before leaving the academic circuit behind and moving to India to become a Buddhist monk. Along the way, he worked as a French interpreter for the Dalai Lama, became a bestselling author, and won France's National Order of Merit.

But his most interesting accomplishment is the one he is most uncomfortable talking about: Matthieu Ricard is the world's happiest man.

In an early 2000s study on the impact of meditation conducted by University of Wisconsin researchers, psychologist Richard Davidson asked Ricard to meditate while covered in sensors and wires. Dr. Davidson noted that Ricard's brain produced gamma waves—which are linked to consciousness, attention, learning, and memory—at levels "never reported before in the neuroscience literature."[7] Further, the monitoring identified increased activity in his left prefrontal cortex compared to his right, which researchers noted might be what gives Ricard a high capacity for happiness. These findings, along with a fair bit of creative journalistic spin, led to Matthieu Ricard being dubbed "the World's Happiest Man."

Even though Ricard is not too fond of the moniker ("It's a good title for journalists to use, but I cannot get rid of it. Maybe on my tomb, it will say, 'Here lies the happiest person in the world'"), the underlying insight should be of interest to everyone. The practice of meditation and, more broadly, of mindfulness led to changes in the brain's functioning around consciousness, attention, learning, memory, and happiness that may contribute to a healthier, wealthier existence.

But what does this look like for those of us who cannot imagine meditating for twelve hours per day for decades (the common practice among those studied)? What about mindfulness for all of us non-monks?

Paraphrasing a quote of unknown origin often attributed to Viktor Frankl, your power is in the space that exists between stimulus and response. This idea—of creating and leveraging *space*—is how you can unlock your own monk-like mindfulness.

In a world of constant connectedness, space is incredibly rare.

How many times have you gone through a day without feeling a single moment was truly yours? You wake up, grab your phone, get a barrage of messages and notifications, head to work, bounce from meeting to meeting, go home, eat quickly while scanning emails, and go to bed.

Or how many times have you felt like the shower was the only few minutes of the day that you had to yourself? No phone, no messages, no emails, nothing; just you, your thoughts, and the water. And, relatedly, how many times have you had an "aha moment" while in the shower? That new perspective on a relationship struggle, a creative idea for a business, an unlock on a big work project.

This is no accident: *Our power is in the space.*

Space exists between stimulus and response. Stimulus and response are loud—they involve inputs, action, and outputs. Space is quiet—it is devoid of external inputs and does not require any outputs. It is stillness, solitude. You can create space literally by going to a physical location to be alone and disconnected or metaphorically by going to that location in your mind. The important part is that you go (and regularly).

Space is not lazy—on the contrary, space is rocket fuel for the mind.

Space is what enables you to think, reset, wrestle with the big, unanswerable questions, manage stressors, and recharge. It is what unlocks you and allows you to listen to your inner voice. It is where ideas connect and mingle in your mind. It is where you are able to think differently, approach problems in interesting new ways, connect spiritually with a higher power, or formulate insights that may change your life.

John D. Rockefeller was one of the most successful—and ruthless—businessmen in history. From humble beginnings, Rockefeller built Standard Oil into a gargantuan conglomerate with immense global reach and outsize influence in all manner of world affairs. At the company's peak, Rockefeller had an estimated net worth of $1.4 billion, a figure that was roughly 3 percent of the U.S. GDP at the time. Rockefeller was known for his tireless work ethic and demanding schedule; it was the only way he was able to remain on top of the incomprehensible web of entities and transactions within his empire.

But he also had a curious and noteworthy habit: He could be found every afternoon milling about in his gardens, with no work, books, or notepads in sight. Rockefeller—one of the hardest-working and most powerful men in the world—took multiple daily breaks to simply walk and breathe.

Now, to be sure, most of us do not aspire to be John D. Rockefeller (for a variety of reasons!), but there is an important point to this story: Space is not about turning your back on your worldly possessions, selling your metaphorical (or literal) Ferrari, and going on a quest to find yourself in the mountains. Space is as simple as finding your version of Rockefeller's garden—an escape where you can slow down and breathe new air in your life.

Space is personal and can take many different forms:

- Fifteen-minute technology-free walk in the morning
- Daily prayer practice or reading from a favored religious text
- Free-flow journaling in the evening before bed
- Five-minute breaks between meetings to move around
- Daily cold plunge or sauna to focus on breathing and the internal voice
- Workouts, runs, or bike rides with light music
- Active or passive meditation rituals
- A spiritual gathering

The point: No matter who you are, where you are, or what you're doing, you can embrace the power found in the *space* of your personal mental garden—no monk's vows required.

With an established understanding of the three pillars, we can move to the Mental Wealth Guide, which provides the specific tools and systems to build on these pillars and cultivate a life of Mental Wealth.

20.

The Mental Wealth Guide

Systems for Success

THE MENTAL WEALTH GUIDE that follows provides specific high-leverage systems to build each of the pillars of a life of Mental Wealth. This isn't one-size-fits all and you shouldn't feel compelled to read every single one; browse through and select those that feel most relevant and useful to you.

As you consider and execute the systems for success provided in the Mental Wealth Guide, use your responses to each Mental Wealth statement from the Wealth Score quiz to narrow your focus to the areas where you need to make the most progress (those where you responded *strongly disagree, disagree,* or *neutral*).

1. I regularly embrace a childlike curiosity.
2. I have a clear purpose that provides daily meaning and aligns short- and long-term decision making.
3. I pursue growth and consistently chase my full potential.
4. I have a fundamental belief that I am able to continuously change, develop, and adapt.
5. I have regular rituals that allow me to create space to think, reset, wrestle with questions, and recharge.

A few common Mental Wealth anti-goals to avoid on your journey:

- Failing to connect with a purpose bigger than myself
- Giving up on all learning that does not provide direct financial utility
- Losing all the space in my life as I pursue new activities and growth

Here are ten proven systems for building Mental Wealth.

Mental Wealth Hacks I Wish I Knew
at Twenty-Two

A collaboration with Susan Cain, *New York Times* bestselling author of *Quiet: The Power of Introverts in a World That Can't Stop Talking* and *Bittersweet: How Sorrow and Longing Make Us Whole.*

1. Your purpose in life does not have to be related to what you do for work. Your purpose in life does not have to be grand or ambitious. Your purpose in life simply has to be *yours.*

2. The secret to life is to put yourself in the right lighting. For some, it's a Broadway spotlight; for others, a lamplit desk. Use your natural powers of persistence, concentration, and insight to do work you love and work that matters. Solve problems, make art, think deeply.

3. There's zero correlation between being the best talker and having the best ideas.

4. Choose one creative project at a time and do it as well and as deeply as you possibly can.

5. We know from myths and fairy tales that there are many different kinds of powers in this world. One child is given a lightsaber, another a wizard's education. The trick is not to amass all the different kinds of power but to use well the kind you've been granted.

6. Reflecting on the past is a good way to fuel your growth, but dwelling on the past is a good way to inhibit it. Most people are inclined to either reflection or action. But we all need some of both.

7. Neuroplasticity suggests that experiences can fundamentally alter the structure and function of your brain. Your actions and movements can shape your physical, mental, and spiritual reality. You have that power within you.

8. If you want to get better at anything, do it for thirty minutes per day for thirty straight days. It's easy to over-engineer progress; a little dedicated effort each day is all you need. Nine hundred minutes of accumulated effort is enough for you to make dramatic improvements in literally anything.

9. Solitude matters, and for some people, it's the air they breathe.

10. We put too much of a premium on presenting and not enough on substance and critical thinking.

11. When you're trying to learn something new, attempt to teach it to a friend or family member. See what questions they ask and how those questions expose the gaps in your knowledge. Study more to fill in those gaps. The act of teaching is the most powerful form of learning.

12. At school you might have been prodded to *come out of your shell,* a noxious expression that fails to appreciate that some animals naturally carry shelter everywhere they go and some humans are just the same.

13. Take yourself out for a meal alone once each month. Carry a notebook and pen, bring your favorite book, and leave your phone in your bag. Let your mind run free.

14. The quest to transform pain into beauty is one of the great catalysts of artistic expression.

15. Stop trying to remember things and just write everything down. Use your phone notes app—or, better yet, carry a small pocket notebook and pen. The old-fashioned way still works wonders.

16. Write down three things you're grateful for every single night before you go to bed. Say one of them out loud every single morning when you wake up.

17. Don't consume the news unless you're highly confident it will matter one month from now. Consuming more news has become a reliable way to understand less about the world. Focus on smaller doses of high-signal content, not the constant drip of *Breaking news!* that has become the standard of the industry.

18. Turn whatever pain you can't get rid of into your creative of-
    fering.
19. Creativity has the power to look pain in the eye and turn it
    into something else.
20. You may read thousands of books in your life, but there will
    be only a few that deeply change you. Reread them every sin-
    gle year. Your experience with the book will change as you
    do—you'll get new perspectives. And doing this will remind
    you of how you can fall in love with the same thing (or person)
    over and over again.

How to Find Your Purpose: The Power of *Ikigai*

PILLAR: Purpose

The legendary centenarians of Okinawa, Japan, use the concept of *ikigai* to define their life purpose. You can use the concept with a simple exercise to begin to explore yours as well.

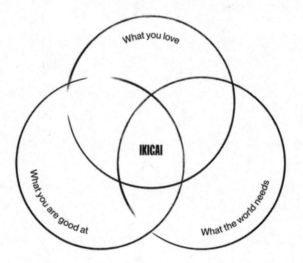

Your *ikigai*—your life purpose—sits at the center of the three overlapping circles:

1. WHAT YOU LOVE: The activities that are life-giving
2. WHAT YOU ARE GOOD AT: The activities that feel effortless
3. WHAT THE WORLD NEEDS: The activities that your current world needs from you

On a blank sheet of paper, write down your answers to the following questions:

1. WHAT YOU LOVE: What activities or responsibilities create joy in your life? What were you doing in the moments when you

felt the most natural happiness? Make a list of the activities
that are life-giving.

2. WHAT YOU ARE GOOD AT: What feels effortless to you that
   may be difficult for others? Where do your natural and acquired skills stand out? What do other people seem to recognize as your attributes or skills? Make a list of the activities
   that you have unique competency in.

3. WHAT THE WORLD NEEDS: What activities does your world
   need from you in this season of life? How you define your
   world will vary across the seasons. Your world may be defined
   narrowly by the inner circle of yourself and your family at certain points, by the broader circle of your community at others,
   and by the broadest circle of the actual world. In the most
   common arc, the definition of *world* starts out narrow, grows
   wider over time, and then ends narrow. It may begin focused
   on the self and family in the earlier years, expand to focus on
   the community and grander scale in the middle years, and
   then go back to the self and family in the later years. When
   you have fulfilled the needs of your current world, you feel
   free to expand that definition on to the next level. This is a
   fundamental reason why financially successful people who
   were driven by a purpose to provide for their families in their
   early years will likely need to adjust to a broader world to
   maintain a sense of clear purpose. Define your current world
   and make a list of the activities that it needs from you.

The intersection of the three lists is a strong starting point for you
to explore and uncover your higher-order life purpose. Remember
that your purpose does not need to be connected to your profession.
Work through the exercise and you'll be well on your way to harness-
ing the power of *ikigai*, just as the Okinawans have.

How to Choose Your Life Pursuits:
The Pursuit Map

PILLAR: Purpose

> How we spend our days is, of course, how we spend our lives.
> What we do with this hour, and that one, is what we are doing.
> —ANNIE DILLARD, *The Writing Life*

Your time here is finite, so choosing the pursuits—personal and professional—that deliver the greatest returns on that time is essential.

You'll come across a lot of advice that says to follow your interests and passions, but I've always found that guidance to be a bit tricky. What do those words—*interests* and *passions*—really mean? I don't know about you, but I tend to lie to myself and say that I have an interest in things that I'm good at, so interest can be deceiving. And *passion* is a heavy term, one that I'm never fully convinced I'm applying correctly when it comes to my life.

My solution: I focus on energy, not interests or passions. Follow your energy, because it is the truly scarce resource. When you have energy for something, you go deep on it, you push to grow, you gain life from it. It fuels you.

So as you contemplate the grand question of your life—how should I spend my time?—energy should take center stage in your consideration. I use an exercise I call *pursuit mapping* to identify the pursuits that are most likely to bring joy and outsize rewards into my life.

Here's how it works (and how you can use it to change your life):

STEP 1: CREATE YOUR MAP

The pursuit map is a blank two-by-two matrix with competency level (from low to high competency) on the x-axis and energy (from energy-draining to energy-creating) on the y-axis.

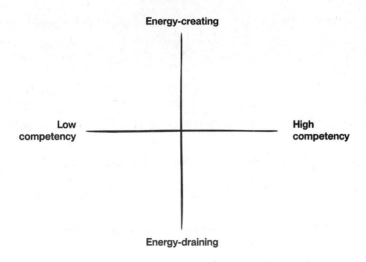

I define the terms as follows:

- ENERGY-CREATING: A pursuit that creates energy in your life; these activities leave you feeling energized—they fill your cup.
- ENERGY-DRAINING: A pursuit that drains energy from your life; these activities leave you feeling drained—they empty your cup.
- HIGH COMPETENCY: A pursuit at which you are skilled; these activities feel effortless.
- LOW COMPETENCY: A pursuit at which you are a novice; these activities feel challenging.

The first step is to place pursuits—both personal and professional—onto this matrix. For the purposes of this exercise, pursuits can be broadly defined (for example, strategy consulting) or specific (for example, market research). This step should include both pursuits you are currently engaged in and those that you may attempt in the future.

For pursuits that you are currently engaged in:

- ESTABLISH ENERGY: How do you feel while engaged in the pursuit? How do you feel after? Do you find the pursuit life-giving?

- ASSESS COMPETENCY: What is your view on your competency level? Ask others who have worked with you on this pursuit for their honest perspectives on your competency level.

Based on your responses and those gathered from others, place each current pursuit on the grid according to the energy and competency levels.

For pursuits that you are not currently engaged in:

- GATHER INFORMATION: Talk to people who are engaged in these pursuits. Ask them about the details of the pursuits to create a baseline estimate of your energy. Remember that the surface-level view of a pursuit may not be accurate—you might think being a lawyer seems great, but are you basing that on the television version of the role or on the actual day-to-day work that is required? Seek to understand the true underlying details of the day-to-day in a given pursuit, not just the surface-level information.
- EXPERIMENT: Choosing the right pursuits involves experimentation. Learn more about your energy for a given activity or pursuit by spending a day engaged in it. Shadow someone to test it out; take on the new role on a trial basis. Gather deeper information through small, reversible actions.
- ASSUME LOW COMPETENCY: With any new pursuit or activity, it is fair to assume you will start out with a low (or modest) competency level. Until you generate evidence to prove otherwise, this is the safe assumption.

Based on the information gathered from discussions and experimentation, place each prospective pursuit on the grid according to the energy and competency levels.

With a populated pursuit map, you can proceed to step 2.

STEP 2: IDENTIFY YOUR ZONES
There are three key zones to consider on your activity map:

1. ZONE OF GENIUS: In his 2010 book *The Big Leap,* author Gay
   Hendricks proposed the novel idea of the Zone of Genius, defined as the range of pursuits where you have excellent competency and high interest or passion. In the context of my
   pursuit-map matrix, I'd consider the Zone of Genius as the
   top right quadrant, where your competency and energy col-
   lide. This is your promised land, the sweet spot of pursuits
   where you will ideally spend most of your time, both professional and personal.

2. ZONE OF HOBBY: This is the range of pursuits that create energy in your life but in which you have a lower competency
   level. This is where you would ideally spend the second biggest chunk of your time. It's okay for certain pursuits to remain in this Zone of Hobby (it's okay to be bad at things!), but
   you will find that pursuits for which you feel a lot of energy
   tend to slowly shift to the right as you improve at them. Pursuits that start in the Zone of Hobby often end up in the Zone
   of Genius over time.

3. ZONE OF DANGER: This is the range of pursuits that drain
   your energy but in which you have a higher competency level.
   It is a dangerous place to spend your time because you will be
   given positive feedback on your performance and feel
   tempted to spend more of your time here as a result. The goal
   is to avoid the trap of these activities or find ways to make
   them more energy-creating for your life.

IDENTIFY YOUR ZONES

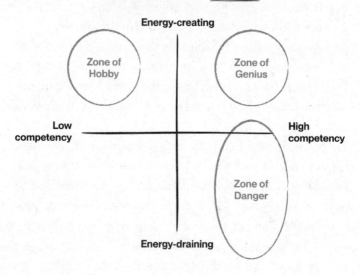

Note: *The bottom left quadrant is what I would consider the dead zone, in that pursuits here should generally be avoided due to being energy-draining and low competency. That being said, there are instances where something becomes energy-creating as you improve at it (for example, many novice runners fall in love with running as they improve their fitness), so writing off these pursuits completely may be a bad idea.*

To assess the likelihood of a pursuit becoming energy-creating as your competency improves, ask yourself, "Do I love the good version of this?" In other words, if you imagine yourself at a modest or improved competency level at the pursuit, does it give you energy?

STEP 3: ALIGN YOUR TIME

By placing the various pursuits on the map and identifying your core zones, you've developed a picture of the pursuits on which you should aim to spend your time.

The changes won't happen overnight; the goal is to slowly work toward incremental improvements:

1. Most of your time is spent on pursuits in your Zone of Genius.
2. Your remaining time is spent on pursuits in your Zone of Hobby.
3. Minimize the time spent on pursuits in your Zone of Danger.
4. Eliminate the time spent on pursuits in the dead zone (with the exception of those that survive the test in the prior note).

If you work in a company, the best approach is to have a clear, candid conversation with your teams and managers about your pursuit map and zones. If you are in a leadership role, encourage the full team to conduct a similar exercise—with everyone's pursuit map, it becomes easier to piece the puzzle together. If you're running into a wall with a company or manager who fails to recognize your perspectives, it may be time for a change. The market will eventually determine which companies survive by allowing for the free flow of talent to the places that allow employees to thrive in their highest form and function.

If you work on your own, be honest with yourself about what daily activities and pursuits fall into what zones. Be ruthless in outsourcing to maximize the time you spend in your Zone of Genius. Your results and performance will improve in line with your ability.

Choosing the right pursuits is a direct path to a more purpose-filled, fulfilling, productive, and successful life. Learn to follow your energy and you won't be led astray. Conduct the pursuit-map exercise and slowly start to work toward a world where your time is invested in the pursuits that provide the greatest rewards.

How to Learn Anything:
The Feynman Technique

PILLAR: Growth

Richard Feynman was an American theoretical physicist born in 1918 in New York City. Feynman was a very late talker—he didn't utter a word until he was three—but it was clear even when he was young that he was extremely observant and intelligent. His parents valued non-consensus thinking; they constantly encouraged young Richard to ask questions and think independently. Feynman taught himself advanced mathematics in his teens and went on to earn a BS from the Massachusetts Institute of Technology and a PhD from Princeton University. He became famous for his work in quantum electrodynamics and received the Nobel Prize in Physics in 1965 for his contributions to the field.

Richard Feynman was certainly intelligent. But there are a lot of intelligent people in the world. Feynman's true genius was his ability to convey complex ideas in simple, elegant ways. He observed that complexity and jargon are often used to mask a lack of deep understanding.

The Feynman technique is a learning model that leverages teaching and prioritizes simplicity to help you develop a deep understanding of any topic.

It involves four key steps:

1. Set the stage.
2. Teach.
3. Assess and study.
4. Organize, convey, and review.

Let's cover each step:

STEP 1: SET THE STAGE

Write down the topic you want to learn about at the top of a blank page and jot down everything you know about it.

Begin the research and learning process on the topic:

* Listen to lectures.
* Read.
* Watch videos.
* Discuss with others.
* Practice by doing.

Start broad, then go deep.

STEP 2: TEACH

Attempt to teach the topic to someone without a base understanding of it. This can be a friend, partner, colleague, or classmate. The only requirement is that it is someone you would consider uninitiated in the topic.

This step requires you to distill and simplify the learning. Avoid jargon and acronyms.

Note: If you don't have a person to teach, do this on another blank page. Write down everything you know about your topic, but pretend you are explaining it to a child. Use simple language.

STEP 3: ASSESS AND STUDY

Ask for feedback and reflect on your performance to form an honest assessment:

* How well were you able to explain the topic to the uninitiated person?
* What questions did the person ask?
* Where did you get frustrated?
* Where did you turn to jargon?

Your answers to these questions will highlight the gaps in your understanding.

Return to step 1 and study more to fill them in.

STEP 4: ORGANIZE, CONVEY, AND REVIEW

Organize your elegant, simple understanding of the topic into a clear, compelling story or narrative. Convey it to a few others, then repeat and refine accordingly. Review your new, deep understanding of the topic.

The Feynman technique is a powerful framework for learning anything. The best entrepreneurs, investors, and thinkers have leveraged this technique whether they know it or not! Their common genius is the ability to break through the complexity and convey ideas in simple, digestible ways.

It's easy to overcomplicate and intimidate—we all know people who do this. But don't be fooled; complexity and jargon are often used to mask a lack of deep understanding.

Use the Feynman technique: Find beauty in simplicity.

How to Retain Everything:
The Spaced-Repetition Method
PILLAR: Growth

Spaced repetition leverages cognitive science to help you retain new information. It plays on the way our brains work to convert short-term to long-term memory. With spaced repetition, information is consumed at increasing intervals until it's committed to long-term memory.

German psychologist Hermann Ebbinghaus was the first to identify the effect of spaced repetition on memory retention. In an 1885 paper, he formulated the Ebbinghaus Forgetting Curve (EFC). The EFC maps the exponential loss of newly learned information.

EBBINGHAUS'S FORGETTING CURVE

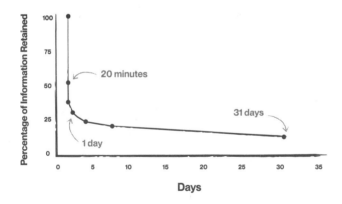

Ebbinghaus observed that each time the newly learned information was reviewed, the EFC was reset at the starting point but with a *slower decay.* The spaced repetitions had the effect of flattening the memory-retention decay curve.

EBBINGHAUS'S FORGETTING CURVE

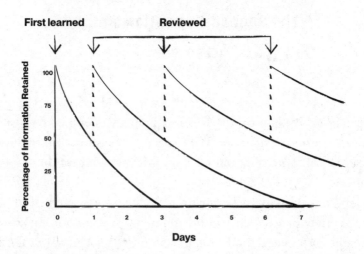

Why does this work? Think of your brain as a muscle—each repetition is a flex of that muscle. By steadily increasing the intervals between reps, you are pushing the muscle with a steadily more challenging load. You're forcing the retention muscle to grow.

Here's how to implement the spaced-repetition method:

Let's imagine you consume some new information at 8:00 A.M. Now you start the repetitions:

- Repetition 1: 9:00 A.M. (one hour later)
- Repetition 2: 12:00 P.M. (three hours later)
- Repetition 3: 6:00 P.M. (six hours later)
- Repetition 4: 6:00 A.M. (twelve hours later)

And so on. The memory is reinforced at increasing intervals. Next time you're trying to retain new information, use the science-backed spaced-repetition method. It works.

How to Think Differently:
The Socratic Method

PILLAR: Growth and Space

In 2009, Stanford business professor Tina Seelig wrote about an interesting experiment she conducted in her book *What I Wish I Knew When I Was 20*. Seelig split her class into fourteen teams and gave them all a challenge: Each group would get five dollars of seed funding and have two hours to make as much money as possible. At the end of the challenge, each group would give a short presentation to the class on their approach and results.

When given this challenge, most respondents will take a linear, logical approach, such as bartering. These options would generate a modest return on the five dollars of seed capital.

A few groups in the original experiment ignored the five dollars altogether and instead thought up ways to make as much money as possible in the two hours of allotted time:

* Made and sold reservations at the best restaurants in town
* Refilled bike tires in the center of campus for a dollar each

These groups made a better return on their initial five dollars.

The winning group also ignored the money, but they took an entirely different approach. They recognized that the most valuable asset was not the money or the two hours they were given for the challenge but the presentation time in front of a class of Stanford students. Internalizing the value of this asset, they sold the presentation time to a company looking to recruit Stanford students for $650, netting a monstrous return on the $5 of initial capital.

The losing groups thought in linear, logical terms and achieved a linear, logical outcome. The winning group thought differently.

Socratic questioning (or the Socratic method) is a process of asking and answering questions that stimulate critical thinking to expose and vet underlying assumptions and logic.

To put it into action, follow this general structure:

* Start with open-ended questions.
* Propose ideas based on these questions.
* Probe these ideas with progressive questioning.
* Repeat until the best ideas are developed.

Here's how you can apply Socratic questioning to think differently:

* START ASKING QUESTIONS: What's the problem you are trying to solve? We often waste time and energy trying to solve the wrong problem. Identify the right problem before you try to solve it. For the students in the business school class, the wrong problem was how to use the five dollars to make the most money; the right problem was how to make the most money given the time allotted for the exercise.
* PROPOSE YOUR CURRENT THINKING ON THE PROBLEM: What is your hypothesis? What are the origins of that thinking?
* OPEN THE FLOOR FOR TARGETED QUESTIONING: Why do you think this? Is the thinking too vague? What is it based on?
* CHALLENGE THE ASSUMPTIONS UNDERLYING THE ORIGINAL THINKING: Why do you believe this to be true? How do you know it's true? How would you know if you were wrong? Identify the source of beliefs on a problem. Be ruthless in evaluating their integrity and validity.
* EVALUATE THE EVIDENCE USED TO SUPPORT THE THINKING: What concrete evidence do you have? How credible is it? What hidden evidence may exist?
* UNDERSTAND THE CONSEQUENCES OF BEING WRONG: Can an error be quickly fixed? How costly is this mistake? Always understand the stakes.
* EVALUATE POTENTIAL ALTERNATIVES: What alternative beliefs or viewpoints might exist? Why might they be superior? Why

do others believe them to be true? What do they know that you don't? Evaluate them on their merits and ask these same fundamental questions about them.

* AFTER ZOOMING IN, ZOOM OUT: What was your original thinking? Was it correct? If not, where did you err? What conclusions can you draw from the process about systemic errors in thinking? In the business school experiment, spending time asking questions to identify this right problem was what unlocked the group to think differently about the assets at their disposal and ultimately come up with a more creative solution.

Socratic questioning takes time. It shouldn't be used on low-cost, easily reversible decisions. But when you encounter a high-stakes decision with the potential for asymmetric rewards in your business, career, or life, it's worth engaging in the exercise. It will empower you to think differently and uncover the path most likely to generate the asymmetric, risk-adjusted returns.

How to Unlock New Growth:
The Think Day

PILLARS: Growth and Space

In the 1980s, Bill Gates began an annual tradition he called Think Week. Gates would seclude himself in a remote location, shut off communication, and spend a week dedicated to reading and thinking.

For Gates, Think Week was a time to be creative and push his thinking with new depth and breadth. It allowed him to exit the demands of an average day on the job and train his sights on the bigger picture.

If you're like me, you don't have an entire week to dedicate to thinking, but you can adapt something with a similar core vision.

The Think Day was my adaptation.

Pick one day each month to step back from all of your day-to-day professional demands:

- Seclude yourself (mentally or physically).
- Put up an out-of-office response.
- Shut off all your devices.

The goal: Spend the entire day reading, learning, journaling, and *thinking*.

By doing this, you create the free time to zoom out, open your mind, and think creatively about the bigger picture.

The essential tools for Think Day:

- Journal and pen
- Books/articles you've been wanting to read
- Secluded location (at home, rental, or outside)
- Thinking prompts to spark your mind

Eight thinking prompts I have found particularly useful:

1. If I repeated my current typical day for one hundred days, would my life be better or worse?
2. If people observed my actions for a week, what would they say my priorities are?
3. If I were the main character in a movie of my life, what would the audience be screaming at me to do right now?
4. Am I hunting antelope (big important problems) or field mice (small urgent problems)?
5. How can I do less but better?
6. What are my strongest beliefs? What would it take for me to change my mind on them?
7. What are a few things I know now that I wish I'd known five years ago?
8. What actions did I engage in five years ago that I cringe at today? What actions am I engaged in today that I might cringe at in five years?

I aim for an eight-hour window split into sixty-minute focus blocks with walks in between.

In a speed-obsessed world, the benefits of slowing down are extensive. It allows you to:

* Restore energy
* Notice things you missed
* Be more deliberate with actions
* Focus on the highest-leverage opportunities
* Move slow to move fast

The Think Day can help. Give it a shot and experience the benefits of intentional solitude.

How to Create New Space:
The Power Walk

PILLAR: Space

There is one simple, entirely free tool that you can use to find and embrace more space in your life: the walk.

Philosophers have long known the power of the walk for mental clarity, creativity, and recovery. Aristotle founded what became known as the Peripatetic school of philosophy—a word that literally translates to "walking" or "given to walking about"—as he had a propensity to walk while lecturing or having conversations. Danish philosopher Søren Kierkegaard wrote, "Above all, do not lose your desire to walk. Every day I walk myself into a state of well-being and walk away from every illness. I have walked myself into my best thoughts, and I know of no thought so burdensome that one cannot walk away from it."

These insights on the benefits of walking are more than just anecdotes; they are supported by a large and growing body of science:

- Stanford researchers found that students performed significantly better on tests measuring creative, divergent thinking during and after walks. In fact, walking boosted creative thinking by an average of 60 percent and the benefits lasted well beyond the walk itself.[8]
- Researchers in Illinois found that children exhibited improved cognitive performance after twenty minutes of walking compared to twenty minutes of sitting quietly.[9]
- University of Hong Kong researchers showed that talking while walking side by side with someone led to deeper feelings of connection, implying that walking meetings may actually create better outcomes.[10]
- A *NeuroImage* study in June 2021 suggested that daily walk-

ing may improve white-matter plasticity in older adults, meaning improved memory-retention curves.[11]

The case for walking is abundantly clear. If there is one single
habit that you can build that will immediately create space, enhance
your creativity, reduce your stress, and improve your overall Mental
Wealth, it is a daily walk.

Find ways to add short and long walks to your daily routine:

* Take a five-minute walk between meetings, after a meal, or
  before an important presentation.
* Go for a fifteen-minute walk first thing in the morning. The
  sunlight, movement, and fresh air have a direct positive impact on your mood, circadian rhythm, metabolism, digestion,
  and more.
* Enjoy longer, passive, tech-free walks when you have the
  time. These walks are thirty to sixty minutes long and are
  done at a slow, leisurely pace with no technology. The mind
  should be free to wander. Allow your ideas to mingle. I'd suggest bringing a little pocket notebook to log anything interesting that comes into your head (it will happen!).

Walking with your thoughts is an ultra-powerful space-creating
tool available to all of us, completely free of charge.

How to Build Clear Boundaries:
The Personal Power-Down Ritual

PILLAR: Space

A power-down ritual is a fixed sequence of actions and behaviors that create space in your life by mentally and physically marking the end of your professional day. The idea originated with author Cal Newport, who penned a blog post on the topic over a decade ago.

An example of my fixed sequence might look something like this:

- Check email for any final requests requiring action.
- Check calendar and task lists for the following day.
- Do fifteen minutes of prep for priority tasks of the next morning.
- Close down all applications and technology for the night.

The benefits of having a power-down ritual that I have observed:

- CLEAR BOUNDARIES: The ritual creates a clear set of boundaries that separate professional and personal activities. We become more present on each side of the boundary.
- ENHANCED MORNING PRODUCTIVITY: By including a bit of prep for the following morning as part of my ritual, I have noticed a clear boost in my productivity on the first task of the following day. I'm ready to hit the ground running.
- IMPROVED MENTAL HEALTH: I feel so much better in the evenings after I have had the power-down. I'm more present with my wife and son, I'm not worried about the random notifications that are hitting, and I'm able to fall asleep faster.

To create your own, incorporate these three key elements:

1. COMPLETE FINAL TASKS: What are the final checks that you need to perform in order to close out the tasks of the day and confirm that there is nothing remaining for you to complete? For most people, this will involve checking email and Slack with a quick scan, plus a sweep of any open projects.
2. PREPARE FOR TOMORROW: What are the focus priorities for tomorrow? What is the first task you want to make progress on when you start work? Do ten to fifteen minutes of prep work to set yourself up to hit the ground running on that priority task.
3. INITIATE POWER-DOWN: Create a mental trigger for the completion of the power-down ritual. Cal Newport had his own magic phrase ("Schedule shutdown, complete"), but you can create your own less nerdy version if you like.

Using those three elements, sketch out what a power-down ritual would look like for you. As with everything, initial action builds momentum. Try it this week and see what happens.

How to Improve Your Mental Health:
The 1-1-1 Journaling Method
PILLAR: Space

Journaling is an extremely powerful tool for creating space and improving mental health. Unfortunately, journaling is a habit that eludes most people. The aspirational self may have thirty minutes of silence in the evenings and the energy to sit down and write at length on a series of complex, interesting prompts. The actual self . . . does not. As a result, most of us assume we don't have the time to create a meaningful, valuable journaling practice.

The reality: Even five minutes of daily journaling can have a profound impact on your mental health.

To build a journaling habit that works in the context of my reality, I developed a dead-simple solution: the 1-1-1 method.

Every single evening, at the end of your day, open your journal (or favorite digital tool or application) and write down three simple points:

- One win from the day
- One point of tension, anxiety, or stress
- One point of gratitude

The whole process takes about five minutes (though you can go longer if you're feeling inspired by anything in particular).

The 1-1-1 method works because of its simplicity:

- One win allows you to appreciate your progress.
- One point of tension allows you to get the topic off your mind and onto the paper. It's therapeutic.
- One point of gratitude allows you to reflect on the most important things in your life.

With a simple structure and a low time burden, the 1-1-1 method is an easy way to start building a journaling practice that will improve your mental health.

To add an additional layer of commitment to make it stick, create a group chat with a few others who want to make journaling a habit in the year ahead. The group chat is used only for sending a *Done* once you complete it in the evening. Use it to keep one another accountable and build the streak.

21.

Summary: Mental Wealth

MENTAL WEALTH OVERVIEW

THE BIG QUESTION: WHAT would your ten-year-old self say to you today?

THE THREE PILLARS OF MENTAL WEALTH:
* PURPOSE: The clarity of defining a unique vision and focus that creates meaning and aligns short- and long-term decision making; the unwillingness to live someone else's life
* GROWTH: The hunger to progress and change, driven by an understanding of the dynamic potential of your intelligence, ability, and character
* SPACE: The creation of stillness and solitude to think, reset, wrestle with questions, and recharge; the ability and willingness to listen to your inner voice

The Mental Wealth Score: For each statement below, respond with 0 (strongly disagree), 1 (disagree), 2 (neutral), 3 (agree), or 4 (strongly agree).

1. I regularly embrace a childlike curiosity.
2. I have a clear purpose that provides daily meaning and aligns short- and long-term decision making.

3. I pursue growth and consistently chase my full potential.
4. I have a fundamental belief that I am able to continuously change, develop, and adapt.
5. I have regular rituals that allow me to create space to think, reset, wrestle with questions, and recharge.

Your baseline score (0 to 20): _____

Goals, Anti-Goals, and Systems

Use the goal-setting framework to calibrate your Mental Wealth compass:

- GOALS: What Mental Wealth Score do you want to achieve within one year? What are the two to three checkpoints that you will need to hit on your path to achieve this score?
- ANTI-GOALS: What are the two to three outcomes that you want to avoid on your journey?
- HIGH-LEVERAGE SYSTEMS: What are the two to three systems from the Mental Wealth Guide that you will implement to make tangible, compounding progress toward your goal score?

YOUR ONE-WEEK JUMP START
Use the *ikigai* exercise to begin to explore and uncover your purpose and how it may connect to your current life endeavors.

Create three separate lists:

1. WHAT YOU LOVE: The activities that are life-giving, that bring joy
2. WHAT YOU ARE GOOD AT: The activities that feel effortless
3. WHAT THE WORLD NEEDS: Define your current world and the activities that your current world needs from you.

Identify the overlap of the three lists—this is a starting point for you to explore and uncover your higher-order life purpose.

Physical Wealth

22.

The Big Question

Will You Be Dancing at Your Eightieth Birthday Party?

THE YOUNG MAN WAS only in his mid-twenties, but he knew that if something didn't change, he was going to end up dead.

Dan Go was raised in a little town in Ontario, the son of two Filipino-Chinese immigrants who had moved the family to Canada in search of more opportunity when he was two. From a young age, he endured considerable psychological strain, the result of severe bullying by other children at school. Recalling the torment of those early years, he said, "They told me I was small, dumb, and never going to amount to anything. When you're a kid, if you're told something enough, you start to believe it's true."

He began heading down a dark, lonely path. Believing his tormentors were right, he dropped out of high school. His self-worth deteriorated and he started taking destructive actions to try to dull his inner pain and struggle—eating, drinking, and partying in ways he never had before. His actions set off a vicious self-fulfilling prophecy—the negative change in his physical appearance further eroded his self-worth, leading to more negative behaviors and a downward spiral. "I was in my early twenties, but I couldn't see a future. I'd wake up, go to the fifteen-dollar-per-hour telemarketing job I hated, eat and drink myself to sleep, and do it again. I couldn't look at myself in the mirror."

At his darkest point, when he no longer saw any light ahead of him, a single chance event changed everything.

His dad got a one-month pass to a local gym and gave it to Dan's brother; he didn't want it and passed it along to Dan.

Reflecting on what sparked him to accept that gym membership—which would be something of a challenge, given his current physical state—Dan stated plainly, "I realized that if I kept living the way I was living, I was going to end up dead."

Dan showed up on the first day and got on a treadmill. Within a few minutes, he was out of breath, drenched in sweat, and bored out of his mind. He couldn't imagine doing it again, but the next day, he convinced himself to go back and try something different. He used every weight machine in the gym, and even though he didn't know what he was doing, he felt a rush of energy from the experience. The next morning, he woke up with a soreness he hadn't felt in his entire life and embraced it as a sign that the weightlifting was working. Days three and four were a struggle as he dealt with the new muscle fatigue, but by day seven, he started to feel more comfortable, able to push himself a little bit harder. By day fourteen, he felt excitement at the prospect of walking into the gym. On day thirty, the day the pass expired, something interesting happened as he got dressed for work: He had to buckle his belt one notch tighter.

In that moment, he knew: His entire life had changed.

The tiny result—a single notch in the belt—was representative of something bigger: Dan Go saw the power in his actions. He had reclaimed control of his life.

As he continued to focus on his health, slowly becoming more scientific about how he approached his training, nutrition, and recovery, reading up on the latest studies and incorporating the new ideas into his routines, he started to see everything in his world changing around him. His brain began to function more effectively; he remembered information, names, people, places. His inner dialogue shifted—he started to think he was capable of anything, and certainly much more than he had ever given himself credit for. "I had this defeatist attitude. Suddenly, that all changed. I had a mindset that the entire world was open to me. I proved that I could press a button with my actions and create change in my world, and if I could do that with my health, I could do that anywhere."

Today, Dan Go is in his forties but looks like he's in his twenties. He is fit and vibrant, a loving husband and father of two beautiful children. He is an entrepreneur building a multimillion-dollar business where he positively influences lives by creating transformations just like the one he went through. Dan Go's future went from dark and uncertain to bright and limitless—and it all started when he showed up on day one and got on the treadmill. It all started when he took control of his actions and built a life of Physical Wealth.

The disciplined pursuit of a life of Physical Wealth is a catalyst for growth: It initiates a mindset shift—it reminds you that you are in control, that you have the power. That mindset shift creates ripples that extend well beyond the core to every area of life.

Just after starting his corporate career in his twenties, Kevin Dahlstrom was struck by a mystery illness that wrecked his health; he had crushing fatigue, panic attacks, and recurrent infections. "It's hard to look at photos of myself from that period," he told me. "I don't even recognize myself." Rather than relying on the symptom-masking treatments that his doctors offered, he took control, spending hundreds of hours researching alternatives and executing a new routine based on exercise, nutrition, and recovery. Within months, his chronic symptoms disappeared, and his athletic physique and vibrant, high-energy personality returned. Through his pursuit of Physical Wealth, Kevin Dahlstrom had regained control—and he had no intention of giving it up again.

Years later, he reached the top of the mountain as a corporate executive earning a seven-figure salary, and it was that feeling of control from all those years ago that he turned to when deciding to walk away from it all. Recounting the decision, he told me, "I made it to the summit of corporate America and realized that life doesn't provide control. The evidence was clear—the most 'successful' people weren't people I wanted to emulate in any way—they had lots of Financial Wealth but zero Physical Wealth. So I hit the eject button."

Today, Kevin Dahlstrom lives his dream life. He estimates that he gave up about ten million dollars in future earnings by stepping off the track, but his vibrant energy and broad smile show he has no regrets. He spends most of his time rock climbing, with his wife and kids, or working on any number of exciting, flexible professional projects that give him energy. Reflecting on the decision he made in his twenties to prioritize Physical Wealth, Kevin said, "A lot of people put off building Physical Wealth thinking that they can do that after they've made it, but it just doesn't work that way. Any kind of wealth takes time and compounding to build, and the control you assume via building Physical Wealth is a catalyst and reminder of the control you have over every other area of your life."

In her book *Imaginable, New York Times* bestselling author Jane McGonigal describes a tool called *futures* thinking that is intended to "inspire you to take actions today that set yourself up for future happiness and success." McGonigal walks readers through a guided exercise in futures thinking that has them envision, in vivid detail, their future selves. What are you wearing? Where are you? What's around you? Who is around you? What do you hear and smell? What do you have planned for the day? The effortful creation of this new future canvas, which scientists refer to as *episodic future thinking* (EFT for short), cements an imagined future in your memory, meaning you can return to this "memory" and use its lessons to make changes or decisions in the present.

In an article for TED, McGonigal wrote, "EFT isn't an escape from reality. It's a way of playing with reality, to discover risks and opportunities you might not have considered. . . . It's a powerful decision-making, planning and motivational tool. It helps us decide: Is this a world I want to wake up in? What do I need to do to be ready for it? Should I change what I'm doing today to make this future more or less likely?"[1]

Most important, imagining the desired future reinforces the need for specific actions in the present to create that end.

Let's try it. Close your eyes and take a deep breath. Imagine you're at your eightieth birthday celebration. All your favorite people are walking in, cards and flowers in hand, big smiles on their faces. You're sitting at the main table, enjoying your favorite drink and meal, when the ambient music starts to get louder. It's your favorite song. Your foot starts tapping on the floor underneath the table, right along with the beat. Memories of wonderful moments with the song flood back into your brain. People start to get up and walk to the center of the room. Everyone is looking over at you.

What happens next?

- Do you get up and start dancing with your loved ones?
- Or are you stuck, forced to enjoy the music from your chair?

The harsh truth is that the answers to those questions were written long before you arrived at your eightieth birthday. Your daily actions along the way determined whether you would be dancing or watching at that party.

That visualization of your future should provide clarity on the present:

- If you continue your current daily actions, will you be dancing or sitting?
- What actions do you need to add or adjust in the present to more closely align your future with your ideal vision for it?
- What would your eighty-year-old self want you to do today?

A life of Physical Wealth is grounded in executing the daily actions—regular **movement**, proper **nutrition**, and thoughtful **recovery**—to live a vital present and build toward your ideal imagined future. Your present self is the primary stakeholder in your world, but your future self is the direct heir of the long-term compounding of your actions in the present.

Your eighty-year-old self would remind you that you get only one body, and the way you treat it today is reflected and amplified in the way it will treat you years in the future.

Few people in the world recognized and acted on this insight with more clarity than star American football quarterback Andrew Luck. During the 2018 season, he was riding high at the peak of his football career. The twenty-nine-year-old quarterback was coming off an injury-riddled 2017 season but was back in fighting form, setting new career highs and leading the Indianapolis Colts to the playoffs. He was given the NFL's Comeback Player of the Year Award and voted to his fourth Pro Bowl appearance. It seemed like his career was back on track and he was destined for Hall of Fame glory. But on August 24, 2019, just before the start of the season, Andrew Luck took the podium at Lucas Oil Stadium and announced his retirement in a teary-eyed speech.

The decision shocked the sports world. By retiring, Luck was giving up over $58 million in contract value from his existing agreement with the Colts, plus lucrative endorsement deals. Colts owner Jim Irsay was quoted as saying that he believed Andrew Luck was leaving up to $450 million on the table by choosing to retire. This is an almost unfathomable sum of money to most of us—and it's even more unfathomable to imagine walking away and giving it up.

And yet that was exactly what Andrew Luck did. Why? The realization that his present and future health was worth more than any contract could offer.

In his six NFL seasons, Luck, who played a hard-nosed brand of football and never shied away from contact, endured torn cartilage in two ribs, a partial tear of an abdominal muscle, a lacerated kidney that left him urinating blood, at least one documented concussion, and a torn labrum in his throwing shoulder. This leaves out any undocumented injuries from his long and illustrious amateur and collegiate career, where he was a Heisman finalist while leading Stanford University to several bowl-game victories and top-ten national finishes. In his retirement speech, Luck pointed to the future: "It's been four years of this injury pain cycle. For me to move forward in my life the way I want to, it [won't] involve football." The constant injuries, pain, and pressure had taken a toll on his life on and off the field. To live the life he imagined for himself and his wife and children, Andrew Luck looked beyond Financial Wealth and saw the bigger picture.

It is fitting to recall the powerful piece of advice shared by one of the wise elders interviewed in the opening section of the book, an eighty-year-old with deep regret for the alcohol-heavy, exercise-light lifestyle he had lived throughout his working life:

"Treat your body like a house you have to live in for another seventy years."

Your body is, quite literally, the house that you're going to live in for the rest of your life. And yet a lot of people treat that house like trash—they drink and eat too much, don't sleep enough, rarely move, and avoid the basic investments and repairs necessary to keep it maintained.

You are in control of the present and future state of your house. Keep the foundation and roof in solid order, fix minor issues as soon as they arise, and make the small daily, weekly, and monthly investments required to ensure it will last a long, long time.

With a body, just as with a home, if you take care of it today, it will take care of you for years to come.

Let's make sure you're dancing at your eightieth birthday party.

23.

The Story of Our Lesser World

IN THE FIRST CENTURY B.C., as Julius Caesar ruled over an expanding Roman Empire, a talented young man named Marcus Vitruvius Pollio quietly served in his army, designing machines for battle to outmaneuver Rome's various enemies. Later in life, he became a well-known scholar of architecture, penning *De architectura,* which is regarded as the first major work on the theory of architecture.

Marcus Vitruvius Pollio firmly believed in the connection between the human form and the universe. His physical design principles reflected that belief; he wrote, "The design of a temple depends on symmetry. There must be a precise relation between its components, as in the case of those of a well-shaped man."[2] He dictated the explicit ideals of a well-shaped man (and their impact on the structural design of the temple) in detail; for example, "The length of the foot is one sixth of the height of the body; of the forearm, one fourth; and the breadth of the breast is also one fourth." The precision and curiosity on display in Marcus Vitruvius Pollio's writings sparked fervent intrigue from the most famous scholar of the Renaissance period: Leonardo da Vinci.

Leonardo's obsession with Marcus Vitruvius Pollio's description of the ideal human form led to his creation of the famed *Vitruvian*

Man drawing—a depiction of the ideal human form in two different positions, one superimposed on the other, that established the perfect measurements. While a few other scholars of the period attempted to create the ideal image, producing loose and free-flowing drawings and diagrams, it was only Leonardo who took on the task with a heightened degree of art and science that was characteristic of all his work.

Around this time, Leonardo famously wrote, "The ancients called man a lesser world, and certainly the use of this name is well bestowed, because his body is an analog for the world." His fascination with human anatomy, lines, proportions, and movements was a crucial part of a thriving Renaissance humanist movement, inspiring a public interest in the human form, an interest that had been lost during the Dark Ages, when the human body had come to be viewed as sinful.

The rippling legacy of Leonardo's obsession is found in a cultural interest in the body and physicality that continues to accelerate today. It is a legacy that runs from Michelangelo's striking *David* all the way through the mirrored walls of our modern-day gyms.

THE NATURE OF THE HUMAN BODY

For thousands of years, Physical Wealth—the internal and external health and vitality of an individual—was ingrained in the human lifestyle. Our earliest ancestors were nomadic hunter-gatherers, meaning they roamed large swaths of land in search of food and shelter. This lifestyle necessitated and contributed to a high level of physical well-being. Men, who were typically responsible for hunting larger game and protein sources, were on the move, running, jumping, climbing, throwing, and more; women, who were typically responsible for child-rearing and gathering edible fruits, seeds, roots, and nuts, were also in constant motion, walking, balancing, carrying, and more. Their survival was based on their ability to do these activities well, and the constant motion also undoubtedly shaped their physical forms, their muscles, bones, and ligaments strengthened through the movement necessary to survive and thrive through reproductive age.

When the Agricultural Revolution took place, around 10,000 B.C., the daily physical demands on the average human changed profoundly. These agrarian tribes did not face the inherent unpredictability of the hunter-gatherer lifestyle; they experienced a more repetitive routine that placed an emphasis on a handful of movements and actions done continuously (such as when they tilled soil) and a diet of staple crops. Anthropologists have observed that remains from agrarian societies show reduced bone density, likely a result of fewer day-to-day physical demands, and a lower overall muscle mass, particularly in the upper body. While aspects of physicality were still a part of life, they took on a lesser role in a more sedentary culture, albeit one with modestly higher life expectancy— 24.9 years for agriculturalists compared to 21.6 years for hunter-gatherers, according to one estimate[3]—due to the decreased risks of daily life.

In the thousands of years that followed, humanity entered a period of war and conquest beyond the scale of the minor turf wars that likely characterized the earliest nomadic and agrarian societies. Empires were built on the backs of enormous armies with complex logistics and supply chains that extended thousands of kilometers and covered perilous territory. Suddenly, the physical archetype of the warrior was thrust into the cultural spotlight, and men trained to ready themselves for military glory, a chance at the immortality bestowed upon great warrior heroes like Achilles. The warrior physique and performance attributes—significant upper body strength to wield heavy shields and weapons and a high degree of cardiovascular fitness to endure long marches and battles—were glorified. Perhaps the most extreme example was found in Sparta, a Greek city-state known for its military might that reached the peak of its power between the sixth and fourth centuries B.C. Spartan males were inspected at birth, and those judged weak were left on a nearby mountain to die. At age seven, boys were taken from their mothers' care and sent to begin their training at the *agoge*, a military camp. For years, they were hardened for a life of war and taught to steel

themselves against pain and suffering. The training was so intense
that Plutarch commented, "They were the only men in the world
with whom war brought a respite in the training for war."

Around this time, the celebration and glorification of the warrior
archetype crossed the chasm into sport. While human beings had
engaged in games and shows of athletic prowess since the dawn of
civilized society, it was the Olympic Games, a creation of the ancient
Greeks, that most notably brought together athletes from a wide
swath of territories and city-states to compete against one another
for glory in a public forum. The first recorded account of the Olympics, in 776 B.C., featured a single 192-meter race.[4] The event was
created as a festival to honor Zeus, the most powerful of the gods,
and held at Olympia, a sacred site in southern Greece. The games
were held every four years and the number and diversity of events
gradually increased. The importance of exercise and diet for physical health and vitality was espoused by famed Greek philosophers.
Plato wrote, "Lack of activity destroys the good condition of every
human being," and Aristotle added, "For both excessive and insufficient exercise destroy one's strength, and both eating and drinking
too much or too little destroy health, whereas the right quantity pro-
duces, increases and preserves it."

The Olympic Games slowly faded after Greece was conquered by
the Roman Empire in the second century B.C., and the celebration
and cultural importance of the human physical form fell out of favor
with the rise of Christianity and the beginning of the Middle Ages.
Author Maria Popova summarized the period: "Under Christian
doctrine, the body was too sinful an instrument to be afforded public celebration or private homilies. The cerebral solemnity of the
cathedral replaced the joyful physicality of the gymnasium, where
crowds had once gathered as much to tone their bodies as to hone
their minds on Plato and Aristotle's philosophy lectures . . . and so it
is that the notion of exercise fell out of the popular imagination for a
millennium."[5]

This period of disfavor lasted for about a thousand years, right up
to the end of the fifteenth century, when Leonardo, Michelangelo,
and a band of Renaissance humanists breathed new life into the

study and importance of the physical human form. Interestingly, it was a lesser-known Italian physician named Girolamo Mercuriale who, in 1573, published *De arte gymnastica* (or *The Art of Exercise*) and formally sparked the modern health and wellness movement that has persisted across the centuries. In this work, Mercuriale wrote, "I have taken as my province to restore to the light the art of exercise, once so highly esteemed, and now plunged into deepest obscurity and utterly perished. . . . Why no one else has taken this on, I dare not say. I know only that this is a task of both maximum utility and enormous labor." His book, which drew upon years of study of the ancient Greek and Roman practices around exercise and diet, served as a primary influence for those pushing the importance of physical education in Europe hundreds of years later.

Another subtle acceleration occurred in 1859 when Charles Darwin published his *On the Origin of Species* and commented on the mechanisms of his theory of natural selection. An English polymath named Herbert Spencer coined the phrase *survival of the fittest* in his own summary of Darwin's work shortly thereafter. Suddenly, physical fitness entered mainstream culture as a status symbol—it was a way to measure oneself against others and rise through the visible or invisible ranks of the primal survival hierarchy.

The Olympics, a sporting tradition long forgotten, were revived through the efforts of a Frenchman named Baron Pierre de Coubertin, a staunch advocate of the physical education traditions and movement. In 1892, he proposed the idea of an international athletic competition to be held every four years, and in 1894, it received approval from the International Olympic Committee, the governing organization of the Olympic Games that still exists today. In 1896, the Olympics were held in Athens, Greece, with participation from 280 all-male athletes from twelve nations across forty-three events.[6] By the time of the eighth games, in 1924, their expanded popularity and scale were evident, with 3,000 athletes (male and female!) from forty-four nations participating. In 2004, the Olympics returned to Athens for the first time since their revival in 1896. Eleven thousand athletes from 201 countries competed in the events. One was an American swimmer named Michael Phelps who won a record-tying eight medals and went on to become the most decorated Olympian of all time; another was a little-known Jamaican runner named Usain Bolt, who failed to make the finals in his Olympic debut but would go on to be considered the greatest sprinter of all time.

Sport and the obsession with human physical performance had officially become part of the cultural zeitgeist.

OUR MODERN OBSESSION

At present, it's hard to go a single day without encountering a new health or wellness fad promising the youth, strength, beauty, or vigor we have been wired to seek. From diet programs like Atkins (carbohydrates are the devil!), South Beach (eat foods with a low glycemic index), keto (carbohydrates are the devil again!), vegan (eat only plants), and carnivore (eat only meat) to exercise regimens like CrossFit, Peloton, and hot yoga, we are bombarded by information and snazzy marketing, all claiming to be the best.

The health and wellness industry has become big business. In 2020, the Global Wellness Institute estimated that the global wellness economy had reached $4.4 trillion,[7] with industries that include:

* Personal care and beauty: $955 billion
* Healthy eating, nutrition, and weight loss: $946 billion
* Physical activity: $738 billion
* Wellness tourism: $436 billion

With each new fitness gadget promising perfect abs and each new miracle health food promising youthful vigor, we are forced into a silent battle against the overwhelmingly strong and savvy energy of the world's best marketers. Their jobs depend on convincing you that you need all of it to live a healthy, happy life—and they are very, very good at their jobs. They shine a light on the imperfections of your current world, show you what your perfect world could look like, and then position Gadget X or Health Food Y as the only thing standing between you and that perfect world.

Let's cut straight to it: It's (mostly) nonsense.

The Pareto principle—more informally called the 80/20 rule— refers to the idea that 80 percent of outcomes come from 20 percent of causes. It originated with Vilfredo Pareto, an Italian economist who observed that 80 percent of the land in his native Italy was owned by just 20 percent of the population. When he later noticed that 80 percent of the peas in his garden came from just 20 percent of the pea pods, Pareto hypothesized that this was something of a "magic" distribution in nature.

Put simply, the 80/20 rule says that a small number of inputs drive most of the outputs.

The market around the entire health and wellness space follows this rule: Most of the results are driven by a few simple inputs— completing basic daily movement, consuming whole, unprocessed foods, and prioritizing sleep and recovery.

This is not to say that there's zero value in the seemingly endless list of health products, services, foods, and beverages—I've used, tested, and enjoyed many of them on my own journey—but it is to say that they should always be secondary and never confused with the primary building blocks of Physical Wealth.

In a world that wants you to chase everything everywhere all at once, you must narrow your focus. Chasing the secondary before finishing the primary is playing the game on hard mode. To avoid this, you must develop a baseline understanding of the core pillars that unlock easy mode and perform them consistently in your journey to Physical Wealth.

24.

The Three Pillars of Physical Wealth

BRYAN JOHNSON IS A highly successful entrepreneur. In 2013, he sold the payment-processing company he'd founded to PayPal for $800 million. For most people, this would have been the end of the story: An entrepreneur achieves his dream of building a transformative company, sells that company for a life-changing amount of money, and sails off into the sunset.

But Bryan Johnson is not most people.

The forty-five-year-old is spending over two million dollars a year on a single, focused pursuit: not dying.

According to Johnson, every human has a chronological age (the number of years since birth) and a biological age (the adjusted age of various cells, tissues, and organs based on their relative physiological appearance and performance). While you cannot change your chronological age, your biological age is influenced by your genes as well as a range of controllable factors, including your environment, diet, exercise, recovery, and sleep habits. Beginning in 2021, Bryan Johnson began collaborating with a team of over thirty doctors and experts to not just slow but actually reverse the progress of his biological age. The idea was to use Johnson as a human guinea pig for a long list of monitoring, treatments, and interventions, ranging from the well-established principles of medical orthodoxy to the farthest-out concepts on the outer fringes of longevity and health research.

The program, which Johnson and the team call Project Blueprint, is freely accessible on his website, and Johnson posts regular updates on his latest testing, experiments, and results on social media pages. At the time of this writing, he reaches millions of followers around the world.

Among other things, Johnson's testing regimen includes:

- Checking daily vital signs, body weight, BMI, waking temperature, and sleep performance
- Regular testing of biofluids (including blood, stool, urine, and saliva)
- Regular full-body MRI scans, ultrasounds, colonoscopies, and bone-density scans

He starts every day with a routine that has become the stuff of legend among biohackers:

- Wake up at 5:00 A.M., take vital signs, and consume first round of morning supplements.
- Conduct morning light therapy and meditation.
- Make and drink pre-workout concoction; consume second round of morning supplements.
- Perform rigorous workout involving a variety of movements and heart-rate zones.
- Take shower and perform skin-care routine.
- Eat post-workout meal (vegetables, lentils, nuts, and other vegan ingredients cooked on the stove).
- Conduct more light therapy and consume third round of morning supplements.

Johnson's diet is as regimented as his mornings; his meals are eaten during a feeding window from 5:00 A.M. to 11:00 A.M. and consist of four components:

- The Green Giant: Pre-workout morning concoction of water, spermidine (greens powder), amino acids, creatine, collagen peptides, cocoa flavanols, and cinnamon
- Super Veggie: High-protein vegan combination of black lentils, broccoli, cauliflower, mushrooms, and a variety of accompaniments, including garlic, ginger root, and more
- Nutty Pudding: Pudding rich in healthy fats composed of macadamia nut milk, macadamia nuts, walnuts, chia seeds, flaxseed, Brazil nuts, cocoa powder, berries, cherries, and more
- A Variable Third Meal: Generally a vegetable-heavy salad or stuffed sweet potato

While researching his unique (okay, extreme!) approach, I had the opportunity to spend an afternoon with Johnson at his home. Given my background as an athlete and my personal interest in health and wellness, I was excited to meet the man who was pushing the public discourse on these topics into new territory. It was more than a personal-passion visit; as someone whose mission is to deconstruct the complex and make it simple and accessible, I wanted to see if it was possible to do that with Johnson's protocols and routines. This mission, it turns out, is one that resonates with Johnson, who is going to extraordinary lengths to distill his ideas into free content that he shares across his social media platforms.

During the afternoon, I got a glimpse into his daily life, tried his Nutty Pudding (delicious), and ran through a few of his fitness and recovery protocols. I came to appreciate that his approach is built on a few simple tenets:

- His rigorous training regimen is built on a basic tenet of daily movement.
- His detailed eating plan is built on a basic tenet of proper nutrition.
- His disciplined sleep routines, meditation, and other therapies are built on a basic tenet of thoughtful recovery.

I also spent time understanding the routines of other top physical performers across different arenas, including professional athletes and members of the elite branches of the armed forces. Everywhere I looked, I found the same underlying principles: For all the complexity on the surface, there was a common simplicity in the foundation, three core pillars that every routine was built around.

They are the three controllable pillars of Physical Wealth:

* MOVEMENT: Daily body movement through a combination of cardiovascular exercise and resistance training; activities to promote stability and flexibility
* NUTRITION: Consumption of primarily whole, unprocessed foods to meet major nutrient needs, supplementing as necessary to meet any micronutrient needs
* RECOVERY: High-quality, consistent sleep performance and other recovery-promoting activities

While the three pillars of Physical Wealth are simple, they can feel intimidating, particularly when you consider all the detailed information available on each pillar and the extremes to which people seem to take them.

To combat this intimidation, I find it useful to leverage a video-game analogy: There are levels within each pillar, from a baseline Level 1 to an expert Level 3. If you are a new player entering the game at Level 1, there is no need to compare yourself to Bryan Johnson (who is attempting to operate on Level 100 of this 1 to 3 scale!). Instead, focus on executing Level 1 consistently before leveling up to Level 2 and eventually Level 3.

Bryan Johnson may be spending two million dollars a year to live on the cutting edge of health and longevity practices, but you don't need that to build a life of Physical Wealth. You don't need a fancy, complex routine to achieve the outcomes you want—you just need to ground yourself in these three pillars. As you measure Physical Wealth as part of your new scoreboard, they provide a blueprint for the right action to build it. By developing an understanding of these pillars and the high-leverage systems to affect them, you can begin to create the right outcomes.

MOVEMENT: ENGAGE THE BODY

Movement is nothing new to human culture, but the scientific understanding of movement's role in allowing us to live long, healthy lives has accelerated in the most recent decade.

In his *New York Times* bestselling book *Outlive*, Peter Attia focuses on the astounding benefits of movement. "The data are unambiguous: exercise not only delays actual death but also prevents both cognitive and physical decline better than any other intervention. It is the single most potent tool we have in the health-span-enhancing tool kit—and that includes nutrition, sleep, and meds."

In a 2012 paper published in the *Journal of Aging Research,* researchers found that all-cause mortality was reduced by a striking 30 to 35 percent in the physically active as compared to the physically inactive.[8] In a more recent study published in *Circulation,* the journal of the American Heart Association, researchers looked at thirty years of medical records and mortality data from over 116,000 adults. They found that people who followed minimum guidelines for physical activity (moderate-intensity activity for 150 to 300 minutes per week or vigorous-intensity activity for 75 to 150 minutes per week) reduced their risk of early death by up to 21 percent; those who exercised two to four times these minimum levels lowered their risk by up to 31 percent.[9]

In other words, a little bit of exercise goes a long way and a lot of exercise goes a *longer* way.

Within the pillar of movement, there are three primary subcategories of training to understand (each with its own set of benefits for your overall health, performance, and appearance):

CARDIOVASCULAR TRAINING

The term *cardiovascular* means anything related to the heart or blood vessels. Cardiovascular training strengthens these systems through movement.

The two types of cardiovascular training to understand:

* AEROBIC: Low intensity; relies on the oxygen you breathe to sustain activity
* ANAEROBIC: High intensity; relies on the breakdown of sugars to sustain activity

In simple terms, during aerobic cardiovascular training, you breathe harder to take in more oxygen, and your heart pumps faster so it can efficiently deliver oxygen-rich blood to the muscles. Regular aerobic cardiovascular training strengthens this entire process, meaning your heart and lungs become more effective at doing their jobs. Common forms of aerobic training include hiking, biking, fast walking, jogging, swimming, and rowing. Aerobic cardiovascular training is a great entry point for those new to movement, as it can be effectively completed at a conversational pace (a pace where you can hold a conversation, sometimes referred to as *zone 2 training*). This means you can have company and avoid the intense discomfort that can result from higher-intensity exercises if you're just starting out.

During higher-intensity anaerobic cardiovascular training, your lungs cannot provide enough oxygen to meet your body's demands, so the body breaks down stored sugars for energy. Anaerobic training is sometimes referred to as *zone 5 training* and typically involves short bursts of intense activity (biking, rowing, running, lifting, and so on) with extended recovery periods in between. Anaerobic training is significantly more uncomfortable and should be considered only after you achieve consistency in basic aerobic activities.

STRENGTH

Strength training is the use of resistance (for instance, weights and bands) to build overall muscle, power, and strength. The development and preservation of muscle, power, and strength is critical for a healthy, enjoyable life. According to Andy Galpin, a professor of kinesiology at California State University, Fullerton, and an expert in the science of performance, "Resistance exercise and strength training is the number one way to combat neuromuscular aging."

Strength training can be done in a variety of forms depending on access and skill level, among them body-weight exercises (push-ups, pull-ups, squats), free weights (dumbbells, kettlebells), compound barbell movements (squats, dead lifting, bench-pressing, overhead pressing), and machines (equipment that keeps the user in a guided range of motion to target specific muscles).

For most beginners, focusing on proper technique with basic body-weight exercises, machines, and free weights will provide a solid foundation. As you advance in your strength and training capacity, you can progress to more advanced movements and add weight to increase the intensity.

STABILITY AND FLEXIBILITY

Stability is a foundation of proper movement, as it enables the body to move and deliver force efficiently and effectively. According to Dr. Attia, "[Stability] is the cornerstone upon which your strength is delivered, your aerobic performance is delivered, and your anaerobic performance is delivered. And it's the way that you do so safely."

Flexibility training employs static and dynamic stretching to improve range of motion in your body's muscles and joints. Recent studies have shown that static stretching provides a range of health benefits, including improved balance, posture, and physical performance and reduced pain and inflammation.[10]

You can build stability and flexibility through dedicated stretching and movement routines and dynamic activities like yoga and Pilates.

THE THREE LEVELS OF MOVEMENT

The three levels of the movement pillar:

* LEVEL 1: Move your body for at least thirty minutes per day.
* LEVEL 2: Move your body for at least thirty minutes per day; engage in two to three specific cardiovascular training sessions

per week and one to two resistance-training sessions per week.

* **LEVEL 3:** Move your body for at least thirty minutes per day; engage in three or more cardiovascular training sessions per week (for a total of at least 120 minutes of aerobic training and 20 minutes of anaerobic training) and at least three resistance-training sessions per week incorporating stability and flexibility training.

The development of a thoughtful movement routine to cover the three major subcategories is a goal to work toward. The guide at the end of this section provides an example routine (with links to additional videos and tutorials available on the website). Such a routine will allow you to engage the three primary subcategories of movement training to achieve your short-term aims around performance and appearance and build toward your long-term aims around health and longevity. Building a movement routine today will allow you to live a better present and prepare for a better future.

Every single day that you delay is a missed opportunity that you'll never get back. The present and future you imagine are within reach—but only if you take action now.

NUTRITION: FUEL THE BODY

For decades, nutrition has been a focus of the mainstream lexicon of physical performance and appearance, but for many of the wrong reasons. Fad diets with extreme principles pushed by savvy marketers have dominated the cultural understanding of nutrition over the years, but contrary to what these expert marketers might tell you, proper nutrition is quite simple. You don't need any extreme or complex regimens to build this pillar in your life.

There are four core principles that provide a strong foundation of nutrition:

OVERALL CALORIC INTAKE

This is the total number of calories you consume in a day. Your overall caloric intake determines the baseline outcomes of your body weight and muscle development. A surplus of calories (consuming more than you use) leads to weight gain; a deficit (consuming less than you use) leads to weight loss; a balance (consuming exactly what you use) leads to weight stability.

MACRONUTRIENTS

Macronutrients (often referred to as macros) are the major nutrients your body needs to function.

The three macronutrients are:

* PROTEINS: The building blocks necessary for muscle growth, tissue repair, and more
* CARBOHYDRATES: A primary source of energy for our bodies
* FATS: A source of energy that supports cell growth, organ health, and more

Two basic rules that everyone should follow with respect to macros:

1. PRIORITIZE PROTEIN: Protein is essential for all body functions, but many under-consume it. Have a solid source of protein at every single meal.
2. FOCUS ON CLEANLINESS OF SOURCE: Rather than adopting a dogmatic view on the specific balance of the different macronutrients, focus on the *cleanliness of the sources* of macronutrients. This means getting the macronutrients from primarily whole, unprocessed sources (foods in their natural state that have not been modified or had synthetic ingredients added to them). A good rule of thumb is to eat foods that have a minimal number of ingredients, as more ingredients typically indicate synthetic processing.

MICRONUTRIENTS

Micronutrients are the vitamins and minerals that are essential to healthy body functioning, disease prevention, and overall well-being but are needed in much smaller quantities than macronutrients. This includes iron, vitamin A, vitamin D, iodine, folate, and zinc, among others. Micronutrients cannot be created in the body, so they must be consumed through diet or supplements.

HYDRATION

We all need water to survive, yet many of us are chronically dehydrated. The National Academy of Medicine recommends a baseline of thirteen cups (about three liters) of fluid per day for men and nine cups (about two liters) of fluid per day for women. These figures will increase based on your activity level and should be considered a low-end target for hydration.

THE THREE LEVELS OF NUTRITION

The three levels of the nutrition pillar:

- LEVEL 1: Eat whole, unprocessed foods 80 percent of the time. Note: As a frame of reference, assuming you eat three meals per day, this means that roughly seventeen of your twenty-one meals each week are comprised of whole, unprocessed foods.
- LEVEL 2: Eat whole, unprocessed foods 90 percent of the time. Prioritize daily protein intake (about 0.8 grams of protein per pound of body weight) and overall macronutrient consumption and make sure you get the recommended amounts of fluid.
- LEVEL 3: Eat whole, unprocessed foods 95 percent of the time. Prioritize daily protein intake (about 0.8 grams of protein per pound of body weight) and overall macronutrient consumption. Supplement as necessary with key micronutrients for a well-rounded nutrition profile. Get the recommended amounts of fluid.

Nutrition is a controllable lifestyle factor with a long list of positive benefits. As the old saying goes, you are what you eat.

RECOVERY: RECHARGE THE BODY

Sleep is nature's miracle drug, yet it remains severely underappreciated and underutilized.

In the United States, about 33 percent of adults and 75 percent of high-schoolers get insufficient sleep on a regular basis.[11] According to the 2019 Philips Global Sleep Survey, which asked eleven thousand participants from twelve countries about their sleep habits, 62 percent of adults don't sleep well; they averaged 6.8 hours on weeknights, far short of the recommended eight hours.[12] Eighty percent of the participants said they wanted to improve the quality of their sleep.

Sleep was barely mentioned in the mainstream physical performance lexicon until 2017, when Matthew Walker, a neuroscientist at the University of California, Berkeley, published *Why We Sleep,* which quickly became a bestseller and changed the way millions of "I'll sleep when I'm dead" go-getters thought about its role in their lives. According to Dr. Walker's research, sleep deprivation has a variety of negative effects on the brain, including diminished attention, focus, concentration, and emotional control, and has been linked to a long list of diseases, including Alzheimer's, heart disease, diabetes, and certain cancers.

Beyond simply mitigating these negative effects, sufficient sleep improves brain and body function. There are several critical physiological processes that occur while you sleep, including:

* Memory processing and integration, consolidation and connection of new information and learnings
* Brain "cleansing" that involves the removal of toxins that accumulate during the day
* A switch to the parasympathetic (rest and recovery) nervous system, which promotes physically restorative processes
* Emotional restoration and mood rebalancing

Andrew Huberman, a Stanford University neuroscientist and host of the popular *Huberman Lab* podcast, summarized the foundational importance of sleep on a 2023 episode of *The Tim Ferriss Show*: "In the absence of quality sleep over two or three days, you're just going to fall to pieces. In the presence of quality-sufficient sleep over two or three days, you're going to function at an amazing level. There's a gain of function and a loss of function there. It's not just if you sleep poorly, you function less well. If you sleep better, you function much better."[13]

Here are the core strategies that scientists recommend for high-quality sleep performance:

- AMOUNT: Seven to eight hours per night, with a consistent schedule for sleep and wake times.
- ENVIRONMENT: The sleep setting should be dark, quiet, and cool.
- ROUTINE: Winding down with a relaxing routine in the evenings promotes the release of chemical signals that it is time to sleep. Viewing morning sunlight for just five to ten minutes on a clear day or fifteen to twenty minutes on an overcast day and low-angle afternoon sunlight have both been shown to regulate the release of cortisol and the circadian rhythm (our natural chemical internal clock).

While sleep is your primary and secondary tool for recovery, there are a range of other recovery methods, both old and new, that can be used to further improve your body's ability to recharge once your basic sleep needs are met. These methods include, but are not limited to, cold and heat therapy, massage therapy, and meditation and breathing protocols. These additional recovery methods should be considered, experimented with, and prioritized only *after* the basic building blocks of recovery (sleep!) are executed with 90 percent consistency.

THE THREE LEVELS OF RECOVERY
The three basic levels of the sleep and recovery pillar:

- **LEVEL 1:** Seven to eight hours of sleep
- **LEVEL 2:** Seven to eight hours of sleep in an optimized sleep environment (a dark, cool, quiet room)
- **LEVEL 3:** Seven to eight hours of sleep in an optimized sleep environment; a fixed sleeping time window with morning and afternoon sunlight exposure to regulate circadian rhythm and improve sleep quality; additional recovery methods

A thoughtful approach to sleep, rest, and recovery is essential to your performance, appearance, and longevity. The "I'll sleep when I'm dead" mentality is broken and, ironically, a great way to end up dead much sooner. Prioritize your recovery and you will begin to function and thrive on an entirely different level.

You are Player 1 in your Physical Wealth video game. Start on Level 1—move your body for at least thirty minutes per day, eat whole, unprocessed foods 90 percent of the time, and sleep seven to eight hours per night—a baseline that everyone should aim for to live a healthy life in the present and set themselves up for health in the future. From there, define your goals and work your way up through the levels as you see fit. These investments pay dividends for the rest of your life.

With an established understanding of the three pillars, we can move to the Physical Wealth Guide, which provides the specific tools and systems to build on these pillars and cultivate a life of Physical Wealth.

25.

The Physical Wealth Guide

Systems for Success

THE PHYSICAL WEALTH GUIDE that follows provides specific, high-leverage systems to build each of the pillars of a life of Physical Wealth. This isn't one-size-fits-all and you shouldn't feel compelled to read every single one; browse through and select those that feel most relevant and useful to you.

As you consider and execute the systems for success provided in the Physical Wealth Guide, use your responses to each Physical Wealth statement from the Wealth Score quiz to narrow your focus on the areas where you need to make the most progress (those where you responded *strongly disagree, disagree,* or *neutral*).

1. I feel strong, healthy, and vital for my age.
2. I move my body regularly through a structured routine and have an active lifestyle.
3. I eat primarily whole, unprocessed foods.
4. I sleep seven or more hours per night on a regular basis and feel rested and recovered.
5. I have a clear plan in place to allow me to physically thrive into my later years.

A few common Physical Wealth anti-goals to avoid on your journey:

- Allowing my strength and fitness to deteriorate as I pursue financial goals
- Failing to move my body daily due to other life demands
- Being chronically sleep-deprived and under-recovered

Here are six proven systems for building Physical Wealth.

The Physical Wealth Thirty-Day Challenge

PILLARS: Movement, Nutrition, and Recovery

To build a life of abundant Physical Wealth, you need to create daily practices that support that end. The levels within each core pillar of Physical Wealth provide a simple structure on which you can build and advance a routine that works for you.

The Physical Wealth Thirty-Day Challenge is a way to jump-start your journey through disciplined daily practices for one month.

How the challenge works:

* Choose a challenge level from the three options to follow. Bronze is a good place to start if you are new to these practices, while Gold is more appropriate if you consider yourself advanced.
* Use a simple spreadsheet or template to track your daily execution. You can find a tracking template at the5typesofwealth .com/tracker.
* Create accountability by finding a partner (or partners) to take on the challenge with you. Make a group message or system for communicating your performance on the daily challenge. Message *Done* upon completion of each item on the list.
* Once you've completed one level of the challenge, you can consider taking on the next level in the following month.

The three levels of the challenge are as follows:

BRONZE CHALLENGE
* Move your body for thirty minutes per day.
* Eat whole, unprocessed foods for 80 percent of your meals.
* Sleep for seven hours every night.

SILVER CHALLENGE
- Execute a morning routine each weekday.
- Move your body for forty-five minutes per day.
- Eat whole, unprocessed foods for 90 percent of your meals.
- Increase protein consumption (0.8 grams of protein per pound of body weight is a good baseline).
- Sleep for seven to eight hours every night, with fixed sleep and wake times on weekdays.

GOLD CHALLENGE
- Drink sixteen ounces of water when you wake up.
- Execute a morning routine each weekday.
- Move your body for sixty minutes per day, including at least three strength sessions per week.
- Eat whole, unprocessed foods at 95 percent of your meals.
- Establish and hit full macronutrient consumption targets (protein, carbs, fats).
- Sleep for eight hours every night, with fixed sleep and wake times.
- Complete one additional recovery method per day (e.g., breathing protocols, meditation, cold or heat therapy).

How to Win the Day: A Science-Backed
Morning Routine

PILLARS: Movement and Nutrition

> When you arise in the morning, think of what a precious
> privilege it is to be alive—to breathe, to think, to enjoy, to love.
> —MARCUS AURELIUS

The first hour of your morning sets the tone for the entire day ahead. Thoughtful movement and nutrition during that window will make you feel more energized, focused, and productive and provide a sense of structure and stability in an otherwise unpredictable world.

Here, I'll share the five principles of an effective morning routine, show you how I incorporate them into my mornings, and provide a template you can use to build your own:

MORNING ROUTINE PRINCIPLE 1: WAKE UP
Maintaining a consistent wake time each day has been scientifically proven to provide real health benefits; it regulates the body's circadian rhythm, improves cognitive function, and boosts energy levels, mood, and overall health.

MY APPLICATION: Waking up early is the easiest way to improve your odds of success. You don't have to wake up early to be successful, but you rarely find an early riser who isn't winning. For me, this means 4:30 on weekdays and around 5:00 on weekends (or earlier if my son decides to crawl all over me in bed!). Note: I try to go to sleep around 8:30 on weeknights to get seven to eight hours of sleep.

IMPLEMENTATION PLAN: Set a fixed time to wake up on weekdays and a fixed time to wake up on the weekend (ideally within thirty to sixty minutes of your weekday wake-up time to avoid negatively affecting your natural sleep cycles). If you need an extra boost, place your phone in the bathroom (or at least ten feet from your bed) to force yourself to get out of bed to turn off the alarm.

MORNING ROUTINE PRINCIPLE 2: HYDRATE

Most of us are chronically dehydrated. This affects all areas of health. Morning hydration kick-starts your metabolism, improves memory, and boosts energy. In addition, hydrating in the morning can lead to better digestion and improved skin health by flushing out toxins from the day (or long night) before.

MY APPLICATION: I hydrate in the morning with a cocktail of sixteen ounces of water, greens powder, and electrolytes.

IMPLEMENTATION PLAN: Make sure you drink sixteen ounces of water upon rising. If you want to add a boost to the water, consider adding lemon, electrolytes, or greens powder to supercharge the effects.

MORNING ROUTINE PRINCIPLE 3: MOVE

Moving your body daily should be a nonnegotiable. We were made to move. Daily activity (thirty to sixty minutes) is essential to health, brain function, and happiness. When you're getting started, just move in whatever way you enjoy—walk, dance, hike, run, lift weights, anything you like. Simple is better than complex.

MY APPLICATION: I use my 5-5-5-30 routine: five push-ups, five squats, five lunges, and a thirty-second plank. You can do this while your coffee is brewing or immediately after you wake up. It will give you an instant boost of energy and get your blood flowing.

IMPLEMENTATION PLAN: Choose a few simple movements to start your day. They can be strength exercises (like mine), mobility exercises, or stretches, and they can be easy. The point is to get your body moving and the blood flowing.

MORNING ROUTINE PRINCIPLE 4: GET OUTSIDE

Exposure to natural light in the morning increases your focus, improves your mood via increased serotonin production, and serves as a natural source of vitamin D. By spending time in nature and away from screens, you'll experience reduced stress and improved overall mental clarity.

MY APPLICATION: My thirty-minute walk with my son is a nonnegotiable part of my morning routine. It always leaves me feeling healthy, happy, and creative.

IMPLEMENTATION PLAN: Get outside and walk to start your day. Fifteen minutes is all you need. Leave your phone on silent (or leave it at home). Allow yourself to think freely and breathe.

MORNING ROUTINE PRINCIPLE 5: FOCUS

Most people are not wired to work from nine to five. Modern work culture is a remnant of an earlier age—long periods of the same steady monotonous tasks. If your goal is to create, you must work like a lion. Sprint when inspired. Rest. Repeat.

MY APPLICATION: I always start my day with two hours of focused work on the most important tasks.

IMPLEMENTATION PLAN: Establish your most important tasks for the next day the night before. Go through them during a focused block of work to start your morning.

Summarizing the five core science-backed principles of a great morning routine:

1. WAKE UP: Establish a fixed waking schedule for weekdays and weekends.
2. HYDRATE: Drink sixteen ounces of water (with superchargers as desired).
3. MOVE: Choose a few simple strength, mobility, or flexibility movements to get your body moving and the blood flowing.
4. GET OUTSIDE: Fifteen minutes of movement outside sets the tone for the day.
5. FOCUS: Set a block of time to work on the most important tasks for the day.

If you incorporate your own version of these five core principles, you'll be well on your way to building your perfect morning routine.

The Movement Plan: A Level 3 Training Plan That Works

PILLAR: Movement

A collaboration with Ben Bruno, a personal trainer and strength coach who works with professional athletes, A-list celebrities, high-powered entrepreneurs, and others.

The following is a training-week template that you can use and adapt once you have reached Level 3 in your movement journey. Levels 1 and 2 are focused on daily movement and building the habit; Level 3 is a more advanced combination of the primary subcategories of training—cardiovascular, strength, stability, and flexibility—necessary for your overall health, performance, and appearance.

Each week at Level 3 should consist of three full-body strength workouts, two low-intensity aerobic cardio workouts, and one high-intensity anaerobic cardio workout. The exact days for each workout are up to you, so don't feel pressure to stick to a rigid routine if you have a busy or irregular schedule. Ideally, give yourself a day of recovery between each full-body strength workout.

The composition of a training week is as follows:

- Day 1: Full-body strength plus optional aerobic cardio
- Day 2: Aerobic cardio (sixty minutes)
- Day 3: Full-body strength plus optional aerobic cardio
- Day 4: Aerobic cardio (sixty minutes)
- Day 5: Full-body strength plus optional aerobic cardio
- Day 6: Anaerobic cardio (twenty minutes)
- Day 7: Light recovery and rest

FULL-BODY STRENGTH

Your full-body strength sessions will incorporate a warm-up routine, static stretching, and dynamic stability and mobility work. While the specific strength routine you follow is your choice, you can find a recommended full-body routine at the5typesofwealth.com/movementplan, including video tutorials for each movement.

AEROBIC CARDIO

Your aerobic cardio sessions are longer, low-intensity workouts. For the average person, the most effective and repeatable form of aerobic cardiovascular training is low intensity, sometimes referred to as zone 2 training. Scientifically, zone 2 is the level of exertion in which the body is using oxygen to convert fat into fuel. While the zone 2 heart rate will vary from person to person, zone 2 can be estimated as the level at which your heart rate is elevated but you are still able to have a conversation and breathe through your nose (roughly 60 to 70 percent of your maximum heart rate). Alternatively, you can estimate that heart rate by subtracting your age from 220 (which establishes your maximum heart rate) and multiplying that by 60 to 70 percent (which gives you your zone 2 heart rate).

Select a format (hiking, biking, fast walking, jogging, swimming, rowing, et cetera) and perform a proper warm-up to get the body prepared. Select an intensity level where you have an elevated heart rate but can still carry on a conversation.

ANAEROBIC CARDIO

Your anaerobic cardio session is a focused, high-intensity workout. Anaerobic training is high intensity (sometimes referred to as zone 5) and involves short bursts of intense activity (biking, rowing, running, lifting, et cetera) with extended recovery periods in between.

This type of training is important for building VO_2 max—the maximum amount of oxygen the body can use during a period of intense exercise. VO_2 max is arguably the most useful indicator of overall cardiorespiratory fitness and has a dramatic impact on health and longevity. In fact, a 2018 study found that a modest increase in VO_2 max from the bottom 25th percentile to the 25th–50th percentile was associated with a 50 percent reduction in all-cause mortality, and a jump from the bottom 25th percentile to the 50th–75th percentile was associated with a dramatic 70 percent reduction in all-cause mortality.[14]

Select a format (bike, row, run, stairs, et cetera) and perform a proper warm-up to get the body prepared. Alternate between rounds of all-out effort and periods of rest for at least twenty minutes. For example, one minute of hard effort followed by two to three minutes of slow movement or rest is a good baseline. Your heart rate should spike during the bouts of effort and come down to a low baseline during the recovery periods.

LIGHT RECOVERY

The recovery day is an essential part of the weekly routine. Light movements—such as walking, easy hikes, or other low heart rate outdoor activities—are great for your recovery day as long as they aren't putting strain on the body. Recovery day is a great time to engage in your favorite recovery protocols, such as cold or heat therapy, massage, and foam rolling. Make sure you prioritize high-quality sleep.

For more information and resources related to the training plan, please visit the5typesofwealth.com/movementplan.

Note: Consult with a physician prior to undertaking any meaningful change to your current routine. While the program is backed by science and many years of training experience, it is generalized, and individuals should review their health and circumstances with a professional prior to taking on a rigorous fitness program.

The Common-Sense Diet: Principles and Foods

PILLAR: Nutrition

A collaboration with Ben Bruno, a personal trainer and strength coach who works with professional athletes, A-list celebrities, high-powered entrepreneurs, and others.

The common-sense diet is a set of eight simple principles that provide a general structure for high-quality nutrition that will fuel your performance, improve your appearance, and optimize your long-term health and longevity.

THE COMMON-SENSE DIET PRINCIPLES

1. Eat well most (about 80 to 90 percent) of the time. Save junk-food splurges for the stuff you really love. Prioritize single-ingredient, whole, unprocessed foods.
2. Stop eating before you're stuffed (eating to 80 percent satiety is a good rule of thumb).
3. Make sure to get enough protein for your body goals. A good baseline is 0.8 grams of protein per pound of body weight for someone who is physically active.
4. Avoid foods that make you feel and perform poorly. Everyone is different in this regard, so find what works and doesn't work for you.
5. Drink plenty of water and fluids but limit alcohol.
6. Eat whole vegetables, fruits, or both at every meal, the more the better.
7. Find a meal frequency that works for your life. Don't buy into the dogmas of one right way to do it.
8. Don't take your diet so seriously that you miss out on life experiences.

Quality Food Sources to Consider

To assist you on the journey, here is a list of high-quality, nutrient-dense foods categorized by macronutrient. Note that this list is not intended to be comprehensive but to provide a starting-point grocery list for improved nutrition.

PROTEIN SOURCES:

- Meat, including beef, poultry, and lamb
- Fish
- Eggs
- Greek yogurt
- Cottage cheese
- Tofu
- Protein powder (from high-quality sources with minimal added ingredients)

CARBOHYDRATE SOURCES:

- Grains, including rice, oatmeal, quinoa, barley, and farro
- Potatoes and sweet potatoes
- Whole fruits and vegetables
- Beans, lentils, and peas
- Raw honey

FAT SOURCES:

- Nuts and nut butters
- Butter or ghee from grass-fed animals
- Extra-virgin olive oil
- Avocado oil
- Coconut oil
- Chia seeds, flaxseed, hemp seeds

Additional Nutritional Information

MACRONUTRIENTS

Proteins and carbohydrates each contain four calories per gram; fats contain nine calories per gram. To calculate your total caloric intake, multiply the grams of each macronutrient consumed during the day by the appropriate number and add them together. For example, if I consume 200 grams of protein, 300 grams of carbohydrates, and 100 grams of fat, that equals 2,900 calories (200 grams of protein at 4 calories per gram plus 300 grams of carbohydrates at 4 calories per gram plus 100 grams of fat at 9 calories per gram).

Various dietary schools debate the relative ideal proportions of each macronutrient, but a grounding in protein (around 0.8 grams and up to 1 gram per pound of body weight for someone engaged in strength training) is a good starting point. Protein is highly filling, which means you're less likely to overeat in other areas, which will make achieving goals easier. The mix of carbohydrates and fats can be tailored to individual fitness or aesthetic goals, but most people will benefit from distributing their remaining calories across carbohydrates and fats.

You can use the free online calculators at calculator.net/calorie-calculator.html to determine a baseline level of caloric intake for your overall physical goals. You can find a free macronutrient calculator at calculator.net/macro-calculator.html to determine a baseline macronutrient profile across various models (I would recommend beginning with the balanced model for most people).

Micronutrients

There are six essential micronutrients according to the U.S. Centers for Disease Control and Prevention: iron, vitamin A, vitamin D, iodine, folate, and zinc. Active individuals may need other micronutrients, such as vitamin E, vitamin B_{12}, magnesium, potassium, and calcium.

Most of these micronutrients are found in whole, unprocessed foods, but some (like vitamin D) are harder to get in sufficient quantities from food alone, and may require supplementation.

There are a variety of meal-tracking applications that will estimate the micronutrient profile of your diet. If you are concerned about your micronutrient intake, consider asking your physician to order a blood panel, or order it yourself through a service (there are many options, depending on your geography and price sensitivity).

Quality nutrition defends against negative outcomes and promotes positive outcomes. Following the eight principles of the common-sense diet and prioritizing the foods from the list in the major macronutrient categories will allow you to achieve a very strong nutritional baseline as you work toward your Physical Wealth goals.

How to Become a Pro Sleeper:
Nine Rules for Sleep

PILLAR: Recovery

Sleep is the most effective tool in your arsenal to achieve optimal health, performance, and recovery.

To become a professional sleeper, follow these basic, science-backed rules:

1. KEEP A REGULAR SCHEDULE: Sleep regularity is important. Set a fixed bedtime that you stick to and try to wake up around the same time every single morning (even on weekends).

2. VIEW MORNING SUNLIGHT: Spend at least ten to fifteen minutes viewing sunlight every single morning (on a walk, ideally). Note that even on an overcast morning, there is sunlight, but you may need to increase the time of exposure to get the same benefit. There is significant scientific evidence that it will help you establish and maintain a healthy circadian rhythm.

3. CONTROL YOUR SLEEP ENVIRONMENT: Your sleep environment should be cool and dark. Use blackout curtains or an eye mask if natural light is a problem.

4. AVOID FOOD RIGHT BEFORE BED: Eating right before bed may disrupt your natural body functions, hormones, and sleep cycle. If you are hungry before bed, keep the meal light and avoid carb-heavy, insulin-spiking meals.

5. AVOID CONSUMING EXCESSIVE LIQUIDS BEFORE BED: Waking up to use the restroom in the middle of the night can be very disruptive. To avoid this, limit liquid intake in the sixty minutes before going to bed.

6. AVOID CAFFEINE IN THE AFTERNOONS: The post-lunch coffee may contribute to your inability to fall asleep at night. Avoid

caffeine within eight hours of your bedtime to ensure it is out of your bloodstream.

7. CUT BACK ON ALCOHOL: Alcohol disrupts sleep (and health) in a variety of ways. Avoid alcohol and your sleep will improve.

8. CREATE A WIND-DOWN ROUTINE: Develop a consistent routine for relaxing and winding down before going to bed. Dim lights in the house an hour or two before bedtime, shut off your work devices, spend time with your family or friends, or read your favorite book. You can include natural sleep supplements, such as magnesium and theanine, which have been proven to support healthy sleep cycles, in the wind-down routine.

9. AVOID SCREENS BEFORE BED: If you have trouble falling asleep at night, avoid screens within an hour of bedtime. Designate your sleep environment as a screen-free zone.

If you follow those rules with 90 percent consistency for thirty days, you will improve your sleep and feel the benefits in your life.

How to Promote Calm: Science-Backed Breathing Protocols

PILLAR: Recovery

Stress is not black-and-white—like most things, it exists on a spectrum. In fact, when it comes to performance in important moments, *too little* stress is just as bad as *too much* stress.

The Yerkes-Dodson Law is a simple model of the relationship between performance and stress. It was proposed in 1908 by psychologists Robert Yerkes and John Dodson, who reached their conclusions after doing a study on Japanese dancing mice. In simple terms, the Yerkes-Dodson Law says that stress and performance are positively correlated only up to a certain point, after which more stress reduces performance.

There are three states to be aware of:

1. LOW STRESS: This is a state of low arousal. This state is necessary for recovery.
2. OPTIMAL STRESS: This is the optimal state of arousal. It's the Goldilocks level—not too hot, not too cold, just right. When you're in this state, you are well positioned to perform important tasks.
3. HIGH STRESS: This is a state of high arousal, the overstressed position we so often find ourselves in. It may lead to a complete shutdown from system overload.

In an ideal world, you would operate in the state of optimal stress during important tasks and then quickly shut that off and operate in the state of low stress at other times. In reality, most people find themselves tipping over the edge into the state of high stress too often and fail to reset to the state of low stress frequently enough to recover.

To execute a stress reset and promote the low-stress recovery state, try these three science-backed breathing techniques:

THE 4-7-8 METHOD

A particularly effective method for triggering the calm state necessary to fall asleep, the 4-7-8 method is one that I use almost daily.

How it works:
- Breathe in through your nose for four seconds.
- Hold your breath for seven seconds.
- Exhale for eight seconds.
- Repeat two to three times.

THE LION'S BREATH

Another effective approach is derived from ancient yogic traditions in India.

How it works:
- Sit in a comfortable position on the floor with a slight forward lean and your hands on the floor.
- Focus your gaze on the tip of your nose.
- Inhale deeply through your nose.
- Stick your tongue out and down to your chin.
- Exhale forcefully with a "Ha!" sound. (Note: Limit the forcefulness of the exhale if you're a beginner.)
- Repeat two to three times.

THE PHYSIOLOGICAL SIGH

The physiological sigh, previously mentioned as a way to moderate stress in your system for effective public speaking, is a remarkably effective approach for promoting calm. First described in the 1930s and reinvigorated by the research of UCLA neurobiologist Jack Feldman and Stanford biochemist Mark Krasnow, we do it naturally when levels of carbon dioxide in the bloodstream get too high. It creates a relaxing sensation by releasing a lot of carbon dioxide very fast.

How it works:

- Inhale through your nose twice, first slowly, then quickly.
- Long exhale through your mouth to a natural stop without forcing the breath.
- Repeat two to three times.

Stress is a necessary part of life. If you can learn to harness it—to operate in the optimal stress environment for important tasks and the low stress environment for recovery—you will always perform at your best. Try these three science-backed breathing protocols and you'll be well on your way to turning stress from your sworn enemy into your good friend (or at least your friendly acquaintance!).

26.

Summary: Physical Wealth

PHYSICAL WEALTH OVERVIEW

THE BIG QUESTION: WILL you be dancing at your eightieth birthday party?

THE THREE PILLARS OF PHYSICAL WEALTH:
* MOVEMENT: Daily body movement through a combination of cardiovascular exercise and resistance training; activities to promote stability and flexibility
* NUTRITION: Consumption of primarily whole, unprocessed foods to meet major nutrient needs, supplementing as necessary to meet micronutrient needs
* RECOVERY: High-quality, consistent sleep performance, and other recovery-promoting activities

The Physical Wealth Score: For each statement below, respond with 0 (strongly disagree), 1 (disagree), 2 (neutral), 3 (agree), or 4 (strongly agree).

1. I feel strong, healthy, and vital for my age.
2. I move my body regularly through a structured routine and have an active lifestyle.
3. I eat primarily whole, unprocessed foods.
4. I sleep seven or more hours per night on a regular basis and feel rested and recovered.
5. I have a clear plan in place to allow me to physically thrive into my later years.

Your baseline score (0 to 20):

Goals, Anti-Goals, and Systems

Use the goal-setting framework to calibrate your Physical Wealth compass:

* GOALS: What Physical Wealth Score do you want to achieve within one year? What are the two to three checkpoints that you will need to hit on your path to achieve this score?
* ANTI-GOALS: What are the two to three outcomes that you want to avoid on your journey?
* HIGH-LEVERAGE SYSTEMS: What are the two to three systems from the Physical Wealth Guide that you will implement to make tangible, compounding progress toward your goal score?

YOUR ONE-WEEK JUMP START
Complete seven consecutive days of your first Physical Wealth Thirty-Day Challenge.

Choose a challenge level from the Physical Wealth Thirty-Day Challenge in the Physical Wealth Guide. Bronze is a good place to start if you are new to these practices, while Gold is more appropriate if you consider yourself advanced.

Use a spreadsheet or template to track your daily execution. You can find a tracking template at the5typesofwealth.com/tracker.

Find a partner (or partners) to take on the challenge with you. Create a group message or system for communicating your performance on the daily challenge. Message *Done* upon completion of each item on the list.

Financial
Wealth

27.

The Big Question

What Is Your Definition of *Enough*?

IN A SHORT POEM about his late friend Joseph Heller, a famous American author best known for his work of satirical genius, *Catch-22*, Kurt Vonnegut shared an anecdote that offers a powerful piece of Heller's wisdom.

As the two enjoyed a party at the home of a billionaire, Vonnegut asked Heller, "Joe, how does it make you feel to know that our host only yesterday may have made more money than your novel *Catch-22* has earned in its entire history?" Heller replied, "I've got something he can never have . . . the knowledge that I've got enough."

I first came across this poem in May 2021 shortly after the conversation with an old friend that had changed my life. The message, amplified by my deeply reflective mental state in the moment, immediately struck a chord.

When Heller spoke those words—"the knowledge that I've got enough"—what did he really mean? What's so special and valuable about that knowledge, about that idea of *enough,* that he had the audacity to claim it was worth more than the billions of dollars that their host had accumulated?

To answer these challenging questions, it helps to invert them:

What happens in the absence of that knowledge? We are gripped—even possessed—by a constant, incessant, obsessive quest for *more*.

Once asked by a reporter how much money was enough money, business tycoon John D. Rockefeller replied, "Just a little bit more."

The quest for more is the modern-day equivalent of the Sisyphean struggle. We push the boulder up the hill, working harder and longer to achieve whatever summit we're chasing, only to have the boulder roll back down to the bottom and force us to begin anew. Hedonic adaptation—that biological predisposition to return to a baseline after positive events—means that no financial win ever quite satiates.

Your current definition of *more* becomes your future definition of *not enough* as you set your sights on the next level that you convince yourself will bring happiness and contentment.

I've seen it happen repeatedly both in my own life and in the lives of those around me. That thing you once longed for becomes the thing you can't wait to upgrade. It's the phenomenon that leads people to take out a new line of credit for that home addition they don't really need, to overextend themselves to buy the new car, to go into credit card debt for that fancy new watch, or to allow their health or family to fall apart while they chase some professional promotion.

In 1869, Mark Twain penned an open letter to Cornelius Vanderbilt, a business tycoon who at the time was the richest man in the world. He wrote of the *poverty of more,* saying, "Poor Vanderbilt! How I pity you . . . You are an old man, and ought to have some rest, and yet you have to struggle, and deny yourself, and rob yourself of restful sleep and peace of mind, because you need money so badly. I always feel for a man who is so poverty ridden as you . . . It isn't what a man has that constitutes wealth. No—it is to be satisfied with what one has; that is wealth."[1]

Many billionaires who have amassed extraordinary riches lack some of the most basic markers of a happy, fulfilling life. Consider the shocking fact that, at the time of this writing, the ten richest people in the world have a combined twelve divorces among them. The Pyrrhic victory: winning the battle but losing the war.

History is littered with stories of billionaires who strive for the next rung of the ladder and take on undue risk, only to lose it all. In the past five years alone, we've seen several entrepreneurs go from being celebrated on the cover of *Forbes* to being jeered in the corner of a prison cellblock. Sam Bankman-Fried and Elizabeth Holmes were touted by many as being part of a new class of generational founders, their names expected to be plastered alongside those of Jobs, Gates, Zuckerberg, Musk, and Bezos. Unfortunately, despite early successes that appear to have been legitimate, their chase for *more* led to a steady deterioration of ethical standards that resulted in eventual criminal charges and convictions.

The fair counterpoint to the rebuke of *more* is that the world needs some of these "crazy ones"—a term made famous by the 1997 Think Different Apple ad campaign—who push for more at all costs and wind up creating new and incredible things. To be clear, it is not the crazy ones themselves but the social and cultural pressure that says you need to be one of them that causes the trouble.

The chase for more is societally celebrated, while the contentment with enough is easily misunderstood as a lack of ambition. The worthiness of your life is not established by the numbers on your bank or brokerage statement, and it never will be. You set the terms of your own pursuit. You define the rules of your game. It's perfectly reasonable (and even advisable) to embrace a different way, to ground yourself in the diverse pillars that define a truly wealthy existence: time, people, purpose, health. In doing so, you begin to live your financial life on your terms, not the ones that your hunter-gatherer mind or modern social pressures force on you.

The solution to your quest for more: defining and embracing the beauty of your *enough*.

Lagom is a Swedish term that translates to "just the right amount." *Lagom* is what we are searching for—the knowledge of enough, of balance, of equilibrium. The challenge is that *lagom* isn't static; it tends to be an ever-increasing target. As you get closer to achieving it, your confidence swells and resets to a higher level. This subconscious reset—from "I'll be happy when I have [$X]" to "I'll be happy when I have triple [$X]"—creates the upward spiral of expectations that you need to avoid.

You will never have true Financial Wealth if you allow your expectations—your definition of *enough*—to grow faster than your assets.

There is no perfect antidote. Hedonic adaptation means our chase for more is genetically hardwired, but forcing the definition of *enough* out of the subconscious mind and into the conscious mind is a start.

After my son was born, in May 2022, I started to contemplate exactly what my Enough Life would look like—that is, the life of *lagom,* where I have just the right amount of Financial Wealth. Rather than allowing my Enough Life to exist in some abstract, secluded region of my mind, I pushed it into the light.

I imagined it. I defined it.

You should do the same: What does your Enough Life look like?

* Where do you live?
* What do you have?
* What are you and your loved ones doing?
* What are you focusing on?
* How much financial cushion do you have?

Importantly, the Enough Life doesn't have to be simple or spartan; it can be as ambitious or lavish as you see fit. My Enough Life has a vacation home in a beautiful location, mainly because I want to be able to host family and friends to make incredible memories, but it is devoid of luxuries I have no interest in (private jets, yachts, mansions, supercars, fancy jewelry, and so on). The point is that it is *your* Enough Life—not someone else's, not influenced by social or cultural pressures, not prone to the subconscious escalation of lifestyle creep. By defining it, by writing it down and keeping it top of mind, you force it into the conscious mind. This doesn't perfectly halt the natural upward movement, but it does convert an irrational, subconscious movement into a rational, conscious one.

Your aim then becomes building Financial Wealth—through **income generation, expense management,** and **long-term investment**—up to the point where it enables that Enough Life that you have defined. Beyond that point, the aim shifts to balancing your energy across a broader range of pursuits. Once you've reached this point, the Enough Life, you no longer need to focus on money and instead you can prioritize more time, relationships, purpose, growth, and health.

There's a beautiful parable that brings this to life:

A wealthy investment banker goes on vacation to a tropical fishing village. As he walks along the docks one afternoon, he comes upon a small, run-down fishing boat with several large fish on its deck.

"How long did it take you to catch those fish?" he asks. The fisherman looks up from his work and smiles at his new visitor.

"Only a little while."

The investment banker is taken aback by this response. He likes the fisherman and wants to help. "Why don't you fish for longer so you can catch more fish?"

The fisherman shrugs and explains to his new friend that he has all he needs. "Each day, I sleep late, fish a little, and spend time with my children and beautiful wife. In the evening, I go into town, drink wine, play the guitar, and sing and laugh with my friends."

The investment banker is puzzled. He wants to help his new friend, who, in his opinion, is clearly confused. The investment banker has helped many businesses and has an MBA and other fancy credentials to his name, so he lays out a plan for the fisherman: "First, you spend more time fishing so you can catch and sell more fish. You use the proceeds to buy a bigger boat, which allows you to catch and sell even more fish. Then you buy a fleet of boats. You hire a team. Vertically integrate! As the CEO of a large, growing enterprise, you could move to the big city. You would take your company public and make millions!"

The fisherman looks confused, but smiles. "And then what?" he asks.

The investment banker laughs at the silly question. "Well, then you could retire to a quiet town! You could sleep late, fish a little, and spend time with your children and beautiful wife. In the evening, you could go into town, drink wine, play the guitar, and sing and laugh with your friends."

The fisherman smiles broadly, thanks his new friend for the advice, and wanders off slowly in the warm afternoon sun.

The popular interpretation of this parable is that the investment banker is wrong, and the fisherman is right. My own interpretation is that this story isn't about the fisherman being right and the banker being wrong—it's about identifying what success and purpose look like to you and building a life that meets that definition. It's about defining your Enough Life and then working to embrace it.

Maybe both the fisherman and the banker are happy with their choices and priorities. I'll let them decide, and the same goes for you.

In a powerful scene in the movie *Cool Runnings*, the story of the unlikely journey of a Jamaican bobsled team to the Olympics, the team's coach, played by the late John Candy, observes to one of the stars of the team: "A gold medal is a wonderful thing, but if you're not enough without it, you'll never be enough with it."

As an ambitious person, you spend most of your life playing a game; everything you do is in anticipation of a future filled with more:

- "I can't wait until I have [$X] so I can get that new car."
- "I can't wait until I have [$Y] so I can get that new house."
- "I can't wait until I have [$Z] so I can get that second house."

When the future arrives, you just reset to the next material goal.

It's natural, but it's a dangerous game, one that you will lose eventually. If you convince yourself that your satisfaction, fulfillment, and happiness are contingent on the next financial milestone—the next *more*—you'll never find it.

That was what Joseph Heller meant when he spoke those words—"the knowledge that I've got enough"—to Kurt Vonnegut all those years ago.

Because "if you're not enough without it, you'll never be enough with it."

28.

The Financial Amusement Park

IN 1485, A YOUNG merchant named Jakob Fugger had an opportunity. The twenty-six-year-old had recently become a partner in his family's burgeoning trading firm and was given the authority to strike his own deals. While traveling to Austria, he met Archduke Sigmund, a notoriously big spender and the cousin of Frederick III, the Holy Roman emperor. Sigmund needed more money to finance his high-flying lifestyle, but many of the region's bankers were fed up with the archduke; he was no longer considered an attractive risk for a prudent banker in an era when laws against usury (lending money at high rates of interest) restricted the financial upside of such loans.

Jakob Fugger smelled an opportunity. He agreed to loan three thousand florins to the archduke in exchange for one thousand pounds of silver from the local mines that would be sold to him at a discounted price. Archduke Sigmund appreciated the show of faith and met his end of the deal, delivering the thousand pounds of silver on time at a price of eight dollars per pound, silver that Fugger resold at a 50 percent markup, netting a modest yet attractive return on the deal. More important to the young merchant, this small deal cemented his relationship with one of the most powerful families in Europe. Several years later, the archduke was in need of a much larger loan to finance his latest misstep, so he turned to Fugger, who again stepped up, this time with one hundred thousand florins and an even more aggressive set of repayment terms and conditions. The archduke again met his end of the deal, and Jakob Fugger was officially vaulted into the ranks of the wealthy elite—he had established himself as a merchant and banker willing to take on risk (assuming he felt adequately compensated for it).

Over the years that followed, Jakob Fugger's money dramatically influenced the course of world history. His financial support was sought by kings, emperors, and explorers alike. When Ferdinand Magellan needed financing for his voyage around the world, Jakob Fugger was there. When Spain's King Charles I sought to become Holy Roman emperor, Jakob Fugger was there. And when free-spending Pope Leo X needed a large sum of money to finance the building of St. Peter's Basilica, Jakob Fugger was there (repayment of this loan required a massive sale of indulgences—sin-forgiveness tickets—to regular citizens, a practice that drew the ire of a reformer named Martin Luther, who went on to lead the Protestant Reformation).[2] Fugger's money—and, by extension, his power and influence—shaped the course of the European continent.

His innovative use of accounting methods—he was one of the first to use double-entry bookkeeping, and he established the now standard practice of consolidating multiple operations into a single set of financial statements—allowed him to keep tabs on the entirety of his financial empire, which was vast during his later years. By the time of his death, Jakob Fugger had amassed a fortune equal to $400 billion in today's money and that represented approximately 2 percent of Europe's GDP at the time. The astonishing figures have led some to refer to him as the richest man who ever lived.

Greg Steinmetz, a journalist and author of a comprehensive book on Fugger (appropriately titled *The Richest Man Who Ever Lived*), wrote, "[Fugger's] deeds changed history more than those of most monarchs, revolutionaries, prophets and poets ever did, and his methods blazed the path for five centuries of capitalists. . . . He was the first modern businessman in that he was the first to pursue wealth for its own sake and without fear of damnation."[3]

Jakob Fugger was, in many ways, the antithesis of the central idea behind *The 5 Types of Wealth*. His pursuit of money was the absolute, defining focus of his life. Steinmetz offered a depressing account of the results of this narrow focus: "He had few friends, only business associates. His only child was illegitimate. His nephews, to whom he relinquished his empire, disappointed him. While on his deathbed, with no one at his side other than paid assistants, his wife was with her lover. But he succeeded on his own terms. His objective was neither comfort nor happiness. It was to stack up money until the end."[4] He chased *more* from start to finish, sacrificing everything else in his life to that chase.

To his credit, Fugger was wise in his understanding of himself. When asked when he planned to retire, he said that his thirst for more money would never be quenched, a fact that clearly contributed to his striking financial success. His pursuit of money and his apparent enjoyment of "the money game" around it is a trend that we can trace into the present. To understand the commanding role of money in our lives today and learn how we can use it as a tool rather than letting it control us, we must take a brief trip back in time to understand how we got here.

FOLLOW THE MONEY

Money has slowly transitioned from a tool with a grounding in the reality of the physical world to something that often resembles a fantastical creation of the human imagination. Accordingly, the nature of Financial Wealth has transitioned from largely visible to largely invisible—a transition that creates specific obstacles you need to avoid on your journey.

The origin of money is a contested topic in economic and anthropological circles. The most conventional understanding suggests that barter—the exchange of one product or service for another—predated money and that its inefficiencies led to the creation of money. The primary support for this account is based on a narrative of Adam Smith, the eighteenth-century Scottish economist and philosopher who, in his book *The Wealth of Nations,* envisioned a scene in which a baker and a butcher are unable to make an exchange because the baker does not have anything that the butcher wants. According to his narrative, these inefficiencies with a barter economy led to the invention of money to facilitate, organize, and manage the free flow of goods and services. However, anthropologists have struggled to find any evidence to support this barter-to-money transition; some even suggest the inverse transition, that barter emerged as a supplement to money. The late David Graeber, an anthropologist at the London School of Economics and author of *Debt: The First 5,000 Years,* wrote, "In most of the cases we know about, [barter] takes place between people who are familiar with the use of money, but for one reason or another, don't have a lot of it around."[5]

Regardless of the details of its origin, money was clearly essential to the growth and development of human society. While excavating the remains of the ancient Mesopotamian capital of Uruk (located in present-day Iraq), archaeologists uncovered etched tablets dating back to 3500 B.C. that they believe were used to track debts. These tablets represent some of the oldest evidence of written language, leading some archaeologists and anthropologists to conclude that the invention of writing was a by-product of the need to track and manage the flow of money and commerce.

Money took on a variety of forms in its early years.[6] Sumerian barley, used as money as early as 3000 B.C., is believed to have been the first official currency. A set quantity of barley was exchangeable for a variety of goods and services in Sumer. Cowrie shells, the white shells of small sea snails abundant in the Indian Ocean, were used as currency in several ancient cultures, from Egypt and other African regions to China and Australia, as early as 1200 B.C. Their portability and relative rarity in most parts of the world made them a suitable form of currency across these regions. The simple white shells, which ironically became a 1990s pop-culture phenomenon worn on necklaces by pop icons and teenagers around the world, had some of the greatest reach and longevity of any form of money in the history of humanity.

Anthropologists believe the earliest metal money and rudimentary coins were created in China around 1000 B.C., with modern coinage first developed by the Lydians, an ancient culture in present-day Turkey, in the sixth century B.C. These modern coins were made from precious metals, so they had a degree of inherent value, and they were generally imprinted with the images of emperors or gods as a marker of their legitimacy. As they were small, portable, and difficult to forge, they reigned supreme as the modern form of money for many years.

Up until this point, money had been a largely visible, physical world construct. The quest to amass more wealth meant the accumulation and storage of real, tangible, physical world assets with some degree of inherent value, whether it was barley, cowrie shells, or precious metals. That all changed when Kublai Khan, the grandson of Genghis Khan, began to mass-produce an innovation that changed the world forever: paper money.

A Venetian merchant named Marco Polo traveled through China in the thirteenth century and later offered a detailed account of this discovery: "All these pieces of paper are issued with as much solemnity and authority as if they were of pure gold or silver . . . and when all is prepared duly, the chief officer deputed by the Khan smears the seal entrusted to him with vermilion, and impresses it on the paper, so that the form of the seal remains imprinted upon it in red; the money is then authentic. Anyone forging it would be punished with death."[7] The paper notes were originally backed by silver but eventually became a fiat currency (meaning they were no longer backed by a tangible commodity). In a 2019 article in *The New Yorker*, writer John Lanchester commented, "The problem with many new forms of money is that people are reluctant to adopt them. Genghis Khan's grandson didn't have that difficulty. He took measures to ensure the authenticity of his currency, and if you didn't use it—if you wouldn't accept it in payment, or preferred to use gold or silver or copper or iron bars or pearls or salt or coins or any of the older forms of payment prevalent in China—he would have you killed. This solved the question of uptake."[8] Quite well, I imagine.

Kublai Khan's invention represented a giant leap forward—the first instance where a piece of paper, cheaply mass-produced and with little to no inherent value, was deemed valuable and guaranteed by the force and authority of the government. Paper money slowly spread around the world because it enabled faster, more efficient commerce and growth.

The next giant leap occurred when the Bank of England, a private company formed in 1694 to act as a financier for the British government, printed *banknotes* as receipts for gold deposits. These paper banknotes, which could, in theory, be redeemed for actual gold in the vaults at the bank, became an effective currency. Clever governments and bankers realized that they could stimulate commerce and growth by issuing these paper assets above and beyond the actual gold or silver that was held in the vaults, a system known as fractional-reserve banking that became the standard operating procedure of banks around the world (and remains in place today). This system generally functions well unless all the depositors come and ask for their gold at once, in which case you have the makings of a classic bank run, where a seemingly healthy bank quickly becomes insolvent (a phenomenon we've seen as recently as 2023 with the rapid collapse of the well-respected Silicon Valley Bank).

For hundreds of years, conventional wisdom held that as long as the paper money was, at least in principle, connected to gold, the global economy built on it could continue to function and thrive. Up through the early twentieth century, all the world's major economies operated on a so-called gold standard, meaning the currency was backed by gold, and a certain quantity of paper money could be taken to the government and exchanged for a fixed amount of gold. In the United States, this meant that any citizen could exchange $20.67 for one ounce of gold. The value of the paper currencies was tied to gold.

But while the system worked in the good times, it began to show major cracks in the bad. During the early years of the Great Depression, panicked citizens redeemed their paper currency for gold and hoarded the precious metal, depleting the reserves in the vaults of the major global powers. In 1931, the Bank of England abandoned the gold standard, and in 1933, concerned that the flight to gold would make the economy grind to a screeching halt at a time when it needed to move, President Franklin Delano Roosevelt announced the United States would do the same.

These groundbreaking decisions untethered paper money from its connection to gold and shifted money from a system rooted in the physical world to a system tethered to something intangible—a system whose only constraint was human imagination.

That shift paved the way for the creation of a seemingly infinite variety of financial instruments and tools, a trend that further accelerated with the advent of computers and the internet, which brings us to the present and into a modern money game governed by bits and bytes rather than barley, shells, gold, and banknotes.

THE DANGERS OF THE MODERN MONEY GAME

Jakob Fugger and John D. Rockefeller had to manage their financial and business empires via a network of paper ledgers and accounts, but most of the financial wealth of today exists on computers and cloud servers. Cash-based economies are dwindling; using cash is increasingly viewed as a sign of dated infrastructure (as in certain developing countries) or illicit activity.

The modern money game is played in a digital world, where money exists merely as numbers on a screen (in fact, the total amount of money in the world is multiple orders of magnitude higher than the total amount of coins and notes). A transaction between two parties used to involve a physical exchange, but it is now as simple as pressing a button and watching the numbers go down on one screen and up on the other. When you consider the amount of money in your account, it may feel tangible, but it is no more than a number on a lit-up screen. Your trust that you will wake up tomorrow and the number on that screen will be correct—and that it is worth something—keeps the system flowing.

The modern money game looks very much like, well, a game.

If the old game was the boring bank with simple cash exchanges and a limited array of deposit and investment options, the new game looks more like an amusement park with an almost unlimited variety of rides, most of which have no minimum height requirement to participate. It is a creation of the human imagination, designed to draw you in. Financial apps spend millions to make their products addicting; your desire for novelty, dopamine, and entertainment is their profit opportunity.

Unfortunately, while the options are seemingly endless, many of the fancy investments and financial instruments are singing a siren song and luring you into danger.

You walk around the amusement park and hear the subtle, devious drone from its attendants:

- "My course on flipping houses is the key to your financial independence."
- "This cryptocurrency is going to fly."
- "That passive real estate investment is a sure thing."
- "These NFTs and fractionalized trading cards look like a steal."
- "If you miss out on this opportunity, you'll regret it the rest of your life."

In a financial universe that tempts your imagination, focus on what is real. The simple, boring basics that you will read about in the coming chapter still stand out as the way to build the life you want. You don't need to ride every ride or play every game. You don't even have to do it better than anyone else—it's not a competition.

To succeed, all you need to do is stick to the basics and play *your* game long enough.

29.

The Three Pillars of Financial Wealth

THOMAS STANLEY WAS BORN in the Bronx, New York, in 1944. He grew up in a humble, lower-middle-class household; his father worked as a subway driver and his mother was a secretary. Stanley attended college and then graduate school, earning a PhD in business administration from the University of Georgia before settling into a life as a professor at Georgia State University. As a professor, he developed a fascination with the habits and practices of the wealthy, so much so that he decided to leave his stable career in academia to research and write about America's millionaires. In 1996, Dr. Stanley coauthored a book based on his research and findings. *The Millionaire Next Door* quickly became a global phenomenon, selling over three million copies to date.

The book offered a novel perspective on the path to financial wealth. You do not need to have an extraordinarily lucrative job, own a business, or receive a large inheritance, he wrote; it could be achieved through the adoption of a set of basic financial-wealth-building principles. It dispelled the notion that the wealthy all lived in gated mansions with fancy foreign cars—a lifestyle incomprehensible to most ordinary people—and replaced it with the idea that there was a millionaire living right next door.

While the specific strategies in the book may spark debate among financial minds, its central premise—that anyone can build a life of Financial Wealth—is empowering. Allow that premise to serve as your foundation as we construct a simple model for the path that anyone can follow.

Financial Wealth is built on three pillars:

* INCOME GENERATION: Create stable, growing income through primary employment, secondary employment, and passive streams
* EXPENSE MANAGEMENT: Manage expenses so that they are reliably below your income level and grow at a slower rate
* LONG-TERM INVESTMENT: Invest the difference between your income and expenses in long-term, efficient, low-cost assets that compound effectively

This simple model is universally effective because it converts short-term net cash flow into long-term wealth. As you measure Financial Wealth as part of your new scoreboard, the three pillars—income generation, expense management, and long-term investment—provide a blueprint for the right action to build it. By developing an understanding of these pillars and the high-leverage systems that affect them, you can begin to create the right outcomes.

INCOME GENERATION AND EXPENSE MANAGEMENT: CREATING THE GAP

The gap between your income and your expenses is the most important tool in your financial independence tool kit—and it's a tool that you get to create.

Income is the cash inflow from primary employment, secondary employment, or passive income streams (rental properties, dividend stocks, et cetera). Expenses are the cash outflows of day-to-day life (food, shelter, transportation, et cetera), debt service (interest and principal payments on outstanding loans), experiences (vacations and events), taxes (if not automatically deducted out of income), and luxuries (material purchases, gifts, et cetera). The gap that you generate—the difference between your income and expenses—is the foundational asset on which Financial Wealth is built. The larger the gap, the larger the asset base to invest and compound.

Building a robust income engine composed of strong, stable, growing income streams should be the primary focus on your journey to generate this gap. The reason is simple: You can cut your expenses only so much, but you can increase your income forever.

A basic model to establish a robust income engine:

1. **BUILD SKILLS:** Marketable skills (sales, design, copywriting, software engineering, and so on) are assets that you can create and compound. Every new skill is built on top of existing skills to create a unique portfolio.
2. **LEVERAGE SKILLS:** Strategically deploy the marketable skills to convert them into income. The means of deployment exists on a risk spectrum from stable, lower-risk, time-for-money primary employment to volatile, higher-risk self-employment and entrepreneurship.

You build skills and then leverage those skills to establish a robust income engine for your present and future Financial Wealth goals.

As you build that engine, manage expenses to live well within your means. This does not mean that you should give up on everything fun and live a spartan lifestyle, but you should implement the basic tenets of expense management:

* **CREATE (AND STICK TO) A BUDGET:** Plan your monthly expenses and track your performance against them. Automate the savings and ensure you have a rainy-day fund that will cover about six months of expenses to cushion against any unexpected turbulence.
* **MANAGE EXPECTATIONS:** The greatest risk on your journey to financial independence is expectation inflation, often referred

to as lifestyle creep. Never allow your expectations to grow
faster than your income.

Those who are willing to live below their means in their early
years are highly likely to reap the rewards in the future. It's easier to
be frugal in those early years, as there is a natural growth in expenses
from family or related considerations in the later years.

Your goal is for the gap between income and expenses to grow
over time, meaning your expenses should never grow at the same
rate as your income. Avoiding lifestyle creep and excessive debt burdens creates a gap that grows at an accelerating rate, which enables
incremental investment to accelerate over time. If you invest appropriately, this is a surefire setup for a future of abundant Financial
Wealth.

LONG-TERM INVESTMENT: COMPOUNDING THE GAP

The first rule of compounding: Never interrupt it unnecessarily.
—CHARLIE MUNGER

In an ancient fable, a young inventor arrives at a king's court and
presents the king with his latest invention, a game he calls chess.
Pleased with the new game, the king offers the inventor any reward
he desires.

The young inventor replies, "Your Highness, I do not ask for
money or jewels; I simply ask for a little rice. A single grain on the
first square, two grains on the second, four on the third, eight on the
fourth, and so on, for the full sixty-four squares of this chessboard."

The king, surprised to have gotten such a great bargain, smiles
and summons his treasurer.

As the treasurer begins to issue the rice to the inventor, it becomes clear that the king has underestimated the request. On the
final square at the end of the first row, there are 128 grains of rice.
On the final square at the end of the second row, there are 32,768

grains of rice. By the middle square of the third row, there are 524,288 grains of rice. Realizing he has been duped, the king signals to his guards, and the young inventor is executed, a cheeky smile plastered across his face.

The cruel king was smart to act when he did, for if he had allowed the process to continue, he would have owed the inventor over eighteen quintillion (that's 18 with 18 zeros after it!) grains of rice.

This infamous story is perhaps the most vivid visualization of one of the greatest forces in our natural world, a force that we must all understand and put to work on our journey to build a life of Financial Wealth.

That force: compounding.

Compound interest is interest calculated and paid on both the initial principal balance and all of the accumulated interest. Compound interest is what allows an investment to grow at an accelerating rate (just as the rice grains did on the king's chessboard). As a simple example, imagine $1 invested today at a 10 percent compounded annual return. By year 10, it's about $2.60. By year 20, it's about $6.70. By year 30, it's about $17.40. By year 50, that $1 has grown to over $117. A visual representation of this compounding is striking: The growth comes slowly at first, then all at once.

COMPOUNDING

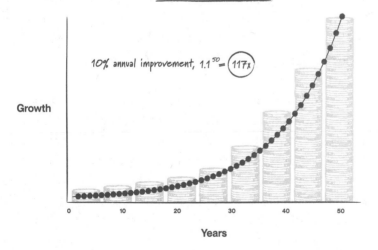

10% annual improvement, $1.1^{50} = (117x)$

Growth

Years

Benjamin Franklin summarized compound interest in his quint-essentially pithy manner: "Money makes money. And the money that money makes, makes money."

Warren Buffett is history's most famous investor. Interestingly, it was his rejection from Harvard Business School that may have set his career on its legendary trajectory. He enrolled at Columbia instead, and there he met and studied under the legendary investor Benjamin Graham. At Columbia he learned the core tenets of his investing philosophy: intrinsic value, margin of safety, and, most important, the power of compounding. During his long and illustrious investing career, Warren Buffett amassed a net worth of over $130 billion, a figure made even more stunning by the fact that the vast majority of this wealth was built after his sixtieth birthday. According to most estimates, he reached $1 million at age thirty, $25 million at age forty, $375 million at age fifty, and $1 billion at age fifty-six. That means that it took him roughly thirty-two years (from when he started working for Benjamin Graham at age twenty-four up to his fifty-sixth birthday) to earn his first billion but just thirty-seven years to earn his next *$129 billion.*

Warren Buffett created one of history's greatest compounding machines, got out of its way, and allowed it to work on his behalf.

When it comes to leveraging compounding to build Financial Wealth, we all need to take a lesson from Buffett: Time, not average annual returns, is the most important factor. Morgan Housel, the bestselling author of *The Psychology of Money* and *Same as Ever,* adds clarity to this point: "All compounding is, is returns to the power of time, but time is the exponent. So that's to me what you want to maximize."[9]

The most common and most attractive way to harness the full power of compound interest is to invest in and hold liquid market assets, such as stocks or low-cost diversified funds. When you hear financial advisers or experts referring to compounding, investments in these market-based assets are typically what they mean. People spend countless hours and considerable energy worrying about selecting the perfect mix of stocks or assets to generate a slightly higher return, or they pay advisers to do that for them when the math suggests that simply buying, holding, and compounding a diversified market index fund will generate the most attractive time-, energy-, and risk-adjusted long-term outcomes. Unless you're a professional investor with a specific edge and a track record of outperforming the market, it's unlikely that you will consistently beat an index fund, so you're almost always better off taking common returns and allowing your time in the market to be the uncommon factor that drives your outsize rewards.

Nick Maggiulli, author of the bestselling book *Just Keep Buying*, is a vocal proponent of the long-term buy-and-hold investment strategy. When I asked him about his best advice to his younger self, he focused on the importance of saving and investing heavily in your early years. Starting early and investing often is a tried-and-true approach for building Financial Wealth. The philosophy's effectiveness, Maggiulli noted, is driven by two factors: "Money invested earlier in time typically grows more than money invested later in time [and] compounding money is easier than saving money." Starting early places the time exponent Morgan Housel highlighted firmly in your corner.

Paraphrasing a well-known proverb: The best time to start was twenty years ago; the second best time is today.

Average returns compounded over long periods produce extraordinary outcomes[10]:

* If a twenty-two-year-old invested $10,000 in the S&P 500 index in January 1980, she would have a retirement nest egg of well over $1 million today (assuming reinvestment of dividends along the way).
* If that same person invested just $100 per month after the initial investment, she would have a portfolio of well over $2 million today.
* If she ratcheted up her monthly investment to $1,000, she would have a portfolio of over $10 million today.

Remember, these figures do not require special investing knowledge, edge, or insight! The only requirement is that you start and let time work for you rather than against you.

Albert Einstein famously referred to compound interest as "the eighth wonder of the world": "He who understands it, earns it; he who doesn't, pays it." He was correct. By starting early and focusing on regular investments, you set your compounding machine in motion. Once it is in motion, take a page from the Warren Buffett playbook:

Get out of the way and let the magic of compounding work on your behalf.

THE FIVE LEVELS OF FINANCIAL WEALTH

There are five clear and distinct levels to the Financial Wealth journey:

- LEVEL 1: Baseline needs are met, including food and shelter.
- LEVEL 2: All baseline needs are exceeded, and modest pleasures become accessible. This includes meals at restaurants, simple vacations, and spending on education.
- LEVEL 3: Baseline needs are no longer top of mind, and the focus is on saving, investing, and compounding wealth. More significant pleasures, such as multiple vacations, are readily available. More aggressive asset compounding generally begins at this level.
- LEVEL 4: Most reasonable pleasures are readily available. Asset accumulation accelerates, and assets begin to generate passive income to cover some lifestyle expenses. This is the level of moderate financial independence, as you can reduce your active income and continue to live the same lifestyle.
- LEVEL 5: All pleasures are available. Asset accumulation reaches escape velocity, and assets generate passive income in excess of all lifestyle expenses. This is the level of complete financial independence, as you can remove all active income and continue to live the same lifestyle.

Each person begins the journey at a different starting point, but any path upward through the levels requires a disciplined focus on the three pillars of income generation, expense management, and long-term investment. Every person who has reached Level 5 has, in some form or function, followed this simple model: increased income, managed expenses, and invested in long-term compounders. In some cases, the compounder of choice was a business that people invested their time, energy, and excess cash into, and the sale of that business generated the financial windfall that vaulted them into the upper tiers. In other cases, the compounder of choice was a simple low-cost market index fund that they invested their excess cash into on a regular basis, patiently compounding their wealth and methodically moving up the levels as the assets accumulated.

Each level has its own stresses, problems, and headaches. While the traditional money problems you feel at the lower levels dissipate as you climb the ladder, new problems arise and replace them. Patrick Campbell, the founder of ProfitWell, a bootstrapped start-up that he sold for over $200 million, referred to this as a *champagne-problem cycle*. Campbell, who grew up in a working-class family and was new to a life of extreme wealth, noticed he'd gone from one set of problems that felt relatable to a new set of problems that might have sounded ridiculous to most people. The new problems aren't about basic needs, like providing food and shelter for your family, but about your identity, who you are, who you want to be, and more. Money solves money problems, but it will not, in a vacuum, solve anything else.

The point is this: Financial Wealth does not solve your problems; it simply changes the types of problems you face. The most important and fundamental questions about your life will remain, irrespective of the level you achieve. It is entirely up to you to determine how you can leverage the Financial Wealth you have built to create and increase other types of wealth—Time, Social, Mental, and Physical—as you seek to build a comprehensively wealthy life.

Finally, it is important to note that the levels of Financial Wealth are entirely individual, because they are a by-product of *your expectations*—the needs, pleasures, and lifestyle that you want to lead. They are a by-product of your definition of *enough*. This means that the dollar figures necessary to achieve any given level are unique to you.

If you embrace the simple model—focusing on income generation, expense management, and long-term investment—while staying true to your personal definition of *enough*, you will be on a clear path to rise through the five levels of Financial Wealth. With an established understanding of the pillars and levels, we can move to the Financial Wealth Guide, which provides the specific tools and systems to build on these pillars and cultivate a life of Financial Wealth.

30.

The Financial Wealth Guide

Systems for Success

THE FINANCIAL WEALTH GUIDE that follows provides specific, high-leverage systems to build each of the pillars of a life of Financial Wealth. This isn't one size fits all and you shouldn't feel compelled to read every single one; browse through and select those that feel most relevant and useful to you.

As you consider and execute the systems for success provided in the Financial Wealth Guide, use your responses to each Financial Wealth statement from the Wealth Score quiz to narrow your focus to the areas where you need to make the most progress (those where you responded *strongly disagree, disagree,* or *neutral*).

1. I have a clear definition of what it means to have *enough* financially.
2. I have income that is steadily growing alongside my skills and expertise.
3. I manage my monthly expenses so that they are reliably below my income.
4. I have a clear process for investing excess monthly income for long-term compounding.

5. I use my financial wealth as a tool to build other types of wealth.

A few common Financial Wealth anti-goals to avoid on your journey:

* Focusing on my pursuit of financial goals at the expense of the other types of wealth
* Allowing my definition of the Enough Life to subconsciously expand

Here are eight proven systems for building Financial Wealth.

How to Define Your Enough Life: Finding Your *Lagom*

The life of *lagom* is the Enough Life—where you have just the right amount of Financial Wealth to live out your ideal days.

Unfortunately, for most people, it tends to exist in the abstract, where it is prone to the subconscious inflation that is so damning to your fulfillment and happiness. A few years ago, to avoid falling victim to this, I clearly defined my Enough Life. I shifted it from a concept that existed in the abstract to a vivid image in the front of my mind.

Here are the prompts I used to define my Enough Life:

* Where do you live? Are you living in a house, apartment, or something else? What specific characteristics do you love about the place where you live? Do you spend all your time in one place or live in different places?
* Whom do you live with? Are you close to family or far away?
* What are you doing on an average Tuesday? What are you spending your time on? What are you working on? What are you thinking about?
* What material things do you have? What are the objects or possessions that truly bring joy to your life? What do you have the flexibility to spend money on freely?
* What does your financial profile look like? What amount of money enables that life? How much cushion do you have in your finances? What are you earning, saving, and investing each month? How much of a safety net do you have?

Sit down and write out your responses to these questions. Remember that this is a personal exercise; your Enough Life is entirely individual and not subject to the judgment of others. One person's Enough Life may involve several luxury homes to host family and friends, while another person's may simply be the freedom to take two family vacations each year. Just as in the case of dharma, your Enough Life does not have to be grand or impressive—it simply must be *yours*.

If you are married or have a life partner, you should conduct this exercise individually and then come together to compare your responses. My wife and I made a date out of it (which was quite fun!).

Once you have a clear, vivid image of your Enough Life, you can use it as a tool for planning:

- What is the gap from your present reality to that future reality?
- What are the key steps and actions necessary to bridge that gap?

The Enough Life exercise is one that can be completed every few years. In all likelihood, your definition of *enough* will increase over time as your reality comes closer to your definition. That is to be expected. The goal is simply for it to be a conscious upward movement that can be measured and monitored, rather than a subconscious one that can accelerate out of control.

Your life of *lagom* is waiting—define it, imagine it, then start working to build it.

Financial Wealth Hacks I Know at Forty-Two
I Wish I Knew at Twenty-Two

A collaboration with Ramit Sethi, author of the international bestselling books *I Will Teach You to Be Rich* and *Money for Couples* and host of the popular Netflix show *How to Be Rich.*

1. Frugality, quite simply, is about choosing the things you love enough to spend extravagantly on—and then cutting costs mercilessly on the things you don't love.
2. Ask $30,000 questions, not $3 questions. We're obsessed with tiny financial decisions that make no real difference in our lives. They keep us busy and small. The amount you spend on coffee will not change your life, but focusing on $30,000 questions will. Focus on investment fees, asset allocation, negotiating salary, mortgage interest, and student loan interest. These $30,000 questions will make a difference in the long run.
3. Always have six to twelve months of emergency funds in cash. When times are good, work hard and fast to put away emergency funds. This one action alone will alleviate much of the angst you feel when thinking about money.
4. Make a rule to save a specific percentage and invest a specific percentage of your gross annual income. Establish an automatic deposit into accounts at these percentages so that you stick to it. My rule is to save 10 percent and invest 20 percent, but you can start at 5 percent and 10 percent (or whatever figure you see fit).
5. Spend only what you have. Avoid accruing interest on credit card debt. Treat your credit card like a debit card—assume the money is leaving your bank account when you swipe it. Pay it off entirely every month.
6. Always plan ahead. Rich people always plan before they need to plan.

7. Buy the best and keep it as long as possible. Sometimes buying cheap ends up being expensive, and spending a little (or a lot) more for quality saves money in the end. For example, I enjoy buying high-end electronics because they last longer, high-end clothes because they don't tear or rip as easily, and high-end cameras for their reliability. Some of these items can be passed on for generations.

8. Treat everything like a test. When I signed up for a new cell-phone plan, I picked the most expensive one and set a calendar reminder to check in on it in three months. During that time, I tracked my usage and then downgraded accordingly. You should do this with everything: your cable, Netflix, gym memberships, magazine and online subscriptions. The best time to do it is the month before you have to renew. That way you have all the power. You'll have plenty of time to review your options and decide whether to switch services or not. And, because the company will want to keep you as a customer (remember, their customer-acquisition cost is often in the hundreds of dollars), they'll be more likely to give you what you ask for.

9. Be frugal with yourself and generous with others.

10. If an investment or financial opportunity seems too good to be true, assume that it is. Remember: There's no such thing as a free lunch.

11. Okay, but index funds really are a free lunch. Lowest costs, better returns, lower taxes, no effort, less risk. I recommend making at least 90 percent of your portfolio through index funds.

12. If someone uses a bunch of fancy words and jargon to try to sell you an investment or financial opportunity, don't buy it. Run in the other direction, fast.

13. Stay invested in the stock market. It's very easy to panic and sell stocks whenever there's a big drop in the market. However, selling your stocks at the slightest fall or when they are down could be the worst financial decision you can make. Stop timing the market. Create an automated direct deposit

for a small amount of money into an investment account every month. Never look at the account. Don't pay any attention to it. A $100 monthly investment into the S&P 500 for the past ten years would be worth about $20,000 today. Let it compound.

14. Tip more around the holidays. Give a small holiday gift to any service-industry workers you regularly encounter (delivery drivers, trash pickup, cleaners, et cetera). It's greatly appreciated by those on the receiving end of it, and it's a simple way to spread some positive holiday vibes.

15. Set money rules for yourself. We all work in different ways when it comes to money. There's rarely any one-size-fits-all approach to spending, saving, and cutting expenses. If you know you have a certain bad money habit, set a rule for yourself to help you avoid it.

16. Negotiate your bills down. It's a little-known fact that you can negotiate many of your bills with a onetime phone call. In fact, you can save hundreds a month on your car insurance, cellphone plan, gym membership (less likely but still possible), cable TV, credit cards. It's simple too. There are only three things you need to do to negotiate with these companies on fees and rates: Call them; say, "I'm a great customer, and I'd hate to have to leave because of a simple money issue"; and ask, "What can you do for me to lower my rates?" It works.

17. Follow the thirty-day rule to save money. Take thirty days to think about any nonessential purchases or impulse buys before you make them. Once the thirty days are up, if you still want to make the purchase, feel free to go for it!

18. Be a conscious spender, not a cheap person. Cheap people care about the cost of something. Conscious spenders care about the value of something. Cheap people try to get the lowest price on everything. Conscious spenders try to get the lowest price on most things but are willing to spend extravagantly on items they really care about.

19. Fight for simplicity in your finances. The more successful you become with money, the more you have to fight for simplicity

in your finances. When you keep things simple, you can take control of your money and become much more decisive.

20. The way you feel about money is uncorrelated with the amount in your bank account. Many of us believe that if we just had $1,000 more, or $10,000 more, or even $100,000 more, we'd stop worrying about money and finally feel good about money. Bad news: No amount will change the way you feel about money. To feel good about money, you need to (a) know your numbers and (b) improve your money psychology by spending unapologetically on things you care about (and paying as little as possible for things you don't).

Seven Pieces of Career Advice I Wish I Had Known When I Was Starting Out

PILLAR: Income Generation

Career advice is a topic area that so often misses the mark. As *Atlantic* writer Derek Thompson once remarked, "With workers across thousands of occupations in hundreds of industries, saying anything that is of use to all of them is practically impossible. The most common counsel is almost always too personal to be broadly applicable."

Advice often suffers from a specificity trap. This specificity is the real problem: Your world looks very different from the advice giver's world, so you can't apply the same protocol or steps and achieve the same outcome.

The best advice, then, provides the general principles, ideas, and frameworks that you can take, mold, and leverage in *your own way*. Accordingly, I sat down and synthesized the advice I would have wanted to receive early in my career (or what I would tell my own son if he were just starting out).

All the items on the list are:

1. Applicable across domains and career paths
2. Useful and relevant across all seasons and stages of your career

Here are the seven pieces of career advice I wish I knew when I was starting out. . . .

CREATE VALUE, RECEIVE VALUE

Financial success is a by-product of the amount of value you create for those around you. The richest people in the world have billions of dollars, but they have each created tens or hundreds of billions of dollars of value and simply captured a small portion of that value they created. If you want to make a lot of money, stop focusing on your investments, stop focusing on your plan, stop focusing on your strategy, and start focusing on how you can create immense value for everyone around you. If you do that, the money will follow.

SWALLOW THE FROG

> If it's your job to eat a frog, it's best to do it first thing in the morning. And if it's your job to eat two frogs, it's best to eat the biggest one first.
>
> —MARK TWAIN

For Mark Twain, the *frog* is the thing you don't want to do. By eating it first thing in the morning, you build momentum from getting the toughest thing done. This wisdom provides one of the greatest hacks to get ahead early in your career: Swallow the frog for your boss. Observe your boss and figure out what she hates doing, learn to do it, take it off her plate (swallow her frog). This is a clear way to add value, put up a win, and build momentum.

DO THE OLD-FASHIONED THINGS WELL

In a world that has lost sight of the basics, there are simple things that still stand out. Some examples: Look people in the eye, do what you say you'll do, be on time (or early!), practice good posture, have a confident handshake, hold the door, be kind (never gossip!). It may sound silly, but these things are all free, are entirely within your control, and will never go out of style.

WORK HARD FIRST, WORK SMART LATER

Over the past several years, it has become very trendy to say that hard work is overrated, that working smart is all that matters. Wrong. If you want to accomplish anything meaningful, you have to start by working hard. Build a reputation for hard work—take pride in it. Then you can start to build leverage to work smart. Leverage is earned, not found. When you're starting out, you shouldn't be focused on leverage. You should be focused on creating value any-where and everywhere. Hard now, smart later. Earn your leverage.

BUILD STORYTELLING SKILLS

An observation from having the privilege of spending time with some incredible leaders: World-changing CEOs aren't the smartest people in their organizations. They are exceptional at aggregating data and communicating it simply and effectively. Data in, story out. If you can build that storytelling skill, you'll always be valuable.

BUILD A REPUTATION FOR FIGURING IT OUT

At every step of your career, you'll be given a lot of tasks you have no idea how to complete. Impostor syndrome will inevitably set in—you'll wonder how you can possibly do this thing that you've never done before (let alone do it well!). There's nothing more valuable than someone who can just figure it out. Ask the key questions, do some work, get it done. If you do that, people will fight over you.

DIVE THROUGH EVERY CRACKED-OPEN DOOR

If someone cracks open a door that may present an opportunity, dive through it. It doesn't matter if the opening is the exact opportunity you want. Become useful now, and the opportunities that excite you will appear later. Every great story starts with a tiny crack. Spot it. Dive through it.

In your career, there will always be a lot that feels uncomfortably out of your control. But as with all things in life, if you focus your atten-tion and energy on what is within your control, you'll always be bet-ter off. Wherever you are in your career journey, if you embrace these seven pieces of advice, you're controlling the things that mat-ter. Do that and I guarantee you'll find a way to win.

Six Marketable Meta-Skills to Build
for a High-Income Future

PILLAR: Income Generation

In the prior section, I presented the basic model to establish a robust income engine:

1. Build marketable skills
2. Leverage marketable skills to convert them into income

This model is broadly applicable: Whether you're a recent graduate just starting out or a seasoned professional late in your career, to establish and build an income engine, follow this basic model.

Meta-skills are the foundational marketable skills upon which other skills can be developed. The most useful meta-skills are those that can be leveraged across the risk spectrum—from lower-risk, time-for-money primary employment to volatile, higher-risk self-employment—in a variety of potential income-generating endeavors.

Here are a few of the most valuable meta-skills to consider building:

- SALES: The ability to sell a product, service, vision, or oneself is a meta-skill for life. Selling is at the core of most success stories.
- STORYTELLING: The ability to aggregate data and formulate a clear, concise narrative. This applies across functional areas and is essential to a variety of career tracks, including traditional, stable career paths like medicine, law, and finance.
- DESIGN: In a world where artificial intelligence will direct much of the doing, design taste and preferences will rise in importance. The ability to direct AI (and humans) to produce

a coherent, beautiful design vision will be essential across
many industries.

- WRITING: You cannot write clearly if you aren't thinking
  clearly. Writing forces a clarity of thought that is useful across
  any major endeavor. The ability to convey ideas in simple,
  concise language is a meta-skill that will provide value in every
  arena.

- SOFTWARE ENGINEERING: Our world is increasingly governed
  by bits and bytes. Those who understand that world will be
  better positioned to thrive. The ability to leverage AI to accelerate efforts is a skill that all software engineers will need to
  develop.

- DATA SCIENCE: Data is becoming modern gold, a currency
  like no other. The ability to analyze, tag, manipulate, and leverage data is going to be an increasingly valuable skill in an
  AI-driven world.

This is not intended to be an exhaustive list, but each of these
marketable skills is attractive in that it can be leveraged to create
stable, growing primary-employment income and higher-upside
secondary-income streams. There are other marketable skills, such
as those around medicine, law, finance, and certain professional services, that have strong income potential but are generally confined
to single, stable primary employment tracks, so they may be more
limited in terms of long-term upside.

If you build a solid foundation of meta-skills, you will create the
conditions for a high-income future.

The Seven Basic Principles of
Expense Management

PILLAR: Expense Management

While you cannot save your way to financial freedom, a rising income alongside disciplined expense management will generate outsize outcomes in the long run. Effective expense management is essential to building financial freedom. Everyone's situation will be different, but there are basic principles that apply universally.

The seven principles of effective expense management are as follows:

1. CREATE A BUDGET: Having a plan is the first and most important step in your journey to financial freedom. Creating and sticking to a monthly budget is a great starting place. Plan your monthly expenses and use an online tracker or tool (there are many free and premium options) to track your performance. Incorporate regular living expenses and experiences, and build a cushion for unexpected items. Gamify your expense management and try to land as close to your budget as possible.

2. AUTOMATE SAVINGS: Always save before you spend. Automate your monthly savings by having a direct deposit go into a dedicated account.

3. TREAT CREDIT CARDS LIKE CASH: Never carry a balance on your credit cards. Pay them off in full at the end of each month. Treat all of your budgeting as though it is cash in, cash out.

4. CREATE A RAINY-DAY FUND: Having a safety net of about six months of expenses in cash is a good rule of thumb to weather life's inevitable storms. Prioritize creating and maintaining that fund. Do not touch it unless absolutely necessary.

5. BUDGET FOR EXPERIENCES: In creating your monthly budget, be sure to factor in experiences and fun as a cushion. Dinners out, movies, travel, and so forth are all expenses that should be factored in as you contemplate the lifestyle you want to have.

6. PLAN AHEAD: Large purchases or expenditures should never surprise you. Plan ahead for weddings, vacations, cars, debt repayment, et cetera. If you plan, you can avoid incurring significant new debt (credit card or otherwise) when large expenses hit.

7. MANAGE EXPECTATIONS AS A LIABILITY: Expectations that grow faster than assets are the most common cause of financial misery. Track your lifestyle expectations and ensure that you are not allowing those expectations to inflate materially as your income grows. Avoid the perils of lifestyle creep, particularly in the early years of your journey to financial freedom, as incremental dollars invested early are worth more later.

Your expenses will change throughout your life. As you accumulate responsibilities (including partners and children), your expenses will naturally grow. It's perfectly reasonable to assume that your expenses will grow over time (particularly given economic inflation).

As a rule of thumb, you want to ensure that your income is growing at a higher rate than your expenses. This will create a larger investable gap over time and lead to strong financial compounding and an accelerated path to financial independence.

If you follow these seven principles and pair them with steadily rising income and a basic, thoughtful long-term investment strategy, you will be on the path to financial freedom.

The Eight Best Investment Assets for Long-Term Wealth Creation

PILLAR: Long-Term Investment

In the modern financial world, investment opportunities are effectively endless. You are constantly pitched the latest and greatest financial gizmo that promises outsize returns and no appreciable increase in risk. Beware of these claims—as the saying goes, there's no such thing as a free lunch!

In an effort to provide a balanced perspective on your most attractive investment opportunities, I have collaborated on this simple guide with Nick Maggiulli, an author and financial writer whose bestselling book *Just Keep Buying* breaks down and explains how to save money and invest.

The eight asset classes covered are chosen for their income-producing and wealth-creating properties. Each of the asset classes provides income and long-term compounding. Asset classes such as cryptocurrency, art, and precious metals are not included, as they do not provide income potential to the investor. The list is not intended to be a recommendation but a starting point for further research. Always conduct your own research prior to making investments.

ASSET 1: STOCKS

Stocks are an easily accessible asset class that represents ownership in underlying businesses. Historically, they have high average compounded rates of return (8 to 10 percent), they are easy to trade, and they require little to no maintenance. They also have significant volatility and may experience material valuation swings that are dislocated from fundamental business changes.

PROS:

* High historical average rates of return
* Easy to trade
* Very little maintenance

CONS:

* High volatility
* Significant valuation swings that may be dislocated from business fundamentals

ASSET 2: BONDS

Bonds are loans from investors to borrowers with payments that are to be made over specific periods. Bonds vary greatly in their risk profile, depending on the underlying borrower; U.S. Treasury bonds are considered extremely low risk due to the government's ability to print money. They have a lower historical average compounded rate of return (2 to 4 percent), but typically offer a consistent income stream (from payments by the borrower) and tend to rise when stocks fall.

PROS:

* Low overall volatility
* Strong principal safety (in higher-quality government-backed bonds)

CONS:

* Lower overall returns, particularly after accounting for inflation

ASSET 3: INVESTMENT PROPERTY

Investment properties are owned residences purchased with the intention of generating income through rent and wealth through the future value appreciation of the property. The ability to secure leverage for the purchase (via a mortgage) amplifies the return profile, meaning the average compounded annual return can be around 12 to 15 percent, depending on the location and market conditions.

These higher average annual returns are offset by the operational challenges of managing a property and tenants and low liquidity in the underlying asset in the event of a market disruption.

PROS:
- Potential for high average returns given leverage profile
- Experience value if properties are used when not being rented out

CONS:
- High potential for headaches from property and tenant management
- Low liquidity in the event of a market crash

ASSET 4: REAL ESTATE INVESTMENT TRUSTS
Real Estate Investment Trusts (REITs for short) are businesses that own and manage real estate properties and distribute the income from the properties to their shareholders on a consistent basis. Investing in REITs is considered a tax-efficient, low-headache way to invest in real estate, as the REITs are required to pay out a minimum of 90 percent of their taxable income as dividends. They historically provide high average compounded annual returns of around 10 to 12 percent and lower correlation to stocks during bull markets. They also historically exhibit equal or greater volatility than stocks, with significant drawdowns during market crashes.

PROS:
- High historical average compounded annual returns
- Provide tax-efficient real estate exposure without management headaches

CONS:
- High volatility, comparable to or greater than stocks
- Significant drawdowns during market crashes

ASSET 5: FARMLAND

Farmland has historically been a significant source of wealth creation and an attractive, income-producing asset. Given this profile, today there are platforms that provide opportunities for accredited investors to own partial stakes in farmland operations. Farmland has low correlation to stock and bond returns and low overall volatility due to the stability of the land value, and it provides inflation protection, as it tends to rise in value in connection to broader market price trends. Investments in farmland tend to be highly illiquid and generally require higher fees and accreditation status.

PROS:

* Low correlation with traditional assets, low overall principal risk
* Strong hedge against inflation

CONS:

* Low liquidity
* Higher fees and accreditation requirements

ASSET 6: SMALL BUSINESSES AND START-UPS

Small business and start-up acquisitions and investments have become very popular in recent years. They offer the potential for outsize returns (potentially 20 to 25 percent) and an environment where historical success may increase the odds of future success, as you become more likely to be brought attractive opportunities. They also carry a significant time commitment, particularly in the case of active involvement in small business operations, as well as a high likelihood of principal loss.

PROS:

* Outsize returns potential
* Success begets success

CONS:
- High time commitment
- Significant potential for failure and principal loss

ASSET 7: ROYALTIES

Royalties are the payments made for the continued use of copyrighted or owned works. Today, there are platforms that match buyers and sellers of royalty streams, providing new investors with access to the market. Depending on the risk profile, royalties may provide average compounded annual returns of from 5 to 20 percent, with low or no correlation to traditional financial assets and a steady income stream. The platforms tend to charge higher fees and many require accreditation status to invest.

PROS:
- Potential for steady income and attractive average returns
- Low correlation to other financial assets

CONS:
- High fees and accreditation requirements
- Potential for sudden shifts in income due to taste preferences

ASSET 8: YOUR OWN PRODUCTS

Investments in your own income-producing products—physical products, digital products, services, and the like—offer the potential for a high degree of control and personal fulfillment. These investments are time-intensive, particularly at the outset, and do not offer any guarantee of future returns, and the majority are likely to fail. When well built with the potential to scale without significant additional time requirements, they offer outsize potential for returns.

PROS:
- Full control and ownership of outcomes
- High degree of personal fulfillment
- Potential for outsize returns if successful

CONS:

- Significant time commitment
- High likelihood of failure

Developing an awareness and understanding of these eight asset classes will provide any investor with a strong overall foundation of knowledge. You do not need to invest in all eight (I invest in only four of the eight!), but the knowledge will leave you well prepared to act on a variety of investment strategies in the future.

The Return-on-Hassle Spectrum

PILLAR: Long-Term Investment

Investment advisers focus on the risk-adjusted return profile of an investment, meaning the average expected returns given the risk profile of the investment. For example, start-up investing may offer opportunities for ten times or even a hundred times investment appreciation, but it is also incredibly risky; the vast majority of start-ups go bust and lose all of the invested capital, so the risk-adjusted return profile of the asset class is more in line with market index investments.

The concept of risk adjustment is part of the calculation that you should be thinking about when you look at long-term investments in the asset classes from the prior section, but it misses one key component:

Choosing the right asset classes for your portfolio means selecting those that provide access to attractive average returns on a risk-adjusted basis, but also on a hassle-adjusted basis.

Mitchell Baldridge, a well-known certified public accountant and writer, refers to a concept he calls "return on hassle"—the idea that the time and energy associated with an investment need to be considered as part of the return equation. For example, a multifamily real estate investment that generates a 10 percent average annual return may sound like a screaming deal, but if it requires you to spend ten hours away from your family each weekend driving to the location, fixing maintenance issues, and dealing with tenant headaches, that 10 percent annual return may not look so attractive. If you can generate a 7 percent average annual return with zero time and energy outlay by auto-buying and holding market index funds, other potential long-term investments must be weighed against that. If the incremental likely return profile exceeds the value of the incremental time and energy requirements, it is worth considering, but if not, it should be rejected.

To illustrate the point, we can reference a chart of data gathered by Nick Maggiulli that maps a variety of potential long-term investment assets from the prior section based on their risk difficulty/hassle and expected annualized returns.[11]

THE RETURN-ON-HASSLE SPECTRUM

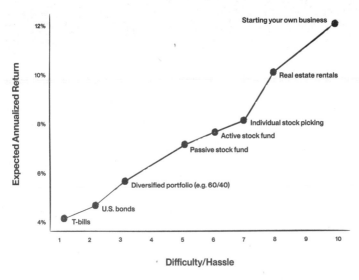

SOURCE: AMERICAN TIME USE SURVEY, OUR WORLD IN DATA

Starting your own business, which occupies the upper right corner of this chart, offers the tantalizing high-risk, high-hassle, high-reward trifecta. The allure of control—the "bet on yourself"—is compelling, but it should not be taken on lightly, as most businesses will fail within their first decade. That said, the alternative, de-risked pathways to entrepreneurship (side hustles, which are covered in the following section) may offer a more manageable risk-reward trade-off for those seeking an accelerated timeline to financial independence.

For most people, the lower middle of this difficulty/hassle spectrum will be the sweet spot. Buying and holding a well-diversified, low-cost market index fund will provide the most attractive balance of returns and energy requirement. Investments in higher-hassle

long-term investments like individual stocks and real estate properties should not be considered without a clear understanding of the
associated time and capital risks as well as a rational perspective on
the "edge" that one has relative to the market in that specific asset
arena.

The Single Greatest Investment in the World

PILLAR: Long-Term Investment

When I was in college, my father shared an insight that I consider to be the single greatest investment advice I have ever received.

He told me to make it a rule to never think twice about investments in yourself:

* Books, courses, and education
* Fitness
* Networking events
* Quality food
* Mental health
* Personal development
* Sleep

These may look like *expenses,* but they can all be considered *investments* that pay dividends in your life for a long time.

As an example, when I started my first job, I chose to live by myself rather than with three roommates. On the surface, it seemed like a silly financial decision—about twice the monthly cost—but it gave me space for deep focus and deep relaxation. I think the investment paid for itself in accelerated career growth within a year.

The bias is to underestimate the value that these investments have. The financial cost is easily quantifiable, so we focus on it and ignore the benefits in other areas of our lives. But if you evaluate the benefits through the lens of the other types of wealth—Time, Social, Mental, and Physical—you will more appropriately account for them and make a better long-term decision.

As a rule of thumb: Never think twice about making investments in yourself.

Think twice about material purchases instead. Try the thirty-day rule: Wait thirty days to complete the order. If you still want it, order it. If not, skip it. This has saved a lot of money on stupid impulse purchases that would have gathered dust. Redeploy the savings into investments in yourself and double the benefit.

Life hack: Always invest in yourself—you'll never regret it.

31.

Summary: Financial Wealth

FINANCIAL WEALTH OVERVIEW

THE BIG QUESTION: WHAT is your definition of *enough*?

THE THREE PILLARS OF FINANCIAL WEALTH:
- INCOME GENERATION: Create stable, growing income through primary employment, secondary employment, or passive streams
- EXPENSE MANAGEMENT: Manage expenses so that they are reliably below your income level and grow at a slower rate
- LONG-TERM INVESTMENT: Invest the difference between your income and expenses in long-term, efficient, low-cost assets that compound effectively

The Financial Wealth Score: For each statement below, respond with 0 (strongly disagree), 1 (disagree), 2 (neutral), 3 (agree), or 4 (strongly agree).

1. I have a clear definition of what it means to have *enough* financially.
2. I have income that is steadily growing alongside my skills and expertise.

3. I manage my monthly expenses so that they are reliably below my income.
4. I have a clear process for investing excess monthly income for long-term compounding.
5. I use my financial wealth as a tool to build other types of wealth.

Your baseline score (0 to 20):

Goals, Anti-Goals, and Systems

Use the goal-setting framework to calibrate your Financial Wealth compass:

* GOALS: What Financial Wealth Score do you want to achieve within one year? What are the two to three checkpoints that you will need to hit on your path to achieve this score?
* ANTI-GOALS: What are the two to three outcomes that you want to avoid on your journey?
* HIGH-LEVERAGE SYSTEMS: What are the two to three systems from the Financial Wealth Guide that you will implement to make tangible, compounding progress toward your goal score?

YOUR ONE-WEEK JUMP START
Use the principles from this section to conduct a simple audit of your current ecosystem:

1. INCOME: What are your current sources of cash inflows? How stable are these sources? Are they growing predictably? Can you increase your cash inflows through building new skills or more effectively leveraging existing skills?
2. EXPENSES: How consistent are your current cash outflows? Are outflows reliably below inflows? Are your expenses grow-

ing faster than your income? Do you have a clear budget and plan? If not, create one and track your progress against it.

3. LONG-TERM INVESTMENTS: Do you have a clear strategy for investing the gap between inflows and outflows in long-term compounding vehicles? If not, create an investment account with a low-cost brokerage and consider establishing an automatic deposit.

This audit will provide a strong starting baseline to build **Financial Wealth**.

CONCLUSION

The Leap of Faith

IN CHRISTOPHER NOLAN'S 2010 science-fiction thriller *Inception,* there is a scene in which the protagonist, played by Leonardo Di-Caprio, is faced with the life-and-death decision of whether to trust a new potential benefactor and seize the challenge presented to him. It is a challenge with the highest possible stakes: the opportunity to return home to his children, whom he hasn't seen in years.

The benefactor, played by Ken Watanabe, seems to sense his counterpart's call to adventure and poses a single, powerful question:

"Do you want to take a leap of faith? Or become an old man, filled with regret, waiting to die alone?"

My life—my entire story—is the result of a leap of faith.

As I sit here writing the final pages of this book, years after the concept first took hold in my mind, I'm struck by just how much its ideas have changed my life and world:

I've built a thriving business ecosystem with a group of wonderful leaders and operators. I create content that positively influences millions of subscribers and followers around the world every single week. I designed a robust health and wellness routine that has allowed me to look and perform better than ever. I have the flexibility and control over my time to pursue energy-creating opportunities. I feel a deep sense of purpose and growth in my day-to-day life.

But above all else, I have my people.

It's 6:30 in the morning right now. I can hear my two-year-old son giggling outside my office doors, my wife no doubt egging him on. When I walk out, he'll run over and pull us into one of his favorite family hugs. This morning, we're packing our bags to make the short drive to Boston, where we'll spend a few days with our parents and siblings. These visits, which were previously annual, are now a frequent occurrence; our decision to leave our stable life in California and move across the country created these ripples of laughter, love, and memories. Since that move, our family has faced unpredictable challenges, health concerns, and sadness, but the important point is that we've faced them all *together.*

I found my people—and I intend to cherish them until my last breath.

So, as I wrap up this writing, I feel an immense gratitude. I am living my dream life because I embraced a better way—I measured the right things, I took the right actions, and I created the right outcomes. I embraced the concepts in *The 5 Types of Wealth.* I'm sure I gave up money by leaving the track I was on, but as far as I'm concerned, I'm the wealthiest man on the face of the earth.

Now it's time for you to do the same.

Measure, make decisions, and design your new life around these five types of wealth:

- Time Wealth
- Social Wealth
- Mental Wealth
- Physical Wealth
- Financial Wealth

Measure your life across all the pillars of a happy, fulfilling existence. Establish your baseline Wealth Score, then come back to it each year to assess your progress and areas of opportunity. Measure for the war and you'll never lose sight of it amid the chaos of the battles.

Make decisions that consider all five types of wealth. Rather than narrowly focusing on Financial Wealth, evaluate a decision based on its impact on all five types of wealth. When you're considering a career change, weigh the impact of the decision on your time, your relationships, and your purpose and growth. When you're thinking about a move, consider the effects on your loved ones and your health. When you're evaluating a big investment or purchase, reflect on the impact it may have on your freedom and mental state. The most important decisions are best made with the full spectrum of your life in mind.

Design your dream life within and across the seasons to come. Use this new model for proactive life design that considers your changing priorities and enables you to focus on specific individual battles without sacrificing your victory in the longer-term war. Navigate life's uncertainty with clarity as you evaluate the trade-offs you are willing and unwilling to make to build the life you want.

You have the tools. You have the information. Only one thing remains. . . .

Do you want to take a leap of faith?

ACKNOWLEDGMENTS

SIR ISAAC NEWTON FAMOUSLY wrote, "If I have seen further, it is by standing on the shoulders of giants." I echo this sentiment: This book was only made possible through the gracious understanding and support of a long list of *incredible* giants who gifted me their shoulders. I would like to take a moment to recognize them here, though words will never do my gratitude sufficient justice.

First and foremost, my wife, Elizabeth, who is without a doubt the most incredible person I've had the pleasure to know. Throughout this process, she was a sounding board, intellectual sparring partner, truth teller, and creative director (her design skills even contributed to the beautiful cover, which I am thrilled with!). Even more impressively, she did it all while being a present, loving mother to our son, Roman. I am a firm believer that who you choose to partner with in life is the most important choice you will ever make— well, every single day I count my blessings that she chose me.

My parents, who combined their high expectations with strong support, a combination that always allowed me to aspire to reach new heights, scale my impact, and dream big. Their love is the foundation of everything in my life, and I am forever grateful for it.

My sister, Sonali, who always set the bar high and showed me what was possible. After years of being separated by age, we find ourselves in the same stage of life, and I can't wait to see our relationship continue to blossom (or Bloom!) in the decades ahead.

My second family, the Gordons—Mary, Steve, Mara, and Samantha—whose support for Elizabeth, Roman, and me is unwavering.

My team, who made this book possible. Blake Burge, my personal Swiss Army knife, who has never met a task he can't take on with positivity and gusto. The type of guy you always want in your corner. Matt Schnuck, a thought partner and friend, who read and reviewed large parts of this book and helped craft the plan to enhance its impact. Christian DiMonda, who created the beautiful, simple visuals that enhance the words throughout. OffMenu Design, my design partner, who created the beautiful website and online resources for the book. Hunter Hammonds, Lucas Gabow, Holly Felicetta, Jess Barber, Sy Santos, and Shane Martin, who all contributed in their own unique ways.

My mentors, advisers, and friends, who have always pushed me to think bigger, but kept me grounded throughout.

My collaborators, including Susan Cain, Arthur Brooks, Ramit Sethi, Ben Bruno, and Nick Maggiulli, who were so generous with their time and insights. Their expertise enriched the quality of this book and the actionability of its guides.

All the incredible people who gifted me with the privilege of telling their stories, from those who are named—Alexis Lockhart, Erik Newton, Dave Prout, Rohan Venkatesh, Hank Behar, Phyllis Behar, Dan Go, Vicki Landis, Kevin Dahlstrom, Greg Sloan, Marc Randolph, and Bryan Johnson—to those who chose to remain anonymous. The hundreds, perhaps even thousands, of conversations brought incredible joy and wisdom into my life and the pages of this book. I am thrilled to be able to share their stories.

My editor, Mary Reynics, who was the perfect partner for this undertaking. At every stage of the process, her critical thinking and pressure testing enhanced the quality of the output. When we first met during the book deal process in 2022, I sensed we would have a great partnership—and I was right. She is special.

My book agent, Pilar Queen, who believed in my concept from the beginning. The first time we met, she said, "Look, I'm going to be honest with you," and my heart sank at what would come next. She continued, "I absolutely love it," and my heart was restored with confidence. Her belief meant the world to me then, as it does now.

And, finally, to all of you, my readers, who give me the energy to write every single day. I consider it the greatest honor to have the opportunity to do this for a living, and I don't take it for granted. Thank you for giving me this great opportunity. Thank you, thank you, thank you.

—Sahil Bloom, December 2024, New York

NOTES

PROLOGUE: THE JOURNEY OF A LIFETIME

1. Jean de La Fontaine, "The Astrologer That Tumbled into a Well," in Charles Denis, *Select Fables* (J. and R. Tonson and S. Draper, 1754).

DESIGNING YOUR DREAM LIFE

1. Arthur C. Brooks, "How to Buy Happiness," *The Atlantic*, April 15, 2021, https://www.theatlantic.com/family/archive/2021/04/money-income-buy -happiness/618601/.
2. Joe Pinsker, "The Reason Many Ultrarich People Aren't Satisfied with Their Wealth," *The Atlantic,* December 4, 2018, https://www.theatlantic .com/family/archive/2018/12/rich-people-happy-money/577231/.
3. Kathleen Elkins, "Warren Buffett Simplifies Investing with a Baseball Analogy," CNBC, February 2, 2017, https://www.cnbc.com/2017/02/02/warren -buffett-simplifies-investing-with-a-baseball-analogy.html.

TIME WEALTH

1. The dataset I discovered was a compilation created by Our World in Data, a website specializing in data visualization, which took the 2009–19 American Time Use Surveys and built a comprehensive view of whom we spend our time with over the course of our lives. They segmented the view across time with family, friends, partner, children, coworkers, and alone. See Esteban Ortiz-Ospina, Charlie Giattino, and Max Roser, "Time Use," Our World in Data, February 29, 2024, https://ourworldindata.org/time-use.
2. Tim Urban, "The Tail End," *Wait but Why* (blog), December 11, 2015, https://waitbutwhy.com/2015/12/the-tail-end.html.

3. Tim Ferriss, "Sam Harris (#342)," *The Tim Ferriss Show* (podcast), October 31, 2018, https://tim.blog/2018/10/31/the-tim-ferriss-show-transcripts-sam-harris-342/.

4. Saloni Dattani et al., "Life Expectancy," Our World in Data, https://ourworldindata.org/life-expectancy.

5. Sophie Leroy, "Why Is It So Hard to Do My Work? The Challenge of Attention Residue When Switching Between Work Tasks," *Organizational Behavior and the Human Decision Processes* 109, no. 2 (July 2009): 168–81.

6. Cal Newport, "A Productivity Lesson from a Classic Arcade Game," *Cal Newport* (blog), September 6, 2016, https://calnewport.com/a-productivity-lesson-from-a-classic-arcade-game/.

7. "Three-Quarters of Parents Too Busy to Read Bedtime Stories," *Telegraph,* February 27, 2009, https://www.telegraph.co.uk/women/mother-tongue/4839894/Three-quarters-of-parents-too-busy-to-read-bedtime-stories.html.

8. Rahul Vohra, "The State of Your Inbox in 2021: Email Burnout and Browsing in Bed," *Superhuman* (blog), April 20, 2021, https://blog.superhuman.com/the-state-of-your-inbox-in-2021/.

9. Emma Seppälä, "Three Science-Based Reasons Vacations Boost Productivity," *Psychology Today,* August 17, 2017, https://www.psychologytoday.com/us/blog/feeling-it/201708/three-science-based-reasons-vacations-boost-productivity.

10. Ashley Whillans, "Time for Happiness," *Harvard Business Review,* January 4, 2019, https://hbr.org/2019/01/time-for-happiness.

11. Marc Andreessen, "Pmarca Guide to Personal Productivity," Pmarchive, June 4, 2007, https://pmarchive.com/guide_to_personal_productivity.html.

12. Tim Ferriss, "James Clear, *Atomic Habits,*" *The Tim Ferriss Show* (podcast), January 6, 2023, https://tim.blog/2023/01/06/james-clear-atomic-habits-transcript/.

SOCIAL WEALTH

1. Emily Esfahani Smith, "Social Connection Makes a Better Brain," *The Atlantic,* October 29, 2013, https://www.theatlantic.com/health/archive/2013/10/social-connection-makes-a-better-brain/280934/.

2. Michael Miller, "What Makes a Good Life?," *Six Seconds* (blog), April 19, 2021, https://www.6seconds.org/2021/04/19/harvard-grant-study/.

3. Vivek H. Murthy, "Our Epidemic of Loneliness and Isolation," U.S. Surgeon General's Advisory, May 2, 2023, https://www.hhs.gov/sites/default/files/surgeon-general-social-connection-advisory.pdf.

4. Viji Diane Kannan and Peter J. Veazie, "US Trends in Social Isolation, Social Engagement, and Companionship—Nationally and by Age, Sex, Race/Ethnicity, Family Income, and Work Hours, 2003–2020," *SSM Population Health* 21 (March 2023): 101331, https://doi.org/10.1016/j.ssmph.2022.101331.

5. Susanne Buecker et al., "Is Loneliness in Emerging Adults Increasing over Time? A Preregistered Cross-Temporal Meta-Analysis and Systematic Review," *Psychological Bulletin* 147, no. 8 (August 2021): 787–805, https://doi.org/10.1037/bul0000332.

6. Kannan and Veazie, "US Trends in Social Isolation."

7. Daniel A. Cox, "Men's Social Circles Are Shrinking," Survey Center on American Life, June 29, 2021, https://www.americansurveycenter.org/why-mens-social-circles-are-shrinking/.

8. Gallup and Meta, "The Global State of Social Connections," Gallup.com, June 27, 2024, https://www.gallup.com/analytics/509675/state-of-social-connections.aspx.

9. Volodymyr Kupriyanov, "2021 Study: Do People Actually Regret Moving?," *Hire a Helper* (blog), June 3, 2021, https://blog.hireahelper.com/2021-study-do-people-actually-regret-moving/.

10. Eleanor Pringle, "The 'Great Resignation' Is Now the 'Great Regret,'" *Fortune,* February 9, 2023, https://fortune.com/2023/02/09/great-resignation-now-great-regret-gen-z-wish-they-had-not-quit-old-job/.

11. Steve Jobs, "You've Got to Find What You Love," *Stanford Report,* June 12, 2005, https://news.stanford.edu/stories/2005/06/youve-got-find-love-jobs-says.

12. Johnaé De Felicis, "What Is a Walking Moai? (and How It Can Improve Your Health, Your Social Life, and Your Productivity)," *Blue Zones,* June 2023, https://www.bluezones.com/2023/06/what-is-a-walking-moai/.

13. Aaron Zitner, "America Pulls Back from Values That Once Defined It, WSJ-NORC Poll Finds," *The Wall Street Journal,* March 27, 2023, https://www.wsj.com/articles/americans-pull-back-from-values-that-once-defined-u-s-wsj-norc-poll-finds-df8534cd.

14. Rogé Karma, "Transcript: Ezra Klein Show with Cecilia Ridgeway," *The New York Times,* September 13, 2022, https://www.nytimes.com/2022/09/13/podcasts/ezra-klein-show-cecilia-ridgeway.html.

15. Christopher von Rueden, "How Social Status Affects Your Health," *The New York Times,* December 12, 2014, https://www.nytimes.com/2014/12/14/opinion/sunday/how-social-status-affects-your-health.html.

16. M. G. Marmot et al., "Health Inequalities Among British Civil Servants: The Whitehall II Study," *The Lancet* 337, no. 8754 (June 8, 1991): 1387–93, https://pubmed.ncbi.nlm.nih.gov/1674771/.

17. Julianne Holt-Lunstad et al., "Social Relationships and Ambulatory Blood Pressure: Structural and Qualitative Predictors of Cardiovascular Function During Everyday Social Interactions," *Health Psychology* 22, no. 4 (2003): 388–97, https://doi.org/10.1037/0278-6133.22.4.388.

18. Adam Grant, "Your Most Ambivalent Relationships Are the Most Toxic," *The New York Times,* May 28, 2023, https://www.nytimes.com/2023/05/28/opinion/frenemies-relationships-health.html.

19. Jancee Dunn, "When Someone You Love Is Upset, Ask This One Ques-

tion," *The New York Times*, April 7, 2023, https://www.nytimes.com/2023/04/07/well/emotions-support-relationships.html.

20. Ed Catmull and Amy Wallace, *Creativity, Inc.: Overcoming the Unseen Forces That Stand in the Way of True Inspiration* (New York: Random House, 2014).

MENTAL WEALTH

1. Michiko Sakaki, Ayano Yagi, and Kou Murayama, "Curiosity in Old Age: A Possible Key to Achieving Adaptive Aging," *Neuroscience and Biobehavioral Reviews* 88 (May 2018): 106–16, https://doi.org/10.1016/j.neubiorev.2018.03.007.

2. Todd B. Kashdan, Paul Rose, and Frank D. Fincham, "Curiosity and Exploration: Facilitating Positive Subjective Experiences and Personal Growth Opportunities," *Journal of Personality Assessment* 82, no. 3 (June 2004): 291–305, https://doi.org/10.1207/s15327752jpa8203_05.

3. Li Chu, Jeanne L. Tsai, and Helene H. Fung, "Association between Age and Intellectual Curiosity: The Mediating Roles of Future Time Perspective and Importance of Curiosity," *European Journal of Ageing* 18, no. 1 (April 27, 2020): 45–53, https://doi.org/10.1007/s10433-020-00567-6.

4. Matthias Ziegler et al., "Openness as a Buffer against Cognitive Decline: The Openness-Fluid-Crystallized-Intelligence (OFCI) Model Applied to Late Adulthood," *Psychology and Aging* 30, no. 3 (January 1, 2015): 573–88, https://doi.org/10.1037/a0039493.

5. "The Right Outlook: How Finding Your Purpose Can Improve Your Life," *Blue Zones*, August 2011, https://www.bluezones.com/2011/08/the-right-outlook-how-finding-your-purpose-can-improve-your-life/.

6. Aliya Alimujiang et al., "Association between Life Purpose and Mortality among US Adults Older Than 50 Years," *JAMA Network Open* 2, no. 5 (May 24, 2019): e194270, https://doi.org/10.1001/jamanetworkopen.2019.4270.

7. Claire Bates, "Is This the World's Happiest Man? Brain Scans Reveal French Monk Found to Have 'Abnormally Large Capacity' for Joy—Thanks to Meditation," *Daily Mail*, October 31, 2012, https://www.dailymail.co.uk/health/article-2225634/Is-worlds-happiest-man-Brain-scans-reveal-French-monk-abnormally-large-capacity-joy-meditation.html.

8. May Wong, "Stanford Study Finds Walking Improves Creativity," *Stanford Report*, April 24, 2014, https://news.stanford.edu/2014/04/24/walking-vs-sitting-042414/.

9. Charles H. Hillman et al., "The Effect of Acute Treadmill Walking on Cognitive Control and Academic Achievement in Preadolescent Children," *Neuroscience* 159, no. 3 (March 31, 2009): 1044–54, https://doi.org/10.1016/j.neuroscience.2009.01.057.

10. Miao Cheng et al., "Paired Walkers with Better First Impression Synchro-

nize Better," *PLoS ONE* 15, no. 2 (February 21, 2020): e0227880, https://doi.org/10.1371/journal.pone.0227880.

11. Andrea Mendez Colmenares et al., "White Matter Plasticity in Healthy Older Adults: The Effects of Aerobic Exercise," *NeuroImage* 239 (October 1, 2021): 118305, https://doi.org/10.1016/j.neuroimage.2021.118305.

PHYSICAL WEALTH

1. Jane McGonigal, "Mental Time Travel Is a Great Decision-Making Tool—This Is How to Use It," Ideas.ted.com, March 10, 2022, https://ideas.ted.com/mental-time-travel-is-a-great-decision-making-tool-this-is-how-to-use-it/.

2. Walter Isaacson, "The Inspiration Behind Leonardo da Vinci's Vitruvian Man," Medium.com, October 30, 2017, https://medium.com/s/leonardo-da-vinci/the-inspiration-behind-leonardo-da-vincis-vitruvian-man-974c525495ec.

3. Timothy B. Gage and Sharon DeWitte, "What Do We Know About the Agricultural Demographic Transition?," *Current Anthropology* 50, no. 5 (October 1, 2009): 649–55, https://doi.org/10.1086/605017.

4. "The Olympic Games," History.com, June 12, 2024, https://www.history.com/topics/sports/olympic-games.

5. Maria Popova, "The Science of Working Out the Body and the Soul: How the Art of Exercise Was Born, Lost, and Rediscovered," *Marginalian*, May 10, 2022, https://www.themarginalian.org/2022/05/10/sweat-bill-hayes/.

6. "The Olympic Games."

7. Global Wellness Institute, "What Is the Wellness Economy?," accessed July 2024, https://globalwellnessinstitute.org/what-is-wellness/what-is-the-wellness-economy/.

8. C. D. Reimers, G. Knapp, and A. K. Reimers, "Does Physical Activity Increase Life Expectancy? A Review of the Literature," *Journal of Aging Research* 2012 (July 1, 2012): 1–9, https://doi.org/10.1155/2012/243958.

9. "Exercising More Than Recommended Could Lengthen Life, Study Suggests," Harvard T. H. Chan School of Public Health, July 29, 2022, https://www.hsph.harvard.edu/news/hsph-in-the-news/exercising-more-than-recommended-could-lengthen-life-study-suggests/.

10. Andrew Huberman, "Stretching Protocols to Increase Flexibility and Support General Health," *Huberman Lab* (podcast), July 27, 2022, https://hubermanlab.com/stretching-protocols-to-increase-flexibility-and-support-general-health/.

11. "Sleep Facts and Stats," CDC Sleep, May 15, 2024, https://www.cdc.gov/sleep/data-research/facts-stats/?CDC_AAref_Val=https://www.cdc.gov/sleep/data_statistics.html.

12. "Are You Sleeping Enough? This Infographic Shows How You Compare to the Rest of the World," World Economic Forum, August 16, 2019, https://www.weforum.org/agenda/2019/08/we-need-more-sleep.

13. Tim Ferriss, "Dr. Andrew Huberman—the Foundations of Physical and Mental Performance, Core Supplements, Sexual Health and Fertility, Sleep Optimization, Psychedelics, and More (#660)," *The Tim Ferriss Show* (podcast), March 10, 2023, https://tim.blog/2023/03/10/dr-andrew-huberman-transcript/.

14. Kyle Mandsager et al., "Association of Cardiorespiratory Fitness with Long-term Mortality among Adults Undergoing Exercise Treadmill Testing," *JAMA Network Open* 1, no. 6 (October 19, 2018): e183605, https://doi.org/10.1001/jamanetworkopen.2018.3605.

FINANCIAL WEALTH

1. Mark Twain, "Observations by Mark Twain," 1869, https://cdnsm5-ss12.sharpschool.com/UserFiles/Servers/Server_520401/File/Departments/Curriculum%20&%20Instruction/ELA/Non-Fiction%20Texts/Observations%20by%20Mark%20Twain.pdf.

2. Larry Getlen, "Meet the World's Richest Man Who Changed Christianity," *New York Post,* July 26, 2015, https://nypost.com/2015/07/26/meet-historys-richest-man-who-changed-christianity/.

3. Greg Steinmetz, *The Richest Man Who Ever Lived: The Life and Times of Jacob Fugger* (New York: Simon and Schuster, 2015).

4. Steinmetz, *The Richest Man Who Ever Lived.*

5. Ilana E. Strauss, "The Myth of the Barter Economy," *The Atlantic,* February 26, 2016, https://www.theatlantic.com/business/archive/2016/02/barter-society-myth/471051/.

6. "The History of Money," *NOVA,* PBS, October 25, 1996, https://www.pbs.org/wgbh/nova/article/history-money/.

7. John Lanchester, "The Invention of Money," *The New Yorker,* July 29, 2019, https://www.newyorker.com/magazine/2019/08/05/the-invention-of-money.

8. Lanchester, "The Invention of Money."

9. Tim Ferriss, "Morgan Housel—*The Psychology of Money, Picking the Right Game, and the $6 Million Janitor* (#576)," *The Tim Ferriss Show* (podcast), March 5, 2022, https://tim.blog/2022/03/05/morgan-housel-the-psychology-of-money-transcript.

10. Nick Maggiulli, "S&P 500 DCA Calculator," *Of Dollars and Data* (blog), 2024, https://ofdollarsanddata.com/sp500-dca-calculator/.

11. Nick Maggiulli, "The Return on Hassle Spectrum," *Of Dollars and Data* (blog), July 25, 2023, https://ofdollarsanddata.com/return-on-hassle/.

INDEX

ABOUT THE AUTHOR

SAHIL BLOOM is an inspirational writer and content creator, captivating millions of people every week through his insights and biweekly newsletter, "The Curiosity Chronicle." He is a successful entrepreneur, the owner of SRB Holdings, and the managing partner of SRB Ventures, an early-stage investment fund. Bloom graduated from Stanford University with a bachelor's degree in economics and sociology and a master's degree in public policy. He was a member of the Stanford baseball team for four years.

sahilbloom.com
X: @sahilbloom
Instagram: @sahilbloom
LinkedIn: @sahilbloom